The SAS 'Deniables'

The SAS 'Deniables'

Special Forces Operations,
denied by the Authorities,
from Vietnam to the War on Terror

Tony May

FRONTLINE BOOKS

First published in Great Britain in 2022 by
Frontline Books
An imprint of
Pen & Sword Books Ltd
Yorkshire – Philadelphia

ISBN 978 1 39909 630 0

A CIP catalogue record for this book is
available from the British Library.

Typeset by Mac Style
Printed and bound by CPI Group (UK) Ltd, Croydon CR0 4YY

Pen & Sword Books Limited incorporates the imprints of Atlas, Archaeology, Aviation, Discovery, Family History, Fiction, History, Maritime, Military, Military Classics, Politics, Select, Transport, True Crime, Air World, Frontline Publishing, Leo Cooper, Remember When, Seaforth Publishing, The Praetorian Press, Wharncliffe Local History, Wharncliffe Transport, Wharncliffe True Crime and White Owl.

For a complete list of Pen & Sword titles please contact

PEN & SWORD BOOKS LIMITED
47 Church Street, Barnsley, South Yorkshire, S70 2AS, England
E-mail: enquiries@pen-and-sword.co.uk
Website: www.pen-and-sword.co.uk

Or

PEN AND SWORD BOOKS
1950 Lawrence Rd, Havertown, PA 19083, USA
E-mail: Uspen-and-sword@casematepublishers.com
Website: www.penandswordbooks.com

Dedication

To the Australian Special Air Service (SAS) trained specialists whose patriotism, experience and knowledge of military covert operations and generosity gave life to this body of work.

To the unnamed men and women of the Australian military and security services who in the past, present and future have and will always put themselves forward as the very silent few who perform the extraordinary with no expectation of recognition or reward, except for having done their job well with pride and passion.

* * *

Any similarities to people living or dead are purely coincidental.

Contents

Preface

Blue on Blue

Not Everyone in the 60s' Wore Beads and Roman Sandals

The routine of observe, report and get chased away from targets was a day-to-day affair. The small team had gotten smaller as there were no replacements and no time to train new personnel. The best tool was a simple compass and regular updating of maps and charts of the areas they had been through. The countryside was littered with unmarked villages both friendly and hostile.

All were considered as hostile and sources of intelligence leaks to the Viet Cong, whom the team were certain knew of their existence.

The mission wasn't finished with just the small targets being taken out, so they continued to search for more transport trails until they uncovered another huge stockpile of munitions. It seemed the opposition had reacted to the last attack, resulting in what was now a huge stockpile of weapons bunched up with nothing going over the Vietnamese border but instead creating a pile-up just five miles inside Cambodia in a valley that had cliffs on each side and a small stream trickling through it.

The SAS team found an ideal spot to set up camp on one of the hill tops with almost perfect cover from aerial surveillance. The enemy below didn't know they were being observed from a vantage point that allowed the SAS a fairly clear view along the valley.

The cache was fairly large and growing, and there were both Viet Cong and Cambodian personnel bivouacked on all sides. They shared this intelligence coup with the Americans via their contact in Saigon. The team was ordered to sit tight and observe when the stockpile looked like it was moving out of the valley and heading towards the border into Vietnam. Within two days the munitions began to move east, a trickle at first until there was more co-ordination of personnel. Spider notified DIO in Saigon, who several hours later advised that the Americans were marshalling a helicopter gunship attack.

It was mid-afternoon, the sky a little hazy but no rain, and the SAS soldiers could make out the head of the line of people carting heavy boxes by hand, on backs and on bicycles. The line had begun to reach the end of the valley and started working its way up an incline before reaching the Vietnamese border.

Then the team of warriors heard the clack of helicopter rotors, when a dozen helicopters breached the top of the rise where the transporters of munitions began to scatter. Too fucking late! The rockets and machine guns began a constant hammering of the ground and through the valley.

The helicopters turned back into the valley and carried out their strafing runs more meticulously by picking out individual targets. By this time the enemy soldiers among the transport labourers had begun return fire using automatic weapons.

This caused the helicopters to break formation and it appeared that they had lost control of the situation and had to regroup.

That decision brought several helicopters right over the top of their position. One of them opened fire with their belly gunner and killed five Australian SAS warriors, who did not return fire.

The SAS team's radioman was on the high frequency radio phone talking to the helicopter flight leader at the time and supporting the mopping up when they were hit. He immediately shouted into the mouthpiece 'Cease fire, cease fire, we are friendlies. You just hit us. We have casualties, call off your stupid fucking choppers'.

Before he could say another word, Major Spider snatched the phone from the radioman's hand and disconnected. His troops were livid; they threatened to use missiles in future to bring down the helicopters.

As the commander on the ground, Major Spider utilised his trained psychologist prowess and by pulling rank he convinced the troop to calm down, that they would deal with this bat-shit crazy matter in a civilised manner. This was no easy task as he was as pissed off as they were.

Brute approached the major with Stocky and Doc close at his heels. Major Spider was aware that these warriors were in shock, the look on their paled faces was one of anger in their deadly, venomous, staring eyes.

'God fuck me to tears major, I tell ya if I ever get my hands on anyone of those fucking murdering cluster fuck Yanks, I will tear their fucking heads off and piss down their ever-loving motherfucking throats.'

'I hear you Sergeant, but not here, not now, our day will come. Right now, we have casualties that need our attention.'

Major Spider saluted Brute and all three warriors returned the salute.

The major knew Brute wasn't kidding and he also knew the big man was capable of doing exactly what he stated.

The bodies of the SAS warriors had been shredded by the multiple wounds from the 50-calibre helicopter weapons. They stripped the remains of any identifying materials and buried them in shallow graves which were located by compass readings and they marked the positions on their maps and charts. The team retreated from the scene leaving the Americans to finish what they had started. The only option was to head back to the landing areas and bug out of Cambodia by trusty Caribou aircraft.

Lest we forget

Chapter 1

Darwin Briefing – Pre-Mobilisation

Australia had agreed with the United States to have a team of Australian Army Special Air Services (SAS) soldiers conduct covert missions into Cambodia. The SAS soldiers would be bivouacked in Thailand.

On the day prior to their departure to Thailand, the Defence Intelligence Organisation (DIO) handlers set up a briefing in the Darwin Barracks for all of the SAS platoon leaders led by Major Pete, nicknamed Spider for his prowess and martial arts abilities, to attend mandatorily. The DIO contact officer, code-named Mr Champion, and the Ministry of Defence representative, Commander Coen, were introduced and provided a very cut down briefing.

The location for the operations had been set up earlier by the DIO with co-operation from the CIA at the Sattahip Marine Base, which had a single north–south runway on the south-eastern seaboard of Thailand adjacent to the Gulf of Thailand coast.

The briefing then focused on a specific operation that laid out the plans for ingress into Cambodia via Thailand with the sole objective of interdicting shipments of weapons that were being smuggled up the Mekong Delta into Cambodia by Russian and Chinese crewed ships. They were then being taken across land into Vietnam, arriving behind the US and allied front lines for back door Viet Cong ambush attacks. The pre-mobilisation planning would commence immediately.

They were given five days to get their act in order and then mobilise to southern Thailand via air into Sattahip Marine Base, which is 280 odd miles west of the Cambodian border. Once they had completed a three-day run-through of the wetland, water, and air training and orientation they could cover in the three days available, all the squads were assembled in parade formation at the Darwin Barracks, then martialled into the parade hall and given an introduction to civilian-dressed members of the Defence Intelligence Organisation (DIO) to whom they would be reporting directly on all future covert operations.

The basis would be plausible deniable under the Commonwealth Secrecy Act, which they all had to read and then sign in front of the DIO members (they had signed similar documents on joining the army). They never got the names of the civilians.

Spider thought for a moment after the signing and whispered quietly to himself 'I think we're fucked from today onwards'.

They were broadly advised that they would carry out special operations disguised as a civilian oil and gas contractor company in a neutral country (Thailand) while acting covertly in sovereign countries (Cambodia) that were not part of the Vietnam War. They would be inserting behind the enemy lines, over borders on land, sea and air as directed.

Chapter 2

Covert Intelligence Operations – Thailand Base

Major Spider and the Team

The Sattahip Marine Base shared a boundary with the U-Tapao airbase. The runway at U-Tapao was lengthened by the US military in the mid-1960s and became one of the airfields used in Southeast Asia by the United States Air force for their B-52 bombing raids over North Vietnam, including air support for the horrendous US Marine battle at Khe Sanh.

Initially kept secret by the Nixon administration, in 1969 U-Tapao was also used for B-52 bombing raids into Cambodia.

Their relationship with the Thai authorities was that they didn't exist as Thailand was neutral and not involved in the Vietnam War. Major Spider was concerned about the security of his operations in someone else's backyard and was informed by the DIO that so long as they *never* ventured outside of Sattahip marine base, Thailand could plead a plausibly deniable case stating that the activities on their base were strictly due to civilian contractors working for oil and gas operators in the region.

The initial SAS contingent mobilised comprising one platoon of twenty fully kitted out soldiers, adding the major himself as commanding officer, plus aircrew for the C-130 transport aircraft. Also, as Major Spider had trained with several of the lieutenants and sergeants in the early days in the CMF volunteer army through to the Puckapunual and Canungra training camps in more recent times, he selected the following personnel as his core inner team who would rotate back to back as needed for the entire period of this operation:

1. Head Pilot David (Dash) Jones with 3,400 flying hours in remote regions. Formerly worked for an Indonesian charter flight company, landing in Papua New Guinea and various small islands.
2. Pilot Officers Mike (Macka) McKey and Paul (Greek) Papas. Both of these pilots had more than 2,000 hours flying time logged with much of it in tropical airstrip locations like Papua New Guinea and Northern Australia.
3. Marine Coxswains Phil (Flipper) Fleckney and Ashley (Hook) Dale.

4. Explosives Specialist Corporal James (Rat) Aims, a mechanic handy with tools and maintenance. Supported the M60 gunner as loader.
5. Field Medic and Communications Specialist Lance Corporal Alex (Doc), McDonald, formally a Commando who had recently been transferred to the SAS. Excellent as an infield paramedic and expert in electronic warfare and communications equipment.
6. Heavy Weapons Specialist or Sniper Sergeant Tony (Brute) Maze, a big strong man and excellent platoon leader.

Threats to Health and Security

On day one in Thailand, Major Spider had the men wear contractor overalls with the same oil company logo printed on the back as the one that been hoisted up onto the aircraft hangar office front. Prior to them departing from Darwin, they had a sign writer paint the Hightower Drilling Contractor logo onto the tail of each aircraft and the designated civilian registration call-sign for radio communications, with civil aviation transponder and radios plus military satellite comms antennae installed.

When you have a bunch of young, strong, virile males and their testosterone kicks in, along with long periods away from home, the attraction that is available just outside the Sattahip base perimeter fence are little brown poverty-stricken Thai beauties, eager and willing to rent their bodies for a couple of local Baht. The *never* venture outside notion was similar to trying to restrain a bucking horse trying to get out of the stall; almost impossible!

Well, the answer to that, Spider thought, was the older guys. However, it turned out they were just as amorous for the physical pleasures outside the wire as the young bucks. Nevertheless, they had a real job on their hands keeping themselves and the younger studs focused by handling the rosters and work details. Spider figured that setting up a ninety-day rotation back to Darwin should do the trick, as there was far less likelihood of leaking intelligence information to the locals or being infected with sexually transferred diseases, malaria or any other tropical malaise.

Everyone returning to Darwin on R&R would receive a full health check on arrival and anyone caught with an STD would be in serious shit as they would be handed over to the DIO security people for a thorough debrief on whom with, when and how often. Their reports would come to Major Spider for disciplinary action. Obviously, they would never return under his command and possibly would be kicked out of the SAS. Being human and understanding the wants and needs of raging male hormones, Spider dropped the hint on many occasions: 'Condoms!' He did not want to lose any of his team on account of a little short-time pleasure.

Operations Begin

Additional information was provided on the locations of known official and unofficial Cambodian landing areas. The latter were possibly used by drugs or weapons smugglers, and also used from time to time by the CIA's so-called Air America contractors involved in ferrying drugs, the profits of which the CIA utilised to finance their private war in the People's Democratic Republic of Laos. Major Spider, along with the other pilots, were provided with current navigation charts and in-transit communications protocols for entry into official airports that were set up for Indonesia Kupang in West Timor, Brunei Darussalam, Singapore's Changi, Butterworth in Penang, Malaysia, and finally Sattahip, Thailand, their ultimate base of operations for airborne and fast boat operations into Cambodia.

They had to airlift their two US fast boats up to Sattahip by C-130 for circuitously prowling up the Cambodian coast, harbours and the myriad of inland river deltas. The flat-bottom boats were the perfect platform for operating in shallow and muddy mangrove waters due to being water jet propelled and reasonably quiet.

They also had listed on the manifest for later delivery two Piper Cub aerial spotter planes that were of Second World War vintage, canvas covered, very slow but light and nimble at very low level. They would have to assemble the detached wings after delivery.

The DIO arranged the local purchase and delivery onto Sattahip base of a 20-ton tiltable flatbed truck with full canvas cover with company logo in case they needed to transport the jet boats, people, ordnance, Piper aircraft or other purposes in order to spread out their so-called oil and gas contracting business away from the base.

All site security was to be inconspicuous and no firearms or uniforms were to be visible. Most of the time on base they wore brown overalls or shorts and T-shirts with rubber sandles on their feet. Sattahip was an old established Thai military and marine base. The Thais did maintain a good security perimeter for their own purposes on the land and water sides. The Thai military were never officially involved at the outset of their arrival at the base, except for the occasional interfacing with them, 'a contractor company hiring their warehouse-hangar space and use of their boat ramp out the back of the warehouse and ad hoc use of the single runway'.

Chapter 3

Transits to and from Darwin and Sattahip

M ajor Spider had made it a point that on arrival the Cubs, Caribou and C-130 remained in the hangar out of sight and mind of curious eyes. The C-130 flights only emerged at night with runway lights on long enough for take-off or touch-down. The Pipers mostly took off at first light before the control tower woke up and came back within a couple of hours due to limited fuel endurance and range. The Caribou flew in and out at ad hoc times, with all aircraft departures turning out over the waters of the Gulf of Thailand for noise abatement and to camouflage the intended direction once they reached cruising altitude.

More often than not, due to the notoriously bad weather in the tropics, their flights to and from Darwin were erratic and required diversion hops into Kupang West Timor, Balikpapan, Indonesia, Brunei Darussalam and the worst-case scenarios of Butterworth Air Force Base in Penang or Singapore's Changi airport.

The only interface at these locations was for refuelling as they never disembarked personnel in order to avoid customs and immigration inspections of their people or cargoes. The Singaporeans and Indonesians were not very happy to allow them to land on a number of occasions, sensing that they were military and not civilian flights, and they had to make a call on the HF radio phone to the DIO for Government intervention, more than likely to pay off some government or military officials.

As Darwin was both an air force base and civilian domestic and international airport, their comings and goings were, for all intents and purposes, indistinguishable from general cargo flights except for where the aircraft was parked, which was well away from the civilian terminals and up against the air force hangar.

Having established their Sattahip base of operations, with aircraft stored and assembled, the hangar offices were turned into barracks and mess rooms. Everyone took turns in preparing meals, which occasionally wound up in food fights as some of the team had no fucking idea of how to prepare a meal. From time to time, they would have someone go into Sattahip village and bring back a load of Thai food, which burned going in and burned coming out. Finally, Brute found an old Thai guy in the village who spoke good English and had worked for the Americans cooking on an offshore oil drilling rig. After discussions with the team, they had the Australian Embassy in Bangkok check with Thai security into the old fart's background. It was all clear, so he was hired. Mess hall problems solved.

It was essential for them to begin their operations role expeditiously with incursions into Cambodia. Ultimately, they were directed to communicate solely with the Vietnam Command HQ – Australian Desk (whatever that meant?) in Saigon.

Apparently, they had been handballed to unfamiliar recipients of their intelligence data and from whom they would receive orders. Having dealt with boffins before, Spider decided to be careful about what specific information he provided or requests he made of them as bureaucrats, as in or out of uniform they usually had a myriad of ways of avoiding a direct answer or would say 'no' until pestered to say 'yes' or 'maybe', which Spider felt impelled to avoid as this left him exposed.

Spider's usual contact, Commander Coen, was a smart operator and he almost always kept them free from uncertainty by making specific, on-the-spot decisions, and then later informing his masters. Spider guessed that he would then face the flak from CIA and Ministry of Defence on their behalf.

The team sat for a week on their arses at the base with the idle jet boats in need of fuel and rations, which finally arrived from a local supplier.

The HF radio phone finally rang on the desk made out of empty crates in the belly of the C-130 where it and the major lived. He staggered over and grabbed it impatiently, then listened for the beep to sound indicating the code script was about to arrive on the screen. He returned by typing in his code on the keyboard and then the familiar voice of Commander Coen of DIO crackled through.

Coen had been posted to Saigon office and would be overseeing the interface with the US Intelligence desk. At last, Spider felt that they were at least plugged into the system again. A series of encrypted text messages followed that included what new encryption mode to respond with. All comms systems were now up and running.

Specific but not detailed mobilisation orders were issued regarding what they saw as key targets. Their job was to work out how to get to them, observe and report with observations (SITCOM) on civilian and combatant movements, the magnitude of stored ordnance, ship identification, photos and recommendations on how they could neutralise the target without being compromised (a nice way of saying don't get caught).

They had not shared their revised charts with DIO and definitely not with the US/CIA. This information was their own security blanket against any leaks from any direction. Spider learned this trick for drawing new chart grids off one of his cadet college officers whose dad had been an officer in the Korean War. The enemy would not be able to interpret their chart location references without the master chart in front of them.

Missions on Wings and Water – Cambodia

Major Spider took up each of the Cub aircraft with the reassembled wings for some one-hour low-level test flights and accidentally on purpose flew southeast over the Gulf of Thailand along the coast of Cambodia, but short of the coastal city of Krong Koh Kong with its airport and harbour. Rat rode along to act as observer/spotter in the back seat.

They could see there were a lot of fishing villages and hundreds of small boats out on the water or beached, plus bamboo fishing net structures out on the water that they could bump into. Many fishing hamlets were not marked on the charts that they were provided with back in Darwin (typical lack of so-called intelligence data). This clustering of boats and structures could cause a problem for them at night when setting out using the jet boat radar. So, they marked their charts and photographed them for later cataloguing.

Night marine probing sorties would be the first action to undertake using radar and visual sightings to observe the density of night movements, local boat identification lights and flags, so they could copy the details onto charts and then gauge the extent of harbour mouth congestion. They had to assume that there would also be Thai vessels out there mixed with Cambodian and possibly some Vietnamese to further complicate matters. Not much point losing one's cover on the first night on the water or you might as well pack up and go home.

On the next day of so-called flight testing, they flew north along the Thai–Cambodian border to look for the unmapped rivers that emptied into the major inland waterway lakes of Tonlé Sap. They located two main water courses close to the Thai border and quite a number of minor tributaries that the jet boats could manage. The only problem would be that they would have to truck the jet boats several hundred miles north without attracting the attention of both countries' border patrols.

The DIO briefing had provided several aerial photographs showing larger coastal freighter vessels entering and leaving the Mekong Delta leading into Lake Tonlé Sap, and interestingly enough they didn't appear to be entering the official South Vietnam port area on the coast or near the listed towns around the lake. This may indicate some back-door operations were under way, which could be an alternate cargo port, drug smuggling shipments or covert munitions delivery for the Viet Cong further upriver.

There were too many tributaries for the US Navy to check them all and their underlying mission was to enter from the Cambodian side, which may be unexpected. Their primary job was to track, document, and report back to DIO. Plus, when necessary, they would interdict (blow them up) using the jet boats and trudging through jungles, their raison d'être.

The first foray into the dark tropical waters was tense in the blackout conditions, with only the quiet purr of the big V-8 engine under the well-silenced hood and the gurgle of the water jet propulsion which left a white luminous telltale wake of startled marine organisms lighting up behind them.

The radar screen was shrouded, so only one observer could press his eyes onto the view slot. The rest of the four-man crew took turns at the helm and spread out around the open deck staring into the darkness at the distant shore and bobbing boat lights. Interestingly, it was noted that there were fewer boats moving about on the water at night, which would be a huge advantage.

At last, the first objective was picked up on the radar, the mouth of the delta, and adjacent port break wall. There were no large vessels out in the open water that would have their own radar. Thank God for that as the crew were fairly exposed, being in a metal boat that would be detected.

After four hours wandering ever closer to the harbour mouth, the crew called it a day when less than a mile off the harbour and about-turned, heading parallel to shore back to base. Thus, they gained an impression of where the villages or other navigation points were and marked up the charts for use later on.

The trusty gyrocompass, clock and boat speed instruments were used, which were accurate enough for the purpose. The following night the remainder of the team went out along the same route and verified the chart markings, plus made a few more observations. They would rely on this chart for the remainder of their time there.

After loading up one of the jet boats onto the truck using a winch, they tied it down under the canvas cover and set off toward the Cambodian border to see if they could cross over to the nearest river, which was about 30km from the south coast and only about 10km inside the border. This river provided a direct line of water to the city of Battambang and the east–west highway, then on to the Lake Tonlé Sap area.

The jet boat had been given a dressing down to make it look old. Some of the superstructure was removed and typical woven cargo containers were stacked on deck to hide the M60 machine guns facing forward and aft. The coxswain position was camouflaged to hide the radio and instruments.

With the Cub spotter flights taking the lead overhead to monitor for best tracks over and around the jungle terrain for the loaded truck to drive through after going off-road in Thailand, they made good time and were unobserved heading over the Cambodian border. The truck made it up to the river edge as planned. It was easier to slide the jet boat off into the water than haul it onto the truck at the base with its 44-gallon drums full of extra fuel. The truck then headed quickly back across the Thai border and onto the hard black top surface of the road leading back to base. It was now time for the jet boat to venture north upriver some distance and ascertain what cover or exposure they would have to encounter in order to penetrate up to the lake as far as those ships had gone.

Back at the base, two of their team (pilot and observer) took off in the Cub at sundown/dusk with instructions to navigate up and over the Cambodian harbour using visual observation points such as villages and fishing boat lights while looking for any larger vessels or alternate ports upriver. They could cover over 150 miles before turning back. Their chart markings would be useful for adding to their marine charts for the jet boats to follow.

Chapter 4

Thailand Base Exposed

Their contact in Thailand, the DIO, the Australian Consulate Official with code name verified, was contacted and they drove up to Sattahip. After exchanging code words, they were handed a copy of a composite topographical chart showing the locations and photos of prospective targets. After the base team had briefed them the DIO men headed out of the gates of the base and disappeared.

In the meantime, the team checked out the remaining jet boat, Piper aircraft and stores in advance of receiving anticipated mobilisation orders.

On the following day Spider received a phone call asking him to come for lunch in Pattaya City at a beachside cafe to discuss 'oil project contracts'. The time and place were agreed and he had one of his key SAS men, Brute, go off base, hire a car locally for cash and then drive him down to Pattaya City, while playing bodyguard just in case that was needed. Both of them were armed with US Army .45 automatic pistols and spare magazines as Spider had the feeling that the Thais or other country agencies were watching them and may pull a fast one – just a hunch!

The short 30km drive from Sattahip base along the coast road to Pattaya City was uneventful and it appeared that they were not tailed. Their rendezvous was specifically designated to be a steak bar on the street parallel with the beach. It was an open-air location with a number of tourists and locals wandering around close by. Not the place for a confidential chat with the DIO man but they had to assume that their masters knew best.

Pattaya City had been a sleepy little fishing village until mid-1959, when several truckloads of United States Marines arrived from bases in Bangkok and many located near the Thai–Lao border for a week's R&R. Almost overnight beach bars and restaurants opened alongside full-body massage parlours. Word spread rapidly through the jungle telegraph and hundreds of poverty-stricken young Thai beauties from the Isan district of north-eastern Thailand arrived in Pattaya City to entertain the military men and relieve them of their cash. From that year forth the village continued to grow and supply entertainment facilities to satisfy all the wants and needs of its visitors.

'Brute,' Spider spoke, 'as we are impersonating oil patch rig pigs it's better we don't address each other with any military rank.'

'Understood major, Oops, just joking, ha, ha, ha. Have you ever worked on the rigs Spider?

'No, you?'

'Yep, I was a ruff-neck for a couple of months some years back in western Queensland, it's hard fucking Yaka. So where do you call home Spider?'

'Right now, Melbourne, although I am originally from Perth with a couple of years in South Australia. My parents split up before I was born. Over the years my mother bounced me around foster care establishments, some of which I ran away from. Where do you call home Brute?'

'South-eastern Queensland. Born and raised a country boy on a wheat farm.'

'What made you join the army?'

'Well, something like you Spider. My childhood was filled with drunken family violence and abuse that got me in a little home town jam. The magistrate gave me a choice, jail or Vietnam, so here I am. So far so good. You married Spider?'

'Nope. You?'

'Not yet but I do know a couple of strong farm girl beauties that sure could rope me.'

'I bet you do.'

They ordered a light lunch of green mango salad and a beer at the counter, paid for with local currency, then sat back like the other tourists and began waiting. Their meals arrived promptly but no DIO man.

'Ya know Brute, I am beginning to think this little adventure is turning into a bit of a cluster fuck.'

'That's about what it looks like me old mate.'

They spent a couple of hours just sitting there and the beers turning flat and warm. They never were intended to be drunk as no alcohol while on duty was the rule of the day.

'Come on Brute, this is a waste of fucking time.'

'I hear ya.'

They headed back to the car and climbed in ready to head back to base with Spider at the wheel, this time with Brute riding shotgun beside him with the .45 on his lap under a paper napkin from lunch.

A European man wearing casual shorts, baseball cap, bright-coloured T-shirt and riding a black motor scooter came alongside next to Spider and tapped on the driver's window, which was by now wound halfway down to let out the hot air that stifled the interior while the air conditioning caught up. The rider said nothing and shoved an envelope through the window opening and took off.

Brute had cocked his weapon ready for action and said 'That is one lucky bastard. He was just seconds away from getting his fucking head blown off'.

'Yea, I was thinking the same fucking thing.'

Actually, the first thing that crossed Spider's mind was 'Is it a bomb?', but, to his relief it was too flat and too small, so they sat there before driving off and opened it. Inside was a short note stating the following:

They had to prepare a detailed tender proposal within seven days for the intended oil and gas contract mobilisation.

A code number was provided for verification of the message.

They both understood the intent and reality of the instructions; 'mobilisation' was the key word. They headed directly back toward the base, only this time they noticed a motorbike sitting back about 100 yards. Every time they stopped in traffic, he stopped, which is unusual as in Thailand the motor scooters and bikes just cut through. Was he a cop or from one of the Thai or other external services?

'We are being tailed Brute; I am going to pull into the next petrol pump.'

'Roger that.'

They pulled into the next petrol station with a refreshment stall to see if he would follow them in. He did. Spider pulled the pistol tucked uncomfortably in his belt and placed it in his pants pocket, firmly gripped in his hand in case it was needed in a hurry. Brute placed his pistol in his belt behind his back and kept his hands on his hips.

The rider got off his motorbike and wandered over to the food stall as if interested. Spider walked right up to him while Brute stepped close behind him, close enough for the rider to feel Brute's breath on the back of his neck. It was evident to the rider that he had just been sucker-punched by thinking they went in for petrol or food and were now standing up close and personal to him. If he did have a weapon, he couldn't grab it or they would have blocked him or worse.

Without a word Spider nodded his head toward the toilet block at the rear of the petrol station. The rider looked down at Spider's hand in his pocket and saw the outline of the pistol, then looked at Brute, who wasn't smiling, and thought better of making a run for it. Behind the toilet block were full smelly rubbish bins and that is where the rider landed on his arse. They frisked him briskly and removed a loaded revolver and some Thai identification cards, which Spider pocketed.

One of them showed a picture of an army officer in uniform but the details were in Thai or Cambodian and they would have to get them translated later. He wasn't offering any explanation in English as to why he was following them, so they took the motorbike keys off him and tossed them onto the toilet roof.

With no further need for his company, they left the surprised and pissed-off Asian guy sitting in a pile of smelly garbage for his trouble. Spider wondered how he was going to explain to whomever sent him after them in the first place.

This type of business can create deviations into places that one should not go, so they got into the car and drove off in a different direction to where they were headed.

Four plus hours later via back roads, they were back in the outskirts of Pattaya City. In a backpacker hotel lobby, Spider phoned the base and arranged for one of the men to get some transport to pick them up at the beach tonight as they could make it in a couple of hours and it would be dark by then. Corporal Rat was able to leave the base and walk down to the local garage and rent a fruit van off a stall owner. A bit on the rough side but the ride back to the garage and walk back into the base was refreshing. No tail on them this time. They left the car parked and locked near the backpacker hotel and Brute would pick it up the following day.

As the motorbike rider may have their hire car number plates memorised, Spider thought it best for Brute to return the car a week later, with all fingerprints wiped clean and an explanation that it had been stolen but now recovered and then pay off the owner for their trouble. The owner told Brute he had been approached by some Asian men looking for the car several days ago, but he didn't know who they were and they wouldn't identify themselves.

They figured it was most likely Thai secret police checking up on Farangs, the Thai slang for white western visitors. However, they were concerned that the base phone line may have been tapped, perhaps their landlords at the marine base may be eavesdropping, or the Australian Consulate staff movements may be monitored and compromised. Possibly a combination of all possibilities was in play, or it was totally paranoia! Nonetheless, additional cautions were taken.

They would have to secure the DIO contacts:

- Validate the letter instructions using the HF radio phone to DIO Australia.
- Have DIO check on what happened in Pattaya City.
- Inform them of their close encounter with the tail and people looking for the hire car.
- Cut off all contacts with Embassy and DIO in Thailand.
- No drives off base without approval.

Bloody wonderful situation, very poor envelope transfer and no wonder their meeting was cancelled. It's more likely that they might also be exposed if that rider was followed. Very clumsy to have been brought up here to be spotted. It would have been more sensible for them to miss the contact, simply drive back to base and receive a HF radio phone call later. Spider's mind turned to the possibility that their set-up in the Sattahip hangar may be compromised, so on return his orders were:

- All meetings and assessments will be carried out on board the C-130 (the bird).
- All documents and photo compilations will remain on board the bird as well as keeping it bottled up and locked down (that means tight as a fish's arse).
- There will be a team on base at all times to keep the base secure and to monitor the HF radio phone.
- All two-way radio frequencies will be changed daily as well as call signs. Radio phone/fax messages only.
- All charts will be divided up into brand new geodetic grids set at an angle rather than north–south.
- Each new grid square will be given a name.
- Only two copies of the new chart layouts will be kept:
  - The master chart will be stored on board the bird.
  - The in-field team will keep the other copy.

If they didn't have the feeling that they were at war, they definitely did now – from all sides. From now on all of them had a touch of paranoia and one could feel it palpably. Nevertheless, the job must go forward and, for the present time, their original orders would stand until otherwise amended by the DIO. Spider made it very clear that any messing around with little brown ladies was now a very serious offence.

All personnel *will* stay inside the wire!

Chapter 5

Chas River Cambodia Mission

Spider and the Boat Crew

Spider hooked up with the jet boat crew back on the Chas River. The journey north turned out to be one way due to the shallow and narrow bends with inhabited clearings of one or more grass huts sighted as they passed by cautiously from time to time. There were no close encounters with local fishing boats during the day or night, just a few log canoes.

There was good visibility without the rain but the crew needed to commit to taking cover somewhere along the river shoreline to take observations during the coming daylight hours, as they were getting close to the city of Battambang to their west and the east–west highway bridge that they had to pass under.

Moving away from clearings and huts with lights, they were traversing on what appeared to be a regularly used channel. Moving across to the opposite shoreline that appeared to be vacant without lights and no boats, hoping the jet boat could push them up into the mangroves and overhanging vegetation, they headed slowly but directly into the unknown.

Having run aground several times on the mud and grounded debris that was always present floating out of the river towards the lake, the boat made its way up a narrow natural opening between the outcrops of mangroves. There was barely enough space to turn the boat around and the engine was raised to a roar several times to skid it around while spraying mud and water into the air and up onto the nearby banks.

The engine was shut down after overheating and everyone discussed the best way to camouflage the boat for the coming daylight. No use getting off and wading around in the pitch black, so the M60 machine gun was moved onto the forward hatch (a just-in-case measure) and the crew set up an ambush position with their rifles pointed out to each side and the other M60 facing out the back.

As night turned slowly into dawn, half of the crew slid off the boat railings and into the thick mud, heaving their boots up and forward until within the mangroves. There was a camouflage net on board the boat, so those remaining behind began to spread it over the upper structure while the shore party used machetes to hack off copious lengths of palm fronds and large lily leaves until the boat resembled a jungle florist shop of sorts.

This would in time become the first of several forward observation posts. From this initial vantage point on the Cas River, about 10 miles upstream from the bridge and city ahead, everyone could sit and watch through the foliage all number of boat movements.

The current from the river washed the sides of the jet boat gun platform and the prevailing sea breeze kept the mosquitoes down to almost bearable. The rations would sustain them for at least one more week. Next time it was agreed they would bring some hand fishing gear as there were schools of fish all around them. Raw fish – hmm.

Spider kept up the daily radio com with the Sattahip base team members, who continued their flights to cover the harbour movements then headed north again out over Cambodia towards the boat's position but not over it. Their observations and photos would be cross-matched with the boat crews once they were all back on base.

At the end of the week the Cub flights had taken photos of a number of middle-sized cargo boats heading up and down the mouth of the Chas River into Lake Tonlé Sap. The base team would cross-check the aerial photos and chart updates, giving them a more detailed picture than expected. The aerial shots had picked up clusters of medium-sized cargo boats similar to the ones they had spotted on the river but were now on the lake. Even with the ships under camouflage nettings they could pick out the outline of either Russian or Chinese shallow-draught coastal trader ships possibly bringing in military ordnance in support of the Viet Cong.

Caribou Arrival at Sattahip

A Caribou twin piston-engine STOL aircraft arrived at the Sattahip base from Darwin as planned, but weeks late. It had been intended to support regional low-level observation and remote landing area check flights. The C-130 aircraft they used for Darwin to Sattahip and return resupply flights was not as nimble and required an extra 1,000 yards of runway.

The C-130 would remain at the base ready to continue the long-distance shuttle of the SAS soldiers and cargoes to and from Darwin as well as being used by Spider as a secure office and communications centre while on the ground at Sattahip. The two-man Cub aircraft were good low-level spotter aircraft but did not have the required range or carrying capacity for platoon-level incursions into Cambodia, so the Caribou was the perfect fit.

Time was now of the essence, so Spider set up a schedule of four-man team ingress drop-off flights by Caribou that would also carry out photo reconnaissance, with, where possible, visual observations covering the river deltas feeding Lake Tonlé Sap in the centre of Cambodia. The jet boat was on its way cautiously downriver, making slow progress past the city of Battambang to its west side and, so far, safely and unchallenged. It passed under the east–west highway bridge, the main obstacle before entering Lake Tonlé Sap and hopefully the tributaries of the Mekong Delta where larger ship targets would likely enter.

The alternate route would be by air and foot, entering from the western side of Cambodia and using the easternmost remote unmapped airstrips and route marching through inhabited jungle. Parachuting in had been ruled out as landing into jungle canopies was more likely to cause serious injuries with no way of extracting the casualties.

Day after day for a month the team developed the high-level photos that ultimately uncovered targets identified by spotting the telltale small cargo boat clusters heading into the lake from the Mekong Delta. Even if they couldn't see the ships clearly, there must be a supply base in those locations. This new intelligence data was sent off to the DIO in Saigon. It was essential for the team to get moving on what appeared to be the larger targets. If there was an ammo dump down there, the US may be able to provide an air strike. If they couldn't enter far into Cambodia, then the team was the closest asset to interdict.

Landing Zones – Cambodia

The Americans had admitted to the DIO about running covert cargo flights from Saigon into Laos, north Cambodia and Burma, utilising Air America, where rough landing areas were hewn out of the jungle, most likely by drug lords. Commander Coen had some way 'encouraged the Yanks' to divulge their high-level photos and topographical maps with precise co-ordinates of their unofficial landing areas in Cambodia, just in case Spider needed to use any of them for dropping off the teams for on-foot surveillance missions.

The Piper aircraft were too small to carry more than a pilot and observer sitting one behind the other and had limited range for embarking on these flights, so the Caribou was prepared for this purpose as it had the range and capacity needed. That meant fitting M60 machine guns on both sides of the hull, waist guns, and stripping out any extraneous equipment to keep it as light as possible. The Americans were also using Caribou as well as other twin-engine aircraft for landing in these airstrips. So far, the North Vietnamese and Chinese had not sent their interceptor aircraft into these areas but there were no guarantees that they would not do so. That is one reason that all flights would have to be low, tree hopping and valley hugging as far as possible to avoid ground and air detection.

Within a day the Caribou on the first mission taxied out with the following crew on board:

- Pilot in command – David (Davy Jones) Henderson
- Co-pilot – Dennis (Wheels) Wheeler
- Waist gunner – weapons specialist-gunner Brute, who hated flying but was a good shot with any firearm you gave him and even better with an M60 machine gun.

At this point, there was only enough time to install the portside M60 machine gun mounting, which left a gaping hole in the fuselage. If this flight encountered any problems with the single gun installation, they would have to can it and revert to status quo on return.

From the hangar Spider watched this bird's navigation lights and the glare on the ground of the powerful landing lights that illuminated the taxiway and orientated it slowly to where it swung sharply onto the end of the runway facing into the light morning warm breeze.

It revved up its two powerful piston engines with brakes full on and then lurched forward as if by sling shot and sped down the unlit Sattahip runway.

It took off at dawn with barely enough visibility and climbed steeply over the water of the Gulf of Thailand in a broad left-hand climbing circle until it had reached 18,000ft and levelled off pointing back north toward the coast.

The flight path took it north along the Thai–Cambodia border until the main highway linking both countries was sighted. The pilot then eased the propeller pitch back to descend slowly at about 1,000ft per minute, bringing the aircraft low enough to be below a regular airline route. It then accelerated to 200 knots after arriving at 1,000ft above the terrain to lose any radar tracking and then manually navigated between the mountain range that extended east to west from Thailand behind and Cambodia straight ahead.

The target airstrip in Cambodia was located directly east some 200km across the border.

The pilot had previous history of flying in the mountain airstrips of Papua and Irian Jaya. With visual navigation required, all eyes focused on reaching and crossing two major rivers, then staring at the maps and charts to locate the hill top airstrip. It was a pretty bumpy ride with random up and down drafts causing the bird to buck and sink.

Brute puked several times out of the opening and left a wet streak down the hull without once letting go of the M60. The pilot and co-pilot were enjoying the unrestricted flying with its twists and turns, pulling up hard after making a turn into a dead-end valley, missing the trees by a few yards and diving down the other side.

Levelling out and easing the speed to 175 knots, the pilots scanned every hill top in the vicinity. The bird circled, then did a figure eight until the short narrow airstrip was located. The crew, now on full alert, surveyed the jungles and tracks in the neighbourhood of the airstrip for signs of life, buildings, vehicles, wind sock, etc.

Apart from the debris of an apparent old air crash at one end of the airstrip, the tracks left the open field and disappeared into the jungle. The Caribou was lined up on approach to land on the gravel runway and buzzed the airfield once to check its length and condition to land. The runway was wide enough and the landing would be up hill, which would be good for stopping before the end and on take-off would help to speed up the departure roll.

Seat belts tightened, all the crew held their breath as the pilot committed to the landing. The gusts of wind from the valley below caused the bird to buck and yaw as the airspeed slowed to 120 knots. The nose now hid the start of the runway but the wheels telegraphed the landing by shuddering and bumping, then the right wheel came off the ground and returned as the pilot yanked the yoke to the right.

The Caribou lost its speed as the nose wheel settled and brakes were applied on and off until the end of the runway was reached and the pitch of the engines lowered until the propellers were feathered. The bird was then roughly swung 180 degrees to face the runway using one engine and one brake. The nose bounced up and down, then settled. Both engines were shut down and Brute was ordered to lower the tail ramp. It was time to go for a reconnaissance to check out the runway, the jungle bordering the field, and browse the remains of the old crashed Beechcraft King Air aircraft.

Brute carried the M60 over his shoulder everywhere he went, expecting an ambush or something to occur any minute. The two pilots were more interested in the condition of the runway as tropical rains could render it unusable and it was a long way to walk home from here. The good thing to observe was that a lot of gravel had been embedded into the muddy under-soil by a number of take-offs and landings and, due to the downward slope, the water had not pooled to loosen the surface.

Checking out the crashed plane, the pilots found that it had severely overrun on landing and buried its nose into the jungle undergrowth. The cockpit was smashed in, the left wing ripped off and the undercarriage flattened. It had been stripped of its instruments and radios and it now appeared to being used as a store or observation facility by someone as it was generally clean inside, half of the seats were still in place, the fuselage door was functional, and the broken cockpit and its windscreen were covered with canvas and palm fronds. Obviously, someone had been here locally to meet the incoming flights. The crew didn't want or need the same attention. Time to start up and skedaddle out of there before the local welcoming party came and began asking questions or worse.

The engines were spun up one at a time and, with the crew in their designated positions, the engines roared at high pitch before the brakes were released. Jerking forward as if its tail was whipped, the Caribou surged forward with dirt and debris raising a cloud behind and the rough gravel threatening to break the undercarriage. The bird lurched into the air at a sharp nose-up angle, just like it was designed to do.

It flew over the edge of the hill causing it to belly lunge downward momentarily and giving everyone on board a weightless feeling until the nose again pointed up and over the coming hills. The pilot eased the bird's nose down and turned it level in a banking manoeuvre with full power to sustain altitude, then swooped into the next valley and up and over the blind end. They returned on the same track as on the inbound run. If they were spotted arriving, then it's likely they would encounter some opposition on the way out. The pilot spoke through the intercom.

'Keep that M60 cocked and loaded Brute, we may get company.'

Chapter 6

Pincer Movement on Air, Land and Sea

Uneventful as the exploratory flight may have been, the experience and the accuracy of the airfield location gave the team a good feeling of confidence to progress their operation even further. Spider planned to deploy the teams at several sites for foot slogging down to the major rivers to take observations and, if possible, join up with the jet boat that had almost reached Lake Tonlé Sap.

Jointly, by air and water, they should be able to identify targets or clear the location all the way across to Lake Tonlé Sap in the middle of Cambodia that, further south-east, linked up with the Mekong Delta in Vietnam, which was fed by a number of other smaller tributaries downriver.

So far, the second jet boat patrolling the southern coast of Cambodia had not identified any worthy targets making their way into or out of the harbour down in the Gulf of Thailand. There were no orders for crossing into South Vietnam and up into the outlet of the Mekong Delta into the Gulf of Thailand. This was US Forces-controlled territory and crossing swords with them could be fatal since, for all intents and purposes, they didn't exist. Their patch was restricted to Cambodia. At least for the time being!

Spider edited the topographical charts with the airstrips marked and asked the team to suggest pet names for all six of them. Typically, the men came up with names of animals, Australian towns, football teams, even golf courses. All were worthy of consideration and better than site A-B-C or 1-2-3. They settled on Melbourne Australian Rules football team names. Locations around them related to areas or positions related to the game such as full forward, centre bounce, half back and so on and included the field being 'goal post'. This was a bit tough on the Queenslanders, who considered Aussie Rules as aerial ping-pong; their game was rugby league but they accepted it all in good-hearted fun.

The next Caribou flight from the base flew north-east into Cambodia and crossed the highway between Battambang and Moung Ruessei, bringing it about 20 miles east and parallel with the Chas River. This flight was heading for one of the unmarked airstrips called 'Geelong Football Club' and had the map and chart co-ordinates directly ahead.

With head pilot David Dash Jones at the controls, they left the base flying at 18,000ft along the Thai coast and then turned abruptly left on a northerly course. They descended rapidly to 1,000ft when they passed over the Cambodian coast and flew inland to the beginning of the Chas River where the jet boat had been launched two weeks earlier. The aircraft continued by circuitously skirting hills and entering valleys, both leaving and returning onto course. Crossing the highway and railway line gave them a firm visual cross-check with their maps and charts.

It appears that the locals below didn't know what this aircraft was about or who it belonged to and showed little if no interest.

The Americans had used the Geelong Football Club airstrip a number of times and reported the local indigenous villagers living below the airstrip as friendlies, so long as gifts were delivered such as T-shirts, building tools, cigarettes and alcohol. There was no trouble buying all of this stuff cheap from the Sattahip town markets. The Caribou carried about half a ton of this on a pallet for the villagers to keep them happy as they needed to have a friendly place to land if required.

Flying over the airstrip at 500ft, a wind sock was sighted laying limp and indicating little or no breeze on approach. The aircraft completed its circuit around the airfield before lining up at about 300ft above an adjacent hill and committing to a direct approach with its wings tilting and levelling from up and down drafts, lowering full flaps and undercarriage, airspeed dropping and nose pointed just above the edge of the hand-hewn airstrip. On crossing the threshold, the wheels touched terra firma and propellers were set to neutral as the nose dropped. A pause, then reverse pitch was set on the propellers as the nose wheel hit the gravel. Carefully putting the brakes on while balancing the pitch of the propellers, the aircraft stabilised into a straight line down the middle of the runway, came to a slow roll and turned abruptly about face at the opposite end of the runway.

'Phew, that was an interesting landing,' the co-pilot Mike 'Macka' McKey murmured as he set about shutting down the starboard engine while idling the port side engine as they didn't intend to stay here any longer than necessary.

The six SAS soldiers in the back sat facing each other released their seat belts and were up on their feet hoisting their backpacks on and slinging their weapons as soon as the plane had begun to about-turn. The rear ramp was already on its way down, stopping about a metre above the dust and gravel below. The first order of the day was to get all of the soldiers off and into the jungle with their heavy packs, which included ammunition, explosives and extra rations for linking up with the jet boat and crew about 20km to the west of the airstrip. Better to be out of sight of the villagers.

A number of locals appeared out of the jungle after carefully satisfying themselves that their presence would be welcome. The pilots and two support crew, SAS soldiers in civilian attire, dropped down from the rear ramp and waved to the villagers. The crate of goodies was unceremoniously shoved out the back of the ramp and thumped onto the ground, loosening the contents for the villagers to grab.

There were smiles and hoots of joy just like it was Christmas. More villagers appeared out of the jungle, this time with women and children in tow.

It took the locals about thirty minutes to settle down and cart off everything, leaving only the crate and strappings. Apparently, they were used to this routine and did not hang about near the aircraft. This was the signal to hoist up the pallet and strapping, climb aboard, and close the ramp ready for take-off.

The still idling port engine's pitch changed as it was throttled up with the propeller still at neutral, and then the starboard engine was started, matching the port engine revs.

Both engines roared as the propellers' pitch increased with the wheel brakes full on. After brake release and take-off roll the Caribou's nose rose sharply and lifted off the ground at a steep angle as it crossed over the adjacent hill at 850ft, after which it levelled off to resume the return circuitous course south-west and back to Sattahip.

It did a sharp right turn coming off the Gulf of Thailand waters and lined up with the Sattahip runway as dusk settled. Then the airstrip would become silent and darkened once more.

Run Through the Jungle

Back in the jungle the SAS soldiers, with Sergeant Brute on point, were making their way west toward the jet boat location. They stopped at the halfway point 10 miles from the airstrip and about 10 miles from the Chas River. Brute sent a message on the HF radio phone with their current location and requested a map link-up point reference to the jet boat on the Chas River. Soon after, the vessel's skipper returned with co-ordinates and advised that the area was hot with onshore and on-water locals moving about. Hence the link up may move or require the onshore team to swim over to the boat.

With co-ordinates set on the onshore team's map, they moved stealthily forward in single file, Brute still on point until it became too dark to continue while loaded up with the heavy packs. At this rate they could easily stumble upon some locals, step on a snake, or onto a booby trap.

It was agreed that Sergeant Brute and Corporal Al Stocky Canham would move forward to rendezvous with the vessel while the others remained in hiding.

This way there would be some observations of the intensity of local movements on shore near where the boat had given its position. About midnight, the two

SAS warriors had come close enough to sight the river from a break in the jungle foliage on a hilltop above it.

There were roads and pathways all over the place. No doubt it was a busy place during the day but at present it was reasonably quiet as the locals had likely bedded down for the night. They could smell smoke in the wind from cooking fires that wafted over the settlements and through the thick jungle foliage.

The two soldiers rested for a while and drank from their water canteens and chewed on some power chocolate bars.

'Where's home for you Brute?' Stocky asked.

'Queensland mate. You?'

'Sydney. Were you conscripted or did you volunteer?'

'No mate, the fucking chief magistrate gave me a choice, army or jail. It wasn't a hard choice.'

'I can understand that.'

'What about you corporal?'

'I volunteered; my dad was in the Royal Navy during World War Two, Special Boats. Actually, he never spoke of it much but I always I thought I would like to, you know, kinda follow in his footsteps.'

'Good for you mate. Well, I guess it's time we made a move. I'll hang around here and keep an eye on this shit. You head back and round up the team.'

'Yes sergeant.'

Brute remained in place monitoring movements while Corporal Stocky returned, leaving his backpack so he could move faster while returning to the waiting team.

Two hours later Stocky returned with the team using the previously sighted trail. They all assembled on the hill top, where they rested and took on board some food and water. Brute had observed and picked out a trail to follow down to the water that had piles of jungle debris washed down from upriver that could be a good spot to link up with the jet boat and not very far from the position previously radioed to them. The skipper of the boat was sent a new message giving ETA by HF radio phone and position of the debris.

The skipper responded with: 'Go-go-go.'

Slithering down the side of the hill was easier than going up; the onshore team arrived early at the pile of debris and were faced with a floating and tangled mass of tree trunks, palm fronds and roots with everything else in between them. With heavy packs, this was going to be a serious problem to cross over.

It was decided to look for a break in the unruly mass and take to the water to meet the vessel. A message was sent for a water pickup.

The skipper replied with 'Gotcha Mate'.

Although heavy, the backpacks were waterproof and with a little luck they would float. Only one way to find out; the first backpacks were slid into the murky water. They didn't sink but the weight kept them low in the water.

All of the onshore team now entered the water and stayed close as they shoved bracken out of the way and slid over submerged logs until they were out on the edge of the smelly mass of rotten debris.

True to form, the jet boat idled forward and along the edge of the debris field. Spotted by the onshore team, it appeared as a dark shadow on the water.

The team was energised and begin to press forward away from the debris field. The vessel came alongside the now stationary bobbing heads in the water and began hauling in the backpacks and then the men. There was no time for social chatter so the new arrivals slumped down on the deck while the boat crew turned the boat around in order to head for a hide they had been moored in for the last few days without being spotted.

By morning the newcomers had had a chance to slip over the side of the boat fully clothed and wash off the smelly sludge that clung to them. This was a perfect observation point and the jet boat camouflage blended into the surroundings.

The shallow water of the mangroves and dense overhanging jungle growth kept prying eyes away. The Coxswain, Phil 'Flipper' Fleckney, sent a HF radio phone message back to Spider at Sattahip base advising 'Rendezvous Complete'.

The message was immediately forwarded to DIO Commander Coen requesting instructions. Within two hours, DIO responded with orders regarding several camouflaged small ships that the most recent reconnaissance photos had highlighted:

> Obtain onshore intel near the identified ships
> SITREP Report ASAP

This may take some time as the ships were on the other side of the lake and they couldn't just motor over there and climb onto the jetty with a camera and clipboard to take notes. Nor did they have time to hoof it all the way around while trying not to get caught in the process. Shit, this was a real challenge. Spider sent a message to the jet boat team requesting their solution. Half an hour later he received the following message:

> Will leave all but two on the boat and make our way across at beginning of dusk until dark.

> If not intercepted and lake edge clear, one man will make shore within a mile of target A.

Boat will likely stand off 100 yards and wait until dawn if no observer.

Will return following dusk to repeat pickup once only (assume busted).

Onshore observer to move in, ID cargo and ship markings, then return to boat.

Boat will return to team for HQ instructions.

He then forwarded this message and its implications to DIO for approval, and received an immediate response:

Mission imperative – Go
Risks understood
Recommend you have egress plan for team to dump and run for flight out

Spider forwarded this message unedited to the team at the boat and got the response he had expected:

Understood – already on our way

The rest of the team was now waiting with all of their kit in the mangrove hide just above the high-water line. They waited and watched as a number of small and large boats passed by oblivious of the well-armed SAS watching them ready to fight or flee their position.

No point in getting into a fight that would just screw the entire mission.

Further back in the mangroves, under the guidance of Corporal Stocky they joined ponchos together with the trusty string that should by now be army issue and using bracken and palm fronds built an A frame to keep out the rain. Also, an improvised latrine was set 5 yards downstream. Shifts were set up every two hours during the day, changing to hourly during the night as one's eyes were strained trying to see movements in the darkened waters. Nerves were also constantly stressed as there were all sorts of noises being heard incessantly. Everyone was a bit jumpy.

The jet boat camouflaged as a small cargo carrier had worked its way slowly across the lake, with its gyrocompass waypoint being set towards the target, while the crew seemed to have sighted a couple of half-sunken boat and barges in the shallows.

Brute's Onshore Sortie

A good place to stand offshore was within 10 yards of the shoreline on the leeward side of a rusty barge hull protruding some 3 yards above the water on its high side with the other side submerged. They looped a single line to the rusty exposed bollard on the hulk, then waited for ten minutes to hear if anyone was close by. With no movement sounds heard from ashore, Coxswain Flipper Fleckney helped Brute slide silently into the water unarmed apart from a bayonet, camera, sketch pad, and a pencil in a waterproof folder. Rations were a plastic bottle of water, chocolate bar, and dry, hard dog biscuits.

Brute's shadowy figure reached the beach and, hunched over, he disappeared from Flipper's view as he ingressed silently into the thin jungle reed edge.

Using his wrist compass as close to his face as he could, as carefully and stealthily as possible he moved through the ever-thinning jungle until there were only sporadically spaced out palm trees. He moved from tree to tree, expecting at any moment to encounter a local villager or barking dog.

Ahead he could make out a compound fence of rusted chain link wire. There were a number of sagging breaks in the mesh, and he passed through without crouching. The glowing cigarette of a security guard in a guard house about 10 yards above the ground caused him to stop and wonder where the other guards were placed.

He stood frozen for about fifteen minutes, sensing in every direction. Then someone began talking out loud some 30 yards ahead and away from the water's edge. Apparently, they weren't expecting visitors so he diverted his direction further back inshore and behind the voices.

Cover became sparse and in front was a road.

To cross over or not to cross over was the question?

Fuck it, he would just have to take a chance. Without faltering, he just stood up and walked out into the open and crossed over to the other side where there was light and he could now see the outlines of people working by torch light. He guessed he was lucky no one saw him or, if they did, they would probably think he was one of them.

Just what the fuck are they working on? he wondered.

He lowered his frame and moved from cover to opportune cover until arriving at a camouflage-netted covered store of some sort.

Not much use going back and tell them that he saw a store without finding out what was in it he figured.

He knelt on one knee, got out his sketch pad and drew a mud map of the shoreline, the rusty fence he had passed through, the road he had just crossed, and the camouflaged store location and port area. Plus, he added a north–south line using his compass for alignment. If he couldn't get any more detail, this would have to suffice if he had to bug out in a hurry.

There was no fencing ahead of him to segregate the store and hinder his progress, but it was highly likely some guards might be roaming about. Better to hang loose for a while and wait and see if anyone patrolled past. He sat among several low bushes for cover, then watched and waited. One armed guard wandered by within a few yards, more intent on lighting his cigarette than on his colleagues with the torches. It was close to midnight and the work crew began to knock off and follow the guard away towards the port area. He had to decide whether to follow them or check out what was in the store.

The store option won as he didn't want to follow these guys home if that's where they were going at this hour. Scurrying low across the now vacant store area, he moved between large stacks of wooden boxes. It was darker in there than outside and he had no torch anyway. Time to be creative: he heaved at the top edge of one box with his bayonet as a crowbar but it was too well nailed down. More boxes, the same outcome.

Continuing to move towards the back of the store, he was startled by a flashlight turning on at the front. Shit, that guard or one of his mates is patrolling in here. Silently, he climbed on top of a stack of boxes and laid flat.

The guard walked right past the base of the same stack without pausing. Satisfied that he had completed his patrol, the guard returned outside in the direction of the earlier workers.

Heading back towards the front of the store, Brute passed an open top crate and felt inside: RPG launchers, possibly Russian. He took one out and headed out by the same route as he had entered. Pausing at a clump of bushes in case he was spotted, he listened for a few minutes. Nothing. He decided to move to the hole in the rusty chain mesh fence. So far so good, he caught his breath and felt his heart racing – not good for a fit man. Anxiety had crept into his physique and needed to be expelled immediately. Taking several deep breaths and a drink of water from his plastic bottle, and half of the chocolate bar for a sugar hit, he trudged on, heading among the palm trees and thickening jungle growth and the boat.

Having reached the shoreline with the barge hulk protruding out of the water, he anticipated being able to see the boat. It wasn't there – gone. Fuck, fuck!

Thirty minutes passed, his rations all gone, and then the burble of the jet boat engine got louder until its outline against the flickering lights from offshore boats became clearer.

With the RPG launcher slung over his shoulder, he entered the murky black water of the lake and frog-kicked his way out to the waiting boat. He hauled himself on board and cursed Flipper the skipper for leaving him.

Flipper turned the boat out and set it on course before responding.

'Sorry pal, a patrol boat was checking out the shoreline and was moving in my direction so I moved offshore until he had passed. Nothing was spotted by the patrol boat so he chugged on down the shoreline about a mile before turning about and patrolling the shoreline on his way back. The patrol boat wasn't in a hurry so no alarm was raised and I headed back here after they had left.'

'OK, I understand. Thanks mate, at least I can have a lift home.' Brute was smiling as he spoke. It was a huge feeling of relief being on board.

The boat maintained the same speed as other vessels out on the water, about 7 knots maximum. That way the patrol boat couldn't pick them out as a different blob on their radar. Travelling in an indirect course back to the other side of the lake, and with dawn coming soon to bring light onto the scene, the jet boat prodded its way into the mangroves using the gyrocompass that was accurate to within a metre or two.

Stuck and grounded, Flipper decided to wait for dawn to finish moving the boat under cover. As it was pretty muddy under the boat, there was no point in either of them trying to hoof it to the shoreline and meet up with the rest of the team, who had heard the boat trying to enter the hide.

By sun up, the jet boat had backed off and re-entered the hide successfully. Sharing the previous night's covert penetration onshore and discovery of the guarded camouflaged store by pure accident, the RPG launcher was displayed for inspection. It was Chinese and not Russian as first thought. There was not any real difference in the model, just in the supplier.

It could be assumed that the store was full of military ordnance of various types as the boxes were of various sizes. The second part of the equation was identifying the ship and that would have to be close up. As there was at least one patrol boat wandering about with a searchlight, the only other way to check the ship out was either onshore, where there were guards in at least one tower and some on foot patrol, or by going for a swim, as the jet boat would be spotted if it got too close.

Corporal Stocky Goes for a Swim

Stocky Canham was originally from London, and emigrated to Australia with his parents when he was 2 years old. He stood around 5ft 8in tall and was built like a brick shithouse, hence the nickname Stocky. He had participated in Olympic swimming trials for Australia.

That evening, with Flipper at the wheel, spotter Ash Hook Dale and the team's best swimmer, Stocky, the jet boat moved out of the hide and retraced the previous night's gyrocompass tracks. This time it stayed offshore about 1,000 yards up current from the ship, allowing Stocky to swim closer and drift down current, hopefully close enough to the ship to read the name. To aid himself, Stocky took along his waterproof backpack with trapped air in it (like an upside-down bucket). That way he could tip it over to sink it if a boat came close and then lift it above the water to let more air into it. There was also plenty of jungle debris floating in the water to hide a swimmer if needed.

Floating down and gauging his angle towards the ship, Stocky eventually came within 50 yards of where he could read the text on the hull, which was above what looked like Thai writing. He would have to try and remember the writing so he could sketch it back at the hide. Drifting past the ship's stern, more text indicated it was registered in Thailand. That was enough detail including the name in text. The boat was waiting by the sunken barge for Stocky to drift down to it but, the same as last night, the patrol boat turned up about 2 miles upstream.

Where the fuck is our man in the water?

Flipper didn't want to wait until the patrol boat arrived. He gunned the engine towards the ship.

'Stocky has got to be in a line between us and the ship – keep a watch for our man in the water Hook, I'm going looking for him.'

The current was stronger in the shallows near shore and Stocky had stopped swimming and was standing waist deep, whistling and waving at them. The jet boat pulled alongside the swimmer, who was dragged roughly over the gunwales and onto the deck.

'Fuck me, you blokes can be rough, but thanks anyway,' muttered Stocky as he began to shed his wet clothes and dry himself off.

The boat spun around and, instead of speeding off, to avoid radar picking them out from the usual vessels moving about the lake, they stayed at 7 knots all the way back to the hide. Meanwhile, Stocky sat inside the cabin and sketched the Thai script and stern identification marks of Thailand while his memory was fresh.

This intel along with Brute's sketched mud map were photographed and sent off to the DIO as soon as they arrived into Spider's hands.

The same boat problems were encountered as the previous evening, getting bogged and having to wriggle the vessel about for some time until they ultimately arrived into the safety of the hide. This time there was a message to send to base and anticipation as to what the orders would be tomorrow. Going in and out of the hide would soon attract unwanted attention, so future excursions would need to include looking for a new hide some miles away from this one. The hide set-up was dismantled in preparation for the move and loaded onto the boat.

Chapter 7

Spider's Logistic Concerns

Spider received the HF radio phone message when it beeped loudly in the belly of the C-130. He was almost ecstatic reading the details on the ship and the RPG, but it soon dawned on him that it was a Thai-registered ship and likely owned and crewed by Thais. Shit, the DIO must read this as the implications for the SAS team being in Thailand and spotting one of their own registered ships supplying Chinese military ordnance under the US noses up the Mekong Delta and through to Cambodia for transporting by land into Vietnam. This was more than serious, plus also complex to deal with politically.

The US military was aware that the Viet Cong had both Russian and Chinese military hardware as their troops had collected examples in the battlefield areas. There had been a surge in Viet Cong activities and the US and its coalition forces were copping a pasting. This was evidence of the Viet Cong being resupplied and that it could dare to expend equipment if it could be readily replaced. Stopping the movement of the cross-border supply of ordnance was germane to the mission in Cambodia.

The Yanks had suspected Cambodia was complicit but had no proof. The satellite photos were not clear enough to pinpoint the source of the ships and the location of port storage areas and ways and means of transporting away from the port.

The next message received from DIO was:

IMPERATIVE
Maintain reporting – all ships in the lake to be ID with port compass position, arrival and departure times.

On land tracing of transport routes required ASAP from Cambodia side of Vietnam border.

US advise they will have the Thai ship tailed when passing out of Mekong Delta.

US will provide ground/air support from South Vietnam border as needed.

Continue reports daily.

Spider got a bad feeling in his bones that the Thai Navy landlords at Sattahip may come knocking on his door very soon. It never happened, thank God, as he wouldn't have wanted to get into a shootout or have the team surrender, along with all of the aircraft. He never shared his thoughts with DIO as the Australian Government boffins would have got involved and security would have been blown.

Radical as it may sound, he had the Piper Cub aircraft wings removed and both loaded into a Caribou with as much fuel as it was safe to carry. All available men would also have to be used to guard the SAS base, carry out spotter flights using empty Caribou aircraft and tracking operations when the transport trails were spotted.

The general idea was to reduce asset exposure at the base and secondly deploy them on reconnaissance operations located at the unmapped airstrips where the first landings had occurred at Geelong Football Club and Collingwood. This was where gifts were handed out to the locals and where the crashed Beechcraft could be used as a store and office. They also planned on visiting a location further east toward the Vietnam border within Cambodia as no locals had turned up, so no interface and gifts were needed to keep them on their side.

Spider decided to retain the one jet boat for tracking the Thai ship if it headed up to Thailand or was called on for other reconnoitring in the Gulf of Thailand. It was up to the US if the Thai ship headed toward China. If it was spotted in the Gulf of Thailand, they would track it to its base port. That just left some bits and pieces of kit in the hangar along with the C-130.

Spider decided to stay put along with a co-pilot and a crewman to act as security guard, HF radio phone monitor and loadmaster when and if they abandoned the base.

This was also the home base for the two Caribou and the jet boat deployed in the Gulf of Thailand waters, and had to be retained as long as possible. Spider thought the truck and Piper aircraft may have to be given up as disposable assets in the long run.

Transport of Munitions to Viet Cong

The SAS team assembled on the edge of the lake had to split up, with two men staying with the jet boat to continue observations on ship unloading movements while the rest were dropped off on the opposite shore near the sunken barge to carry out observations overnight.

The wrap-up of what was going on at the warehouse was that the ships had been observed unloading the armaments at the dock and moving them into the warehouse Brute had discovered. They later distributed the elements of the cargo onto large wooden fishing boats for returning down Lake Tonlé Sap, where the team lost them.

A combination of the C-130 high-level flights, local Cambodian agents in Phnom Penh City and US satellite intelligence images were used to pick up the transport trail using the SAS photographs of the wooden boats.

These boats navigated past Phnom Penh City unchecked, then into the nearby Mekong Delta north against the current to offload at Kratie City. Their cargo was then taken by road transport east toward Snoul village, where the entire convoy then disappeared into the jungle.

Obviously, those running the convoy intended to camouflage the trails used for moving the munitions and weapons over to the South Vietnam border, where they would likely offload them to the Viet Cong at several secret locations that would have to be found.

The US Air Force had previously dealt with some of the cross-border transport trails using carpet bombing just inside the Vietnam border and helicopter gunships for cross-border raids. These were new trails that had to be identified and targeted likewise.

The job was by no means finished after discovering the whereabouts of the on-water routes. The head of the snake needed to be dealt a blow in Cambodia. To disrupt the delivery of munitions into Lake Tonlé Sap, orders were received to destroy several storage warehouses and limpet mine which is a naval mine attached to a target with magnets to the hulls of any Russian-or-Chinese-marked ships, including larger Cambodian wooden fishing boats.

Politically, this was a warning shot from a safe distance from the coalition forces by so-called neutral actors. This was a tall order for a small SAS team and was taken on cautiously as the first shot fired or bomb detonated would put the enemy on alert, and bring them down like a hornet's nest. Therefore, the team planned for receiving the additional stores and limpet mines from the US Vietnam operations in support of a simultaneous attack both on onshore and on water, at multiple locations. There would be no change to the SAS team for security reasons:

1. The attacks relied on having a Russian or Chinese ship in port unloading or anchored and magnetically attaching limpet mines full of Semtex under their stern, which was technically the most vulnerable place close to the engine, fuel, propulsion, and rudder controls.
2. The timer fuse would be pre-set for exploding in seven days ahead, allowing the ships to depart, then navigate down Lake Tonlé Sap and into the Mekong Delta, which emptied into the South China Sea. The ships would mysteriously explode at sea and closer to their home port.
3. The onshore warehouses identified by Brute were intended to be destroyed by secreting timed Semtex C4 charges placed inside boxes of weapons, ammunition or mortars.

4. The planned extraction would be by the jet boat across the lake, or if that was not possible, to hoof it over land to the airstrip and co-ordinate an airlift by Caribou aircraft back to Sattahip base.

Meantime, in preparation for the attacks, the Caribou was tasked to fly down to Vung Tao US base in Vietnam to drop off the two Cubs and pick up the mines, Semtex and additional stores. Refuelled and safely loaded, it took off and on the return leg it turned sharply north across Cambodia on a previously flown mapped trail, flying up, down and around hills and valleys for a round trip to the airstrip on top of the hill to make delivery, then immediately return empty to Sattahip base.

The plane was met by most of the on-ground team spread out around the landing area in the jungle in case of unwanted visitors arriving. They had been in daily contact with the base regarding the ETA of their package of stores, explosive tricks and rations. The trek from the lake and back was uneventful but getting back into the mangrove hide required a chain gang approach for manhandling the heavy ammunition, grenades, limpet mines and Semtex C4 packages onto a stores cache that was constructed earlier in the jungle about 100 yards back from the jet boat location. With conditions turning just right for this operation, raining cats and dogs, with very low visibility, the jet boat set out from the hide in the mangrove on a reconnaissance mission primarily looking out for any ships in the lake and with the cover of rain and darkness coming soon they hoped to be able to get up pretty close to the ship to identify it.

Several hours passed as the boat idled along the north coast of the lake in the vicinity of the dock and stores. They were fully cognisant of the armed patrol boat and its radar that would be lurking about. The bridge and running lights on the patrol boat were lit and were sighted several miles away. Heading east, it chugged past the jet boat as if it were not there due to there being a number of local craft on the lake.

The patrol boat and other boats out on the lake were almost as blind as the SAS Coxswain Flipper, who was trying to see through the rain and not bump into anything in the dark. The patrol boat crew obviously weren't able to use their radar in this rain or it would have been a very different situation for them, being challenged and having to open fire with the M60 against their twin .50 calibre machine guns.

Gritting his teeth, Flipper regained his composure and pointed the boat west in the opposite direction to the patrol boat's course. This direction should align them with the loading dock and any ship moored there for offloading. Soon they spotted the shadowy outline of a ship coming into view with its dimmed lighting casting an eerie glow between rain showers.

The boat's crew, emboldened by the cover and the patrol boat not seeing them at close quarters, idled right up close to the side of the ship and then reversed back about 20 yards to get a glimpse of the nameplate on its bow. It appeared to be in Russian with Cyrillic characters. The name was then written down for future reference. This was enough adventure for the night and the vessel turned south-west across the lake in the usual indirect pattern back to the hide.

Mounting the Attack by Land and Water

Having a Russian ship in port could be the catalyst for initiating the attack planned earlier. They had the resources and the skills to carry out the operation, but needed the go-ahead. The entire team had been in the area for several weeks by now and cooped up in the hide, or stores cache, waiting and watching on board the jet boat rocking in the gentle mangrove waters.

A message was sent to Spider at the Sattahip base for orders, whether they should sit and wait or start the attacks on the ship and shore facilities beginning tomorrow night if conditions were as good as now.

Spider sent off a message to DIO in Saigon as this was a political decision rather than military one. By early morning he received the following message:

Principals notified and concur, proceed as outlined in your plan.

Russian ship has been ID as a regular entering and leaving the Mekong Delta and disappearing up one of the tributaries.

7-day fuse timer setting agreed and will be monitored by US navy/air for direction and last position.

Where possible, look for a Chinese or Thai Ship to set the limpets on and advise of sighting and details prior to receiving orders to proceed.

US will task their satellite to pick up the store warehouse explosions.

Require notification of day and time when each of the limpet mines are set.

Mobilise at your earliest opportunity.

Report your mobilisation timing and status.

Cmdr. Coen RAN.

Chapter 8

The Sabotage Raid

Water Rats

Everyone eagerly awaited dusk and rested but sleep was out of the question. Sergeant Brute would lead the onshore team, who suited up with automatic weapons, backpacks, rations and Semtex C4 with the delay fuses separated. The limpet mine experts, a two-man team headed by Corporal Stocky and supported by Private Philbey, stripped down to swim fins, snorkels and masks, and placed the limpet mines in their waterproof backpacks for floating out to the stern of the ship in port while the remaining warriors stayed on board the boat in case more ships were spotted later.

As afternoon turned into night, light rain was now creating low-level misty clouds across the lake. Not perfect conditions but this would have to do. It was now go time at the hide, so the last meal was finished and the HF radio phone signals for the jet boat's return for extraction rehearsed once more. These included the alternate plan for the onshore teams to rendezvous at the airstrip on the hill, wait three days and nights, then use the HF radio phone to contact the boat crew. If they received no response, they were to call Sattahip base for airlifting out.

The jet boat and swimmer crew were to head further east after depositing the limpet mines on the Russian ship in order to look for any other ship that may be waiting to offload their cargoes, set the limpets and head back to the hide. Flipper would be responsible for forwarding on to the DIO by HF radio phone.

The slow transit across the lake was almost boring except for the adrenalin pumping through everyone's veins. There was a feeling of excitement for the older members who had survived missions in other unnamed places. With no patrol boat sighted so far, the boat nudged in against the half-sunken barge hull until the bow ran aground in half a metre of water. The shore team rolled off the gunnels on each side and without a word headed straight up to the beach and disappeared from sight.

Having lightened the vessel of its passengers, the crew set its sights on avoiding the patrol boat; knowing its line of travel was about 100 yards off the beach, well clear of the barge and other obstacles closer in. Heading out some 500 yards, the boat began a slow, idle speed drift east parallel with the shore to avoid the patrol boat but also to sight it and ascertain its direction and speed. An hour passed slowly, second by second, and out of the haze they saw the patrol boat headed in a westerly direction, passing the moored ship at the wharf. It would be about an hour before it had done its rounds in that direction and returned based on past observations.

Flipper began turning towards the wake of the patrol boat and the Russian ship. He headed toward the stern quarter of the ship, close enough to touch the flaking black tar paint on its hull. Stocky silently nodded then slid over the gunnels and into the water without making a ripple. His sidekick Philbey followed, their backpacks with magnetic limpet mines inside floating ahead of them.

They frog-kicked their way around the back of the ship to the protruding rudder and paused to check the wharf for movements in the flickering lights.

Pulling over the lever to expose the magnetic face of the mine, partly deflating the backpack until neutrally buoyant, they then took a deep breath before duck diving down beside the rudder as a guide in the darkness. When level with the bottom of the rudder, they both kicked hard with their fins forward toward the underside of the stern, where the single-screw propeller was sitting idle just below the level of the lake. This meant that the ship had been unloaded earlier and was now high in the water.

With the sound of a generator engine reverberating inside the hull above them to hide any sound of connecting the mine, there was not much time to dally about. The two swimmers yanked out the limpet mines from their backpacks, placed them up and forward of the propeller with the magnetic side up against the hull, pulled the pre-set time fuse pin and shoved themselves down and backwards toward the rudder.

The stern of the jet boat was backed up and only 2 yards away from the rudder by this time as they were anxious to scat out of there ASAP. The few minutes that this task took seemed like an eternity for the whole crew, so there was little said when the pair boarded and slumped onto the deck with empty backpacks on their laps. The boat slowly picked up speed in order to move outside of the patrol boat's routine course or risk being sighted by workers on the ship or wharf.

As no alarms were heard, and there was no rapid return of the patrol boat, Flipper headed along the north coast some 20 miles looking for another ship. Not being able to see anything through the misty rain, the boat turned southward toward the centre of the lake on a waiting position in case the shore team called for extraction.

The unmistakable rattle of a ship's anchor nearby was heard and brought the crew to action stations, with the M60 pointing out of its covered position on the bow. Voices could be heard echoing on board the ship, and the engine eased lightly to pull on the anchor until it took. Then there was silence apart from the distant murmuring of the ship's generator. As the ship swung with the lazy current and limp wind, the running lights and porthole lights glimmered through the misty rain.

Flipper clicked the boat into gear and idling moved toward the lights until the hull and then bow with anchor chain in the water came into view. Manoeuvring parallel to the ship, close enough to see the name plate, Chinese characters in white paint appeared. This ship was newer in shape and condition than the Russian one. It had possibly been constructed recently with this sort of mission in mind, hence greater caution when approaching it would be necessary.

Their radar would have the jet boat on screen and tracked, so Flipper just maintained course and alerted Stocky and Philbey to slide over the stern and swim for it.

Short notice but there was no need to do preparations as the limpet mines were already prepped. The two swimmers only needed to pull their fins, masks and snorkels on before the jet boat had drifted past the ship's stern.

They had a tough job on this occasion as the open water current moved at about 3 knots, their maximum swimming speed. Being experienced surfers, they knew how to swim in a shore rip, which they both had experienced many times on Bondi Beach in Sydney, and were able to edge sideways as they swam forward holding their floating backpacks. No time to rest or they would miss the ship completely.

On reaching the stern of the Chinese ship, they found that the rudder was below the waterline as the cargo had weighted the ship low in the water. The hull appeared to be clear of barnacles and did not offer much of a hold. Getting tired, the swimmers looked about for something to grab so they could rest. Below an overhanging lifeboat there was a thin rope that was probably used when using the lifeboat for ship-to-shore transits.

The rope dangled in the water with about a metre partly submerged and angled with the current along the hull. Both soldiers grabbed onto it and made a loop on the end so they could put one arm each through and rest to decide on their next move. Meanwhile, on deck, they could hear people moving about, chains being dragged and voices being raised.

It sounded like the ship's crew were getting the cargo covers off and preparing to enter port for unloading.

The feverish action above prompted the two frogmen to come up with plan B. This entailed preparing the mines with magnets exposed and fuse pins removed and making a dash underwater to push the mines onto the deepest part of the hull that they could reach, then up to the surface and floating back with the current. Getting picked up by the jet boat would be difficult but it should wait down current until dawn at least.

The water was a warm 24C, so popping up their empty backpacks and partly filling them with air, there was no chance of exhaustion or drowning.

The jet boat had drifted about a mile down current and daren't head directly to the ship as their radar operator might wonder who they were. Instead, they made several turns, avoiding fishing boats and anchored barges, to hopefully confuse the radar operator into thinking that the next boat coming toward them was different from the last. Flipper checked the previous gyrocompass route line and followed it back towards the Chinese ship position.

There was a bang on the port-side hull and a whistle: they had almost run over the SAS frogmen. The men in the water used the steps on the stern of the jet boat to board and waved to the skipper to get going. Having observed that there were no mines brought aboard, Flipper instinctively knew what the hurry was all about.

It was time to mingle with the other vessels out on the water for the rest of the night. As dawn would be upon them soon, with no contact from the shore teams, they decided to head circuitously back to the hide to wait out the day, then return that night in the dark and wait on station again.

Onshore Attack

The onshore team split up into two-man teams, after checking out the first storage depot seen previously. It was decided that one pair would wait there while the other team headed off to look further out in a wide circle for any more munition stores. Trucks were entering and leaving another compound a couple of hundred yards inland where a much larger depot was situated with guard towers and foot soldiers guarding the perimeter. This would be a much harder nut to crack, so the pairs split up to go in opposing directions around this secured compound.

There were sections of fence in disrepair similar to the first depot, but guards were in the vicinity most of the time. If one team could distract the guards long enough for them to head towards the front, one warrior could scramble across the open ground and into the store with two backpacks full of explosive Semtex C4 charges and time fuses.

A two-man team headed back over their footprints and across the road leading to the front gate. One warrior kept watch while the other gathered some semi-dry palm fronds and leaves. Using one of the time fuses and a length of fuse cable, he set up a rough bonfire with a ten-minute timer to ignite the fuse without exploding if a detonator was used. Both warriors were satisfied that a brush fire might draw some attention away from the back and sides of the compound. They hunched down and re-joined the pair waiting to breach the fence at the side.

The two pairs lay in wait for the signal to move. Brute and his partner, explosives specialist Corporal Rat Aims, would scurry forward through the fence and inside the store. The other pair would provide cover fire if needed. Sure enough, the fire caused consternation out front and the guards in the watchtowers turned spotlights onto the fire. The foot patrols waddled up to the front with nobody attempting to put out the fire.

Even the store workers turned up at the front gates bemused as to what was going on and took advantage of the confusion by lighting cigarettes and chatting.

The opportunity would not last. Brute and Rat dashed across with the explosives, past the rusted-out chain wire fence which they pushed aside, and hunched down to avoid the light beams shining over the roof of the store by the rear tower guards. Entering the store via an open side door, they were faced with high stacks of boxes containing all sorts of ordnance. The target boxes needed to be quickly identified and charges placed into one of each stack of ammunition, mortars or artillery shells.

Five minutes later, cases of mortars were identified fairly easily with 'no open flame' pictures stencilled on the sides. With bayonets in hand, plywood panels were pried open enough to squeeze the small 1lb packs of Semtex and fuses through. Another five minutes and grenade and RPG rockets were located and, being smaller boxes, these were easily pried open and charges placed in them.

All charges had been set for one hour, so it was high time to head out to the waiting SAS team. The commotion out front continued, with workers now being shouted at to put out their cigarettes and bring water buckets to quell the fire. A guard had a fire hose stretched out but it didn't extend past the gate.

Returning to the first store, the guards had run up the road after hearing that there was a fire near the other store. The store workers were standing out front waiting for instructions and paid no interest to the store area. They were probably being coerced to work there. Perfect, now the two onshore teams concentrated on this warehouse and were able to move in unobserved and place their charges similarly to the second store with a forty-five-minute fuse setting.

Due to the limited time available to meet the jet boat, the team sent a HF radio message advising 'Warehouses are hot – Heading for the airstrip – see you there.'

As Brute and the team cautiously scurried away from the immediate vicinity to the distant airstrip they heard and saw what seemed like a beautiful firework show, as multiple colours flashed from the different munitions screaming high into the night sky. The whole fucking world was lit up. Mortars, artillery shells, grenades and RPG were blowing the hell out of the warehouses; tower guards, foot soldiers, and even the poor buggers working in the warehouses would have been blown to bits and pieces. The whole area around the warehouses would have been nothing but chaos and carnage. Death and destruction, it's what war is all about: kill or be killed.

The shore team were in unfamiliar territory and had to dash and dodge their way for four days, covering about 65 miles before arriving at the foot of the hill top airstrip. A further message was sent to Sattahip base with a copy to the jet boat crew: 'Waiting for the bird.'

The boat crew had received the first message from the shore team and understood when they received the second one, advising that the shore team were safely at the airstrip, that they would have to abandon the hide and find a deep enough spot to sink the jet boat, then swim ashore. They had witnessed the fireworks show that had brilliantly lit up that dark Southeast Asian night sky. After stripping the hide of anything that could be considered to be linked to unwanted visitors from across the border, the crew headed to the airstrip to link up with the others some 20 miles and one day away.

The Caribou left Sattahip and this time changed its flight path by heading along the coast and then directly into Cambodia, almost in a straight line to the airstrip with less circuitous valley grabbing. This would be the last time to undertake this trip and by now the Cambodians would be searching every hill and valley for the attackers of the munition stores. The flight was tense as extraction of the entire SAS team and their kit was imperative. The locals would have seen and heard the Caribou on several occasions by now and would likely report the sightings to their authorities, particularly now that an attack had occurred on their territory by unknown perpetrators.

The landing went according to plan with the Special Forces soldiers already assembled and waiting at the top end of the runway as the plane spun around, the twin engines roaring. With the tail ramp now reaching the ground, all rushed aboard. The loadmaster raised the ramp when the last man stepped aboard and over his headset shouted to the pilots 'All aboard, ramp coming up'.

The aircraft jerked forward, mud and stones splattering against the fuselage as it made its final run toward the end of the runway and climbed steeply, levelled, and powered down the valleys by now very familiar to the pilots. This time the crew ensured no radar would pick them up as they headed more or less directly for the Thai border.

Climbing to 1,500ft on passing over the main Thai highway leading into Cambodia, the pilot made all of the right inbound approach radio calls to Sattahip control tower. The Caribou was cleared to land on runway 27 and began its direct approach from the west and landed without attracting any special attention from the Thais on the base.

The aircraft was hand baton signalled by Spider to continue taxiing into the hangar. With engines shutting down, the hangar door closed and the tail ramp lowered. The somewhat exhausted but victorious SAS teams disembarked with their kit. Spider ordered them to hit the showers and get some food into them and, when cleaned up, the team leaders were to report to himself for debriefing so a HF radio phone/fax message report could be compiled and sent to DIO.

Within an hour the following message was sent:

Lake Tonlé Sap mission:
1. Successfully demolished two munitions storage warehouses.
2. Russian and Chinese ships mined with seven-day fuses.
3. No casualties except for disposal of one jet boat.
4. All of the team now at Sattahip.

We await instructions on:
1. Thai munitions ship being tracked by US in case it returns to Thai waters.
2. New targets.

Chapter 9

Link-Up with US Assets

The team rested and sorted out their kits, saw to any cuts and scrapes received and listed any stores requirements so everyone would be ready for further action.

The following response was received late that night:

Mission success noted – well done.

Next mission will be close to Cambodia–Vietnam border to interdict with the land transport of munitions across into Vietnam – Will require flights into landing areas closest to Kratie City on the Mekong and Snoul City near the border of Vietnam.

Suspect there is a series of stores and trails to be ID and destroyed with co-ordination between Australian and USA resources.

Cmdr Coen RAN

It appeared that there would be no R&R flight back to Darwin just yet even though their month away on this assignment was just about up.

Team leaders met Spider in the belly of the C-130 as soon as the message was received for a briefing in preparation for the next joint operation sorties into east Cambodia.

They perused the topographical charts regarding terrain, tracks and waterways and highlighted the locations on the US unmapped landing areas nearest to the two Cambodian cities. The review came up with several landing area possibilities that the Caribou would have to be sent into for two-man patrols to reconnoitre before they committed to operational teams. No good going in without their own intelligence, particularly if this was going to be a deployment for a long period.

Once Spider mobilised the crew, there would be several four-man observer teams sent in using the existing SAS contingent resources due to their familiarity with the Cambodian countryside for the initial ingress. That would mean ceasing the remaining jet boat operations in the Gulf of Thailand unless there was a specific target identified for attention. If the duration exceeded seven days, then fresh exchange teams would be called in early from Darwin using the C-130 to ship them and more supplies.

Spider decided he could do with a distraction from the day-to-day administration at the base and a meeting with the DIO personnel in Darwin would be his excuse to pilot the bird back home, although he had no intention of taking R&R while his men were on the front lines. Plus, he was a control freak and had to stay on top of the ongoing actions on land, sea and air.

Having too many men and a lot of flights in and out of the Sattahip base was prone to raise questions from the Thais and so far they had not approached the team, but that may change if they suspected the visitors had anything to do with the explosions at the stores in Cambodia. Or, in fact, a Thai-registered ship blowing up in Thai waters.

Sunken Ships and Thai Secrets

Seven-day time fuses should be about to blow according to the calendar as the evening of the seventh day came and went. The team sat and wondered if the limpet mines had done their job, were detected and removed, or failed to explode. It would be a full week before they received a coded message advising that the mission had delivered an unexpected outcome.

A ship had exploded close to the Chinese port of Zhanjiang. The Russian ship had disappeared without a trace some hours before in the same area. It can be assumed that both vessels were taking on munitions cargoes in Zhanjiang and sailing down to the Mekong Delta to offload in Lake Tonlé Sap. The shipments were warehoused well away from South Vietnam and the war, before the cargoes were split up and sent by small Cambodian fishing fleets back down to the Mekong or offloaded for transporting on land routes in support of the Viet Cong.

The US Navy had been shadowing the Thai-registered ship, which was heading out of the Mekong Delta and up the Gulf of Thailand – in the team's direction. The ship was not challenged and finally anchored off Chon Buri, not more than a mile from the local Royal Thai Army Base. The US intended to find out who in the Thai military was involved in smuggling military equipment into Cambodia that was destined to support the Viet Cong.

A sting operation was mounted by the Thai secret service and US CIA agents, who began monitoring the ship until it anchored, and the crew were onshore just ahead of a blast in the engine room that sank the vessel in minutes. A well-known retired Thai general suspected of drug cultivation and smuggling was pinpointed as the snake's head and was being paid by the Chinese to transfer cargoes from Chinese freighters before they arrived into the Samut Prakan port near Bangkok and ship them into Cambodia. The general was being paid in Chinese-manufactured drugs and other contraband.

The general, his bodyguards and more than twenty of the ships' crew were swooped upon in a single night raid by the Thai secret service and taken away – never to be seen or heard of again.

Chinese ships had to endure heavy customs searches from that point onward. The Thai smuggling ship remained half sunken offshore, a rusting hulk. Perhaps it served as a reminder to wannabe smugglers or a headstone, but no one asked or knew the cause of its sinking.

Major Spider received a very confidential briefing regarding the fate of all four ships direct from Commander Coen when he returned to Darwin. Coen had phoned Spider late on his first night back in Darwin on his government-supplied apartment land line and asked him to call back on the scrambled sat phone. After ten minutes of Spider fumbling about half-awake as he tried to find the twelve-character phone number, the phone began to ring. Commander Coen was sitting in his secure Darwin office several floors below ground level and before he picked up the receiver he took a long puff on his cigarette, one of the many that now lay in the ashtray beside him.

Spider's voice mumbled over the line 'Good evening, or should I say good morning Commander. What's the nature of this call, I guess it's not social.'

The commander just grunted and said 'Yes, it's late and we are both fucking tired so let's cut to the chase. I have received a report from my opposite in Thailand and it briefly goes like this:

- Chinese operatives in several cities in Thailand have been arrested by the secret police, questioned with malice and disposed of. They were inserted into the country illegally, supervised and paid for by the Chinese Government. The Thais found them through the money transfers, monitoring their movements, and their association with known Thai drug dealers.
- The Thai nationals involved did not survive interrogation, a tough lot who refused to talk. Thai secret services are still looking for a number of associates and have a zero-tolerance approach to their activities.
- The vessel in the harbour will eventually be towed away for scrap but in the meantime it will remain there as a warning to ship owners intending to use the seaway into Thailand. No doubt other routes will be used from now on.
- Feedback on the ships that were mined is that two were sunk out in the South China Sea and two were severely damaged and ended up on south China coastal beaches'.

Chapter 10

East Cambodia Operations

Flying over east Cambodia, the Caribou aircraft meandered around heavy rain clouds, with head pilot David Dash Jones and co-pilot Paul Greek Papas straining their eyes to get a visual fix on a single runway cut out among fairly flat jungle scrub. They circled lower to drop beneath the cloud base but the cloud was almost to ground level. Pulling up at full power to avoid a stall, the plane adjusted its position and ducked down in the next break in the clouds and eventually found the airstrip.

Not wanting to pull up for another go-around, the pilot in command continued the descent with the aircraft nose pointing at the threshold and seeing the end of the runway now only 500ft ahead. The aircraft bucked and shuddered in the below cloud turbulence. With rudder pedals shoved in and out to yaw the aircraft and wash off speed at the same time, the crew deftly straightened the Caribou and hit the gravel one wheel at a time until the propellers were reverse pitched and runway speed got under control enough to make the landing look rough but effective.

The aircraft skidded to a stop just short of the jungle ahead and promptly spun around with the port brake on and the port propeller pitch eased forward. Jones should have been a racing driver, he did a neat turn though. As usual, the rear ramp was on its way down and the SAS soldiers on board were more than glad to get out into the sultry air and shake off wanting to puke due to the sharp turns, plusses and minuses of gravity experienced on the ride down.

On the ground, Brute and Rat with full backpacks and automatic weapons slung loose, now trudged over to the edge of the clearing, looked over their shoulders once and then disappeared into the green foliage. They would make a HF radio phone call in two days regarding the security of this landing zone and surroundings. The co-pilot marked this position on his map for future reference as the position provided by the US was out by several hundred yards. Not good enough in this weather.

After stretching their legs, the remaining soldiers jumped up on the ramp and scurried forward as it began rising. The loadmaster advised the pilots through his head set to: 'Ramp up – go to'.

The twin engines roared, brakes, on and then released. The plane jerked forward and rushed down the rough surface of the airstrip. Seconds later the nose raised and the wheels came off the ground, with the nimble Caribou skimming over tree tops and climbing up into dark clouds and the turbulence contained within them. The aircraft had a second landing area to locate and drop off the remaining SAS soldiers. After about thirty minutes there was a very similar pattern of search and see for the next jungle runway, but this time it was on a hill top similar to the ones used over on the west side of Cambodia for the raids on the Lake Tonlé Sap area.

The co-pilot, Greek, who had New Guinea flying experience, took the controls and, as hills were easier to find, spotted a steeply sloping upward runway to his starboard side. Unlike the gung-ho approach on the flat terrain at the last spot, this runway was dangerous and it needed every bit of his experience to turn between adjacent hills and deep valleys, then line up accurately, wheels down, half flaps. He waited for the shuddering of a stall and put on more power, full flaps and committed to hitting the runway right at the edge of the hillside while ignoring the outline of a crashed aircraft that had missed its approach.

Knuckles bared on the pitch control, the aircraft skidded onto the runway apron just yards in from the edge and trundled drunkenly up the rising angle of the runway until doing a similar turning pirouette to about face downhill. Ramp on the way down, they checked the position on the map which was correct this time.

The remaining two soldiers, Stocky and Philbey, jumped down and almost kissed the ground, knowing how perilous this landing was. They then marched up to the top of the clearing, waved and were gone. The engines roared, brakes off, and down the slope it went, before it momentarily sank out of sight over the edge of the hill in a down draft and swung around into the deep valley to avoid the adjacent hill top.

The sound of the engines soon faded and the soldiers were alone and taking stock of their surroundings.

Feedback from the two landing areas where the two-man teams headed out from on each of their two points of their compass this gave coverage of all four compass points indicated no local habitation but a few foot tracks that native hunters possibly used. The jungle was not as dense as the higher ground to the west, so moving through there was easier but provided less cover.

Major Spider signalled the teams to join up with the rest of their platoons when they arrived on the next Caribou landing planned in two days.

Sufficient supplies would also be delivered to support a three-to-four-week seek and destroy and report operation searching for the munitions supply trails and, if possible, the hidden storage areas that the US forces were keen on destroying as a lot of their troops had recently faced strong and sustained confrontations from the Viet Cong supported by Chinese regulars. This meant that the enemy was emboldened by knowing that they had assured supply lines and could expend resources without having to withdraw.

The remaining jet boat at Sattahip was hauled up and into the hangar for storage alongside the C-130. The extra pallets of stores were covered over with camouflaged waterproof canvas for hiding at each landing area and loaded into both Caribou. The two platoons of keen and rested SAS soldiers already had their kit in rows ready for boarding the aircraft.

An extra ordered-up Caribou had arrived from Darwin as two wouldn't be able to carry all of the men and equipment and still safely land on the difficult runways to the east. Also, another aircraft was needed for backup transport in case there was an emergency bailout or medical case extraction needed.

With the base tied down security wise, Spider took it on himself to fly one of the Caribou on the ingress mission. It would give him an appreciation of the conditions the men would be facing; also a good morale boost for the men seeing the team leader up in the cockpit. In the back of his mind, he was considering staying in the field with one of the platoons. The first objective in his briefing to the men was:

1. Both team locations to move parallel and to the eastern border of Vietnam, which was about 30 miles away, and report back.
2. When they had reached the unmade road between Snoul and Senmonorom towns this must be checked out as a possible artery for moving munitions up and across the Vietnam border.
3. As the team was going to be in hostile countryside, frivolously engaging the enemy must be avoided. If spotted, make a run for it and leave some booby traps to slow the hunters down.
4. Also, the Viet Cong may be operating on this side of the Cambodian border and could lay an ambush, so ears up and tails down.
5. Send an HF radio report on progress daily 'when possible'.
6. Everyone knows the rules; if one of the team is caught or seriously injured, don't wait behind for them, keep going to complete the mission.
7. The US Army has the job of taking out the targets that are identified, so don't get too close to the target area or you will become collateral damage.
8. Heads down and get back to the landing areas in one piece

Each platoon with their stores and kit boarded their designated Caribou and these took off from Sattahip base thirty minutes apart and headed circuitously to their set landing destination. The pilots in command on the departing aircraft were those who flew the first flights into the eastern two airstrips, so there was no learning curve required and the new backup pilots would get their introduction to the difficult terrain by sitting beside them. Spider boarded the aircraft heading for the hill top landing and changed places with Greek Papas, the pilot in command, who moved over to the co-pilot seat, with the displaced co-pilot, Mike 'Macka' McKey, taking the spare jump seat behind the pilots.

All flights were able to take off and land without any additional drama apart from the usual nail-biting landings. At least the compass positions were dead on and helped to reduce the air time over the areas. Both two-man teams were waiting at the landing strips. As ordered, the platoons cached the spare stores in the jungle not far from the landing areas and then headed off in an easterly direction led by Brute and Stocky, who had carried out the area surveys prior to the platoon's arrival. With each man forming a line and spaced apart far enough to just make out the man ahead of them in case of ambush, the platoons moved cautiously forward until dusk when it was time to form ambush-proof positions in the wet undergrowth.

Field Medic Alex Doc McDonald

After one week of bush bashing through virgin jungle, creeks and swamps, the road had been found and crossed and Brute's southern team had at last discovered a well-used track with foot and bicycle wheel grooves in it.

The team had advised the base of its findings with a copy to Stocky's team further north. They continued right up to the Vietnam border, then turned back in case they encountered US troops or Viet Cong active in the area.

Stocky decided to go further north parallel with the gravel road they had crossed over two days earlier to try and identify any new tracks toward the border similar to Brute's platoon about 15 miles further south. Tracks and a village were sighted and considered a possible target.

Stocky's platoon spread out in pairs and moved on both sides of the gravel road to observe any comings and goings and activities within the village and the food plantations at the edges of the jungle. With no specific issues observed, the platoon gathered a further mile past and over several hills and streams. There they set up ambush positions for the night, intending in the morning to move east to the Vietnamese border following the trails probably used by the villagers.

At dawn the platoon split in half and followed one trail each. Unfortunately, one trail was booby-trapped and one soldier had his right hand blown off after setting one off. This crude booby trap had been made up using a bamboo tube stuffed with pebbles and down the middle what appeared to be a bundle of plastic-wrapped cordite normally used in artillery shells. The detonator was taken from a mortar and was set off using a rusty spring being released by stepping on a wooden stick trigger.

The blast shot straight up and ripped the soldier's hand to bits and pieces. It was followed by his terrified and painful scream.

The platoon immediately disbursed further north after the explosion and settled in reasonably thick undergrowth, where they waited and listened for any villagers or enemy coming to investigate the small, crude but effective, explosion.

The wounded man was then attended to by field medic Alex Doc McDonald close to where the booby trap went off by injecting morphine for the pain, tidying up the broken exposed wrist bone and hanging flesh by breaking the sharp edges off the bone with a pair of pliers and using small scissors to trim the flesh.

Then, having flushed the wound as thoroughly as possible with Betadine, he applied sulphur powder antiseptic for good measure. Doc then sewed the skin flap opening shut. Satisfied with that, a dressing was placed on it to keep it dry; he then bound the stub on the end of the soldier's arm with duct tape.

Doc and the wounded soldier then headed off at a run to catch up with the body of the platoon members as he was not wounded enough to be left behind. He stayed in the jungle carrying out daily observations for two weeks until he was transported out on the Caribou with his platoon members. On return to Darwin, he was sent to the Darwin Hospital on the coast not far from the airport and the orthopaedic surgeon there advised that the wound had healed perfectly and with help from physiotherapy he could be fitted with a prosthetic hand at some point.

Former Commando McDonald was praised for a job well done by surgeons at the Darwin Hospital.

Chapter 11

US Soldier Stood on a Mine

Major Spider to the Rescue

Brute's platoon in the south area had identified a munitions store and an air strike was co-ordinated through the US Air Force. After the munitions had exploded, blowing the shit out of everything within a several hundred-yard radius, the SAS troops provided support mopping up on the ground and took on the remnants of the Viet Cong that had become disoriented. Some were wounded during the bombing and had scattered in all directions. There were a few unarmed Cambodians that had taken to the bush but were valued as not worth pursuing, job done.

During all of the mayhem and confusion after the bombing and explosion a US platoon had made its way on foot over the border to assess the damage and they made themselves known by firing a few shots into the air, then shouting 'Americans, Americans'.

The SAS called out 'Australians, Australians', and several faces showed through the jungle and smoke haze. The SAS warriors explained how they had called in the air raid as their team was in the area after crossing over a river from Cambodia into Vietnam while following a shipment of weapons destined for the Viet Cong.

An alarm was raised down the track for everybody to stand still. A big black US soldier had stood on an anti-personnel mine of some sort with his left foot, heard it click and instantly froze; lifting his foot would cause the mine to pop up and explode, taking off his legs and maybe gutting him in the process. It was patterned after a Bouncing Betty mine.

His yelping and hollering could be heard from quite a distance, and Spider headed over to see what was going on. He immediately heard from this soldier's sergeant that there was possibly a mine under this guy's boot and he was fucked if he knew what to do about it. Maybe just leave the soldier there and get out of range.

Having previous experience in other war zones with clearing booby traps, Spider figured that if the soldier's boot stayed on the mine striker it wouldn't go off as it hadn't done so yet. So, he set about removing the guy's boot laces, firmly held down on his foot with his right hand and, with him being a left-hander, he carefully cut around the sewn leather edge of the soldier's boot with his left hand until the top of the boot and some of the sock could be lifted carefully up the soldier's shin to his knee.

The next thing was to clear the earth around the mine and have a look at what type and size he was dealing with. It was a crude Viet Cong bamboo device with a pop-up bottom charge fused and crammed with a bunch of old bullet casings, steel scraps and poisoned bamboo skewers.

Spider figured the safest method was to slide a length of his trusty coil of Aussie farm fence wire under the mine, up and around then under the soldier's foot arch while maintaining downward pressure. Then he twisted the wire tight with the loop now holding the boot sole and mine striker spring down.

Spider laid low with his head close to the soldier's foot and asked him to slowly lift it ever so slightly to check if there was any slack in the wire loop so he could tighten it further. As there was no noticeable movement between the mine and boot sole, he tied one end of a ball of string that he used for tying ponchos together for rain cover. He quickly got onto his knees, crawled behind a tree stump about 3 yards away and then said calmly 'OK soldier boy, you can now carefully lift your foot and step away'.

Soldier boy subsequently fainted and fell backwards, the mine didn't go off and his shocked sergeant dragged him away after a brief pause.

All clear, Spider planned to set off the mine later by pulling the string and freeing the wire loop over the boot sole. Backtracking past the tree stump and pausing about 10 yards away, having fed out most of the ball of string, he climbed over and behind a fallen tree trunk where the team were waiting. Giving the string a sharp pull, the mine hissed and then popped above the ground, exploded and brought down jungle leaves from the canopy above like rain and tore into lower shrubs all around them including the log they were sheltering behind.

No one ever heard again from that one-boot guy or his sergeant as they noisily hightailed it away through the jungle. Tut tut. The things people do for their neighbours. As all of this crashing about the bush and an exploding mine would have woken the dead, the SAS warriors also took off in the opposite direction to the Americans.

Most of their observe and report missions were far less exciting and to some extent boring as they counted boats going up and down the river deltas. Having identified a number of water-and land-borne ordnance storage depots and delivery trails, the Americans carried out airstrikes and they went back to confirm potency and collateral damage.

The Americans avoided hitting the Chinese and Russian cargo ships overtly, likely for diplomatic reasons. However, as the war dragged on and the Americans and coalition forces were taking increased losses, they were ordered to take out two cargo ships by attaching limpet mines to their hulls with timers set to explode somewhere out in the South China Sea.

Blue-on-Blue Attack

The routine of observe, report and get chased away from targets became a day-to-day affair. The small team had gotten smaller as there were no replacements and no time to train new personnel. The best tool was a simple compass and the regular updating of maps and charts of the areas they had been through. The countryside was littered with unmarked villages, both friendly and hostile.

All were considered as hostile and sources of intelligence leaks to the Viet Cong, whom the team were certain knew of their existence.

The mission wasn't finished, with just small targets being taken out, so they continued to search for more transport trails until they uncovered another huge stockpile of munitions. It seemed the opposition had reacted to the last attack, resulting in what was now a huge stockpile of weapons with nothing going over the Vietnamese border. Instead it was creating a pile-up just 5 miles inside Cambodia in a valley that had cliffs on each side and a small stream trickling through it.

The SAS team found an ideal spot to set up camp on one of the hill tops with almost perfect cover from aerial surveillance. The enemy below didn't know they were being observed from a vantage point that allowed them a fairly clear view along the valley.

The cache was fairly large and growing, and there were both Viet Cong and Cambodian personnel bivouacked on all sides. The Australians shared this intelligence coup with the Americans via their contact in Saigon. The team was ordered to sit tight and observe when the stockpile looked like it was moving out of the valley and heading towards the border into Vietnam. Within two days the munitions began to move east, a trickle at first and then there was more co-ordination of personnel. Spider notified DIO in Saigon, who several hours later advised that the Americans were marshalling a helicopter gunship attack.

It was mid-afternoon, the sky was a little hazy but there was no rain and the SAS soldiers could make out the head of the line of people carting heavy boxes by hand, on backs and on bicycles. The line had begun to reach the end of the valley and was working its way up an incline before reaching the Vietnamese border.

Then the team of warriors heard the clack of helicopter rotors and a dozen choppers breached the top of the rise, whereupon the transporters of munitions began to scatter. Too fucking late! The rockets and machine guns began a constant hammering of the ground and through the valley.

Then they turned back into the valley and carried out their strafing runs more meticulously by picking out individual targets. By this time the enemy soldiers among the transport labourers had begun return fire using automatic weapons.

This caused the helicopters to break formation and it appeared that they had lost control of the situation and had to regroup.

That decision brought several helicopters right over the top of the Australians' position and one of them opened fire with their belly gunner and killed five SAS warriors, who did not return fire.

The SAS team's radioman was on the High Frequency radio phone talking to the helicopter flight leader at the time and supporting the mopping up when they were hit. He immediately shouted into the mouthpiece 'Cease fire, cease fire. We are friendlies. You just hit us. We have casualties. Call off your stupid fucking choppers.'

Before he could say another word, Major Spider snatched the phone from the radioman's hand and disconnected. His troops were livid; they threatened to use missiles in future to bring down the helicopters.

As the commander on the ground, utilising his trained psychologist prowess and by pulling rank he convinced the troops to calm down, that they would deal with this bat-shit crazy matter in a civilised manner. This was no easy task as he was as pissed off as they were.

Brute approached the major with Stocky and Doc close at his heels. Major Spider was aware that these warriors were in shock, the look on their paled faces was one of anger in their deadly, venomous, staring eyes.

'God fuck me to tears major. I tell ya if I ever get my hands on anyone of those fucking murdering cluster fuck Yanks, I will tear their fucking heads off and piss down their ever-loving motherfucking throats.'

'I hear you Sergeant, but not here, not now, our day will come. Right now, we have casualties that need our attention.'

Major Spider saluted Brute and all three warriors returned the salute.

The major knew Brute wasn't kidding and he also knew the big man was capable of doing exactly what he stated.

The bodies of the SAS warriors had been shredded by the multiple wounds from the 50-calibere helicopter weapons. They stripped the remains of any identifying materials and buried them in shallow graves which were located by compass readings and they marked the positions on their maps and charts. The team retreated from the scene leaving the Americans to finish what they had started. The only option was to head back to the landing areas and bug out of Cambodia by trusty Caribou aircraft.

Chapter 12

Doc's Tale

On the flight back to Sattahip, Spider was seated next to Doc. Silence hung like a black cloud throughout the aircraft, Suddenly Doc started to chuckle.

'What the hell's so funny, Doc?' asked Spider.

'I was just remembering one of the deceased we left behind, a real jovial little fella from Balmain, Sydney. Private Dougie Smith.'

'Sure, I remember him, real talkative little bloke. Sometimes at chow his chin would start wagging and ya just wanted to tell him to shut the hell up, but to keep the peace we just let him rattle on.'

'Well, I was just thinking about the night he went to the wire at Sattahip, just after you issued orders that no one was to cross over, for some short-time fun with the little brown ladies.'

'What happened Doc?'

'Well Dougie was a bit of a butterfly and, feeling his oats, he ventured to the wire which in fact is a chain link fence. Now the little brown ladies still need to eat so the blokes would just hang their dicks through the netted wire, pay a couple of Baht and get a blow job.'

'No shit, this is all news to me.'

'Of course, it is! But don't sweat it. Anyhow this one night Dougie unbuttons his shorts, he wasn't wearing any underwear, slides them down his thighs, pokes his dick through the wire, the little brown lady gets down on her knees, grabs a firm hold of his dick and then somehow sticks a long sharp object through the netted wire right up under his ball bag and demands all the cash he has.

'Seems he told her to go fuck herself so she jams him harder. Now he can't just pull back as she has a death grip on his dick with the netted wire between him and her hand. He knows it could be a Punji stick, which may have a poisoned tip, or it could be a long-bladed stiletto. Whatever it is, he is now in panic mode. He feels something trickling down his leg and knows he hasn't pissed himself. How could he, she is still holding on to him. He figures it's blood.

'Now he is scared shitless, he doesn't want to lose his family jewels, so he reaches down as little and painlessly as he can, pulls his shorts up enough to stick his hands into both pockets and hands over 300 Thai Baht and 5 Aussie dollars and turns his pockets inside out to convince her that's all he's got.

'She snatches the cash, lets go of his dick, pulls the sharp object out from between his legs and disappears into the night.'

'How long ago was this?'

'Oh, a couple of months ago. Anyhow, he comes to me and asks if I would take a look, which I did. She had spiked him enough to break the skin and create a small flow of blood. I sterilised the wound, gave him some Rexona ointment and told him to keep the wound clean, stick a band aid on it and in a couple of days he'd be fine.'

'I'll be damned.'

'Yea, well I warned him to keep his mouth shut about it and say nothing to no one because if Major Spider ever found out about it his arse was grass and the major was a lawnmower. And now the poor guy is dead. Good soldiers, killed for no fucking reason except stupidity, way before their time.'

'The fucking events of war Doc, it's enough to make horses cry. But I understand why you chuckled. It is kinda funny. Bloody little Dougie Smith, RIP soldier.'

'Roger that major.'

The political consequences were to hush up the incident of the 'blue on blue', or whatever the powers that be liked to name it. Some called it friendly fire, probably the most stupid title for such an imbecilic act; there was just nothing friendly about it. Five SAS warriors were needlessly killed by a bunch of scared young helicopter pilots and belly gunners that had lost the plot on this occasion.

Spider naturally took umbrage to this shocking incident and threatened the Americans in Saigon with counter-action using one of their own stinger, shoulder-launched missiles. As the commander on the ground, he was ordered to report to US headquarters in Bung Tao, so he flew one of the Caribou over with co-pilot Macka McKey and Brute. They were all wound up tight and ready to kick Yankee arse.

An Australian general met Major Spider at the airport. On arrival at the US HQ, Spider spoke to Brute and warned him to stay cool, adding he was no good to anyone doing time in a US army brig.

'Let me say one thing Major Spider. The nation that forgets its defenders will forget itself. Don't let those motherfuckers forget that we laid to rest five brave souls in that stinking fucking Cambodian jungle.'

Spider was then escorted into a conference room full of US brass. He was carpeted, yelled at and threatened by the US brass for about an hour. Not once did those pompous pricks offer an apology, explanation or excuse for their people shooting and killing five brave SAS soldiers. The Australian general just stood there listening like a fucking galoot and said nothing, he just escorted Spider in and then out of the building without more than a 'Follow me, say nothing, and then go back to base'.

Spider didn't give up the missile launcher, as they had disarmed and buried it. The Yanks would have to live with the uncertainty that these crazy Aussie SAS would shoot down one of their helicopters – or maybe not? One will never know.

All gave some, some gave all.

Back Home and Demobilised

No Closure for Major Spider

This saga continued on from the 1969 mobilisation into Cambodia until the final departure in 1972, when the SAS had finally packed up most of the stores and equipment at the Sattahip base, hauled the sole jet boat into the C-130, and organised for the truck to be returned to its former Thai owner. With all personnel on board and spread between aircraft types, all the birds took off from Thailand at ten-minute intervals for the last time. Due to the cargo weight, all aircraft refuelled at Brunei Darussalam airport and again at Kupang in West Timor before the final leg into Darwin.

Spider maintained contact with his living team members, all of whom share a special bond. This saga has never been told before as there still remains a cloud of secrecy as the Australian Government attempts to open up diplomatic and trade negotiations with the Cambodian Government.

It was Spider's personal duty to make contact with all of the wounded men to ensure that they received the best of medical care.

He visited the deceased members' families and provided them with an explanation of what happened to their loved ones (as nobody else did). He maintained contact with these families over a number of years until he was satisfied that they were coping and back on their feet. As for himself, the military sent him a letter advising that he was no longer required under this government act. However, he was to remain in reserve and continue his soldier training as a CMF major and finish his university education, entering into normal industry doing normal things but all the time having a feeling that this was only the beginning of his military life. In the background the Vietnam War ground down and was lost by the players in the coalition. What a waste of life, and for what?

One very sad outcome of the Cambodian operation was the death of five brave SAS soldiers and the refusal of the Australian Government of the day and the military to repatriate their remains for military burial and some form of closure for their families. The excuse they broadcast was that the Australian Government was in the process of pursuing good relations with the Cambodians and they did not want to upset those efforts.

Another disturbing footnote to the Australian involvement in the Vietnam conflict was that the remains of those military personnel who were killed in action between 1962 and 1966 were not repatriated by the government that sent them into the war zone unless their families paid the bill. This disgraceful, unethical decision was changed in 1966. However, the remains of some twenty-five soldiers remained in South Vietnam until some fifty years later, when in 2015 the Australian Government led by Prime Minister Tony Abbot repatriated them along with several others from Malaysian and Singapore grave sites.

How true were those words from Brute?

The nation that forgets its defenders will forget itself.

Epilogue

The Vietnam War

The French quit what became known as the First Indochina War against the communist-led Viet Minh in 1954 after losing the battle of Dien Bien Phu, ending almost a century of French colonial rule in Indochina.

As a result of the peace accords in Geneva, Switzerland, Vietnam was divided into North Vietnam and South Vietnam at the 17th Parallel. In August 1954 Ho Chi Minh was appointed Prime Minister of North Vietnam. He had formed the organisation Viet Minh in China in 1941 to fight for independence from the French.

Most of the financing after the Second World War for the French conflict against the Viet Minh was provided by the United States, who assumed financial and military support for the South Vietnamese state and this led to what became known as the Second Indochina War or the American War. The conflict involved Vietnam, Laos and Cambodia from November 1955, and ended with the fall of Saigon in April 1975.

North Vietnam was supported by China and the Soviet Union, while South Vietnam was supported by the United States, South Korea, the Philippines, Australia, Thailand, New Zealand and other anti-communist allies.

United States involvement in South Vietnam escalated under President John F. Kennedy through the Military Assistance Advisory Group (MAAG). A thousand US advisors were dispatched in 1954, there were 16,000 in 1963 and this had increased to 23,000 by 1969.

On 2 August 1964 the United States naval vessel the USS *Maddox* was allegedly fired upon by North Vietnamese torpedo boats that were supposedly shadowing it where it was stationed, 10 miles off the North Vietnam coastline in the Gulf of Tonkin. A reported second attack occurred two days later on 4 August, against the USS *Turner Joy* and the *Maddox* in the same location; both vessels were supporting the South Vietnam Navy. The circumstances of the attacks were suspicious.

Congress approved the Gulf of Tonkin Resolution on 7 August 1964 and granted the current President, Lyndon Johnson, to take necessary measures to repel any armed aggression against the forces of the United States to prevent further attacks.

President Johnson interpreted this to mean that he had a blank cheque and approval to expand the war. In February 1965 the United States began a prolonged bombing campaign of North Vietnam that included both military and civilian targets. The bombing became known as Operation Rolling Thunder.

By the end of 1965 Johnson had escalated the US troop contingent in South Vietnam to approximately 190,000 and in December 1967 the count was 500,000 and still rising.

In April 1965 Australian Prime Minister Robert Menzies and his liberal government, after discussions with the US, dispatched an infantry battalion for service in Vietnam. In 1962 he had sent thirty military instructors to provide military training to the South Vietnamese forces.

Large sections of sparsely populated eastern Cambodia were being utilised as sanctuaries by the People's Army of Vietnam (PAVN) and the Viet Cong. They would withdraw from the fighting in South Vietnam to rest and reorganise without being attacked.

The Cambodian sanctuaries were also being utilised to receive and store large caches of weapons from North Vietnam, which were being supplied by China and the USSR through the city of Hanoi. These weapons were being transported down the notorious Ho Chi Minh Trail that meandered through Laos and into Cambodia for the resupply to the PAVN and the VC. The United States bombed the Ho Chi Minh trail in both Laos and Cambodia to little avail as the weapons were still arriving by sea transport into Cambodia from both China and the USSR, and even rogue traders from Southeast Asian countries that were in it for the cash.

Violence and Lies

More than 500,000 tons of bombs were covertly dropped on Cambodia with a complete disregard for civilian life. President Richard Nixon was elected in January 1969, with his presidency lasting until August 1974. Later in 1969 Nixon issued orders to his Secretary of State Henry Kissinger, who told General Alexander Haig 'Nixon wants a massive bombing campaign in Cambodia'.

Commencing in March 1969, the carpet-bombing mission known as Operation Menu was carried out over Cambodia for the next four years. Fifty-four B-52 long-range bomber aircraft from U-Tapao Air Force Base in Thailand and another 153 from Anderson Air Force base in Guam were used. These bombing raids were not exposed publicly until 1973.

The Communist Party of Kampuchea (Cambodia), commonly known as the Khmer Rouge, and its leader Pol Pot would not have won power without the United States' military and economic destabilisation due to the bombing campaign against an already fragile Government of Norodom Sihanouk.

The genocide under the dictatorship of Pol Pot became known as the Killing Fields, with 1½ to 2½ million Cambodians exterminated.

An undated NSA (National Security Agency) Publication declassified in 2005 stated there was no attack on 4 August 1964 on either of the two vessels, the *Maddox* or the *Turner Joy*. This lie had led to President Johnson's escalation of the tense situation into war.

On 29 April 1975 Saigon fell and the remaining United States personnel were evacuated. On the following day, which is now known in Vietnam as Liberation Day, North Vietnamese tanks rolled into the presidential palace compound in Saigon and raised that country's flag.

Reports vary on civilian deaths caused by both sides but range from 2 million to 3½ million. United States casualties numbered 58,300, including both combat and non-combat deaths, those missing in action and in captivity. In addition, more than 153,000 Americans were wounded in action.

Unexploded ordnance, especially bombs dropped by the United States, continue to detonate and kill civilians. The defoliant Agent Orange and other chemicals have caused illnesses in as many as 3 million Vietnamese civilians; both of these killing commodities continue their deadly attributes to this day.

A total of 60,000 Australian military forces from the air force, navy and ground forces served in Vietnam. A total of 521 were killed and over 3,000 were wounded.

Under Prime Minster John Gorton, in 1970 Australia began to withdraw its military forces and completed the process in 1973.

Chapter 13

Mindanao Muslim Madness

There is a stretch of ocean in Southeast Asia that is potentially the most dangerous in the maritime world today for piracy and crime on the high seas. A militant Muslim group calling themselves Abu Sayyaf operate in the Sulu-Celebes Sea and base themselves around several islands in the south-western part of the Philippines. They have been operational for approximately forty years, and Libya, Syria and Saudi Arabia have extended training in Islamic theology to the organisation.

Abu Sayyaf is officially known by ISIS as the 'Islamic State – East Asia Province'. It is a jihadist militant organisation and follows the Wahhabi doctrine of Sunni Islam. Since its inception the organisation has been involved in bomb attacks in Manila, kidnappings, assassinations of politicians, extortion, rape, child sexual assaults, forced marriages, drive-by shootings, tourist beheadings and drug trafficking.

From January 2002 until February 2015 fighting Abu Sayyaf became a mission of the United States military's operation Enduring Freedom as part of the global war on terrorism.

The organisation has been labelled as terrorists by Australia, Japan, Canada, Indonesia, Malaysia, the Philippines, the United Arab Emirates, the United Kingdom and the United States.

Mindanao Hostage Recovery

Eleven French Hostages Taken from North Malaysian Resort

It was a beautiful clear morning at around 5am at a nice tropical holiday resort on an island off the remote north-east Malaysian coast near the town of Kuantan. Four fishing boats sat drifting offshore and the crews were watching the movements of the resort staff as they began arriving for work on motor scooters as they had always done. Nothing seemed out of the ordinary except for there being one fishing boat that had landed a mile further north in a small cove out of sight off the roadway.

The five-man crew on the boat had gone ashore two days earlier and sat among the palm trees to monitor the comings and goings of the local Malay staff to establish when there was a break in arrivals and that no other movements were expected. In this case there was a forty-minute break between the arrivals of workers' groups. This gap would be the signal over a CB radio from shore to the four boats languishing in the low swell offshore to start their engines and move in line abreast up to the beach in front of the resort accommodation apartments that were constructed on piles over the shallow calm water facing the South China Sea.

There were always the sights and sounds of boats going up and down the coast, so the low noise of these boats would not have attracted any undue attention. The fifth boat crew had scrambled aboard their boat, upped anchor and at full speed headed out to the position where the four boats had been waiting offshore. This boat would maintain watch for patrol boats or land police vehicles heading for the resort.

The sun had risen just over the horizon as the four boats reached the shoreline. The crews were armed with AK-47s but dressed in typical local fisherman robes. Silently the crews split up in predetermined pairs and headed to their specific tourist bungalows over the water.

All hell broke loose as bungalow doors were kicked in and rifle butts smashed into the sleeping occupants, waking them up in pain with screams from the women. The pirates shouted 'Get up, get dressed and get out or we will shoot you dead'.

The pandemonium lasted all of ten minutes until all eleven French tourists were standing on the beach and being herded toward the waiting boats. There was no sign of the Malaysian resort staff at this point as their routine did not take them over to the bungalows as the tourists generally ate in the main building restaurant later in the morning.

All the sparsely clad tourists were pushed and shoved into the boats at gunpoint and remained silent for fear of further gun butts and kicks from the pirates. The French men and women were forced to lie on top of each other on the floor of the boats and could not see where they were being taken. The boat skippers reversed the outboard engines while several of the pirates helped by pushing the bow of the boats loose from the sandy beach. The boats swung out to sea meeting up with the fifth boat, which hung back in the rear in case any of the prisoners tried to jump out.

These tourists had been taken hostage by Mindanao Moslem pirates and were helpless to do anything but obey their orders to stay alive. There were six men and five women whose lives had changed instantly that morning from happy tourists enjoying a holiday at a remote resort well away from the usual noisy haunts to potential terrorist victims.

The lead pirate boat had a hand-held basic GPS aboard, the type many fishermen used when venturing out of sight of land. The boats rose and fell in the chop and swell, which made the prone hostages ill and some began to vomit uncontrollably. Hours passed with the sun and humidity not making the journey any better. The fifteen-hour trip took them over 200km from the Malaysian coast to the Philippine island of Sulu, where the boats pulled into the village cove of Parang (meaning sword). Darkness cloaked the boats' arrival and exhaustion had overtaken the hostages to a point that they had trouble getting out, irrespective of being pushed and dragged over the side into the cool shallow water.

The pirates were well prepared and were met by a number of villagers, who assisted the hostages stagger up the beach and along a well-used track that took them all deeper into the tropical forest above and behind the village. Cages had been constructed using old run-down huts. There were no comforts of home, just plastic buckets that the pigs enjoyed tipping over and eating the contents or just rolling in the excrement. Barking dogs wandered about and could smell the fear emitted by the hostages.

The prison huts were located in the middle of a group of thatched dwellings used by the pirates and other supporting villagers, which were made up of men, women and teenage boys. All of these people carried either AK-47s, hunting rifles, automatic pistols and or machetes. These were the keepers of the hostages and were dominated by the leader of the five boat crews who spoke good English. Luckily, the French also spoke English as it was imperative for them not to be further abused or misunderstood.

The hostages were fed twice a day at sun up and sun down, and buckets of sea water were provided for ablutions once a day in the morning. Interaction with the pirates and villagers was forbidden; only the leader could communicate with them on the rare occasions when he decided it necessary. Photographs of the hostages were taken as proof of life with the current newspaper in front of them. There were arguments among the pirates and villagers from time to time as the days turned into weeks and weeks into months. Apparently, the French Government Consulate in Manila had been contacted by the pirates' representatives with demands for a ransom. However, both the Philippines Government and the French were trying to ascertain where the hostages were being held while stalling the negotiations.

Identification of Hostage Location
The French obtained US satellite survey pictures around the timeline of the hostage taking and spent time analysing and enhancing the clarity. Interviews with the Malaysian resort staff indicated that four or five white-hulled open boats were used to spirit the hostages away. Eventually, five white boats were spotted on the satellite imagery and several exposures were overlaid until a

reasonable fix was obtained on which island in Mindanao the hostages had landed on. The French requested the USA to task their satellite to pass over the island of Sulu and the smaller islands nearby. Sulu was selected as the most likely location given the direction of the five boats and the limited number of inhabitants.

The five boats were difficult to spot as there were a number of fishing boats in coves and bays around the island. The only practical way to gather detailed intelligence was to insert a pair of specialist observers to establish covertly:

- Which island
- The specific location on the island
- If all hostages were in the same place
- How the hostages were being held
- How many guards
- What weapons
- Security patrols, warning system
- The layout of possible recovery terrain
- Ingress/egress plan

Then the intention was to send in a team to extract all the hostages using whatever force was necessary. Time was of the essence due to the veracity of pirates threatening to shoot a male hostage.

The threats were taken seriously by the French but they were not able to mobilise a DGE special operations hit team from France or French Polynesia in time. Other options were considered such as using Philippines security forces but this was rejected due to the likelihood of there being a leak of their intentions to the pirates, who would then definitely shoot the hostages.

Chapter 14

Australian SAS Called Up

Major Spider

At this particular moment in history, there was a joint military training operation between the British Garrison Gurkhas based in Brunei Darussalam, Australian SAS and the Singapore Army. The Australian Embassy in Manila informed the French Ambassador that there were skilled resources in the region should the French wish to request their mobilisation.

Major Spider was currently back in the saddle in charge of an Australian SAS company, putting them through their training paces in the Bruneian jungle in the Tenburong area, and he felt bloody good to be at it again after desk jobs and returning to university to complete his degree in engineering. Several days into the training, Spider received a confidential helicopter-borne and hand-delivered message direct from the Australian Consulate in the Brunei capital city of Bandar Seri Begawan. The message required him to contact the DIO in Australia and receive a briefing on a live operation that required an SAS jungle specialist team.

Having only a minute to digest the message, a satellite phone was promptly handed to him by the consular representative, who spoke into his ear that the DIO was on the other end. Commander Coen's voice bellowed out at Spider as if he was trying to be heard from across a parade ground in Canberra, Australia.

'Major, we have a hostage problem and you have the only qualified skills and team right near where the show is going on. This is a French show as the hostages are their people being held by Mindanao area pirates. There's not much time to stand about pissing into the wind about who, what, where, so your orders are to assemble a ten-man hit team and determine what stores (weapons, comms, kit, etc.) are required.'

Spider responded with a 'Yes Sir, consider it done'.

'The British Garrison barracks in Seri Brunei will kit you out and we will provide all available intel en route. Confirm:

- You and the team's readiness. Ingress will be in two stages:
- Two-man insertion to establish situation and a ten-man insertion for hostage extraction.'

'Understood Commander, over and out.'

Spider requested an additional Black Hawk helicopter immediately from the British Garrison and, while he waited, he called in his men and selected the best ten Australian SAS personnel he had available. At least his group of instructors would make up half of the hit team. Kitting out for this mission went pretty smoothly as the Gurkhas were very well disciplined and Spider had free rein in their ordnance stores and warehouse. Now, the next problem confronting their kitted up and raring to go SAS hit team was: How the hell do we get to this Sulu Island without being spotted?

The Brits had the solution; they had a naval base in the capital Bandar Seri Begawn. Spider got on to the British Embassy in the capital and requested them to organise naval support for the mission, in the form of a helicopter and a patrol boat. It seemed that everyone knew about the hostage crisis and the need to co-operate. All ten SAS team members clambered aboard the helicopter and Spider instructed the pilot to head directly for the port in the capital, which was about a thirty-minute flight. This way they could avoid being seen by the locals.

British Naval Support

Back to Work Warriors
Apparently, the Royal Navy were very experienced in the Mindanao waters as they had conducted regular pirate patrols to protect commercial shipping passing through the seaway. The helicopter pilot spoke over the radio on the military frequency to the captain of the patrol boat while en route and arranged for a hot touchdown and disembarkation of the 'cargo' onto the dock adjacent to the boat. The crew would facilitate a rapid embarkation onto the boat. The helicopter engines roared as it barely touched the dock. They all exited and ran to the gangway of the boat, where its crew briskly ushered them aboard and into the galley area. There they dumped their kit onto the tables. The sound of the helicopter faded as it sped off back to base.

With all ten members of the SAS team secreted on board, the patrol boat's engines roared, mooring lines were hoisted aboard and then they edged out of the harbour and into the South China Sea pointing north. In the ward room, Spider received a briefing on what the captain proposed for their insertion near Sulu Island. Detailed charts of the island and water depths were assessed along with faxed copies of the satellite photos of the island terrain, housing clusters and fishing boats in the coves.

The Royal Navy's mission should look like a routine patrol passing to the west of the island offshore about 20 miles. The plan for the patrol boat was to arrive at night, in blackout conditions, and turn directly towards the island where their radar showed very few or no fishing boats on the water. The closer to the island the better but the pirates were not stupid and would have people watching the coast and the skies for intruders.

At the stern of the patrol boat, the SAS team were issued with three Zodiac-type rubber dinghies:

- Two ten-man Zodiacs fitted with 130hp outboard engines.
- The two-man intel-gathering Zodiac was smaller and fitted with a 30hp engine.
- The two ten-man Zodiacs would stay aboard the patrol boat until called for over the satellite phone.
- The main hit team would tow the second ten-man Zodiac and use it for taking the hostages out.

There could be no diminutive plan of attack and extraction until the first intel pair had inserted and reported back via satellite phone.

The patrol boat and remaining hit team would wait and slowly carry out a routine patrol about 10 miles off the island while waiting for the call. It took three days for the patrol boat to arrive on station off Sulu Island. The weather observed was rain and 1-metre seas, perfect for moving in close as the fair-weather fishing boats did not show up on the radar, thus giving Major Spider and his old mate from the Cambodian missions, Sergeant Brute, the go-ahead for insertion. The weather allowed for less distance to get to see the shoreline and pick a place to sink the Zodiac. They stumbled down the rope ladder on the stern of the patrol boat and onto the Zodiac, where they found that the sailors had placed and tied down their backpacks and weapons. They had started the motor and had it in neutral gear ready for a quick launch before it hit the water.

Sulu Island Landing

Major Spider and Sergeant Brute
Wet as a shag on a rock in the spray from the waves, they pointed the Zodiac in the direction of the island using the hand-held marine GPS provided. It would be very useful for setting the other team's GPS way points, which were travel lines on the GPS screen, before they left the patrol boat. The latest marine GPS equipment provided included an 8in screen, built-in antenna, and maps showing water depths, channel markers, lighthouses and major shoreline objects like water tank towers. They also highlighted reefs, shallows and coastal

harbour details, and were very accurate to within a metre. The old types only gave out compass headings once you set up a map longitude and latitude and not much else.

Spider and Brute discussed the most efficient, safest and logical landing zone for them to ingress the island. They decided on the opposite side (north), from which they would work their way south across the centre of the island until they spotted where the hostages were being held. The maps of the island only displayed roads and villages on the west and south coasts, so entering from the north side and working their way the 30km to the southern beaches should give them fewer encounters with the locals and they guessed that the hostages would be well away from the beach.

The Zodiac scraped on the reef that the waves were breaking over and it started to take on water. Spider and Brute decided it was time to grab their kits and, using their bayonets, sink the Zodiac between the shallower reef outcrops so as not to have someone blunder on to it closer to the land mass. Soaking wet, they both clambered over the jagged rocks in the shallows and eventually, with a few cuts on their hands from the barnacles on the rock surfaces, they headed into the overhanging canopy of the jungle.

Their past jungle exposure was during the Vietnam War, wandering around the Cambodian jungle with plenty of local natives and enemies from across the border. This should be similar terrain and they were ready for whatever was ahead in the dark. Even the locals wouldn't wander about during the night, so they could assume they were alone for the time being.

Having reached the approximate centre of the island at the highest point, they set up an observation post by transplanting some of the low brush and large lily leaves. This spot was selected as they could see lights flickering in several locations below. As daylight ascended it clarified from where the lights had been emitting there were several small clusters of huts in cleared areas and people down there were beginning to move about. This was still about 10km from the west and southern main fishing villages.

The telltale evidence of anything associated with the hostages would be people wandering around with firearms, or guard posts on the roads or tracks.

Intel observation is a somewhat boring job unless you know what is, and what is not, a lead to the target. If Spider and Brute weren't spotted arriving, then the guards should be relaxed, which might just let them get a lot closer by splitting up and one warrior going to one clearing and the other staying put, and then changing places at another clearing. This routine went on all day until they had exhausted the possibilities in this area as there was no sighting of weapons and no sign of holding areas for the hostages, just plantations for fruit and vegetables.

Plan B was to continue moving towards the southern end of the island and setting up another observation point. There was no Plan C yet, so they moved forward along a track just before it got too dark and they thanked their blessings that the covering rain had now stopped. Given that they had observed several narrower tracks through the jungle during the day and that nobody had used them, they decided it would be quicker for them to use this one to speed up the trek south rather than hacking and wrestling their way very noisily through the prickly undergrowth.

The track appeared to lead nowhere in particular and split off from time to time, so they had to choose which route kept them on the high ground and in a southerly direction.

About 5km from the southern coast, as they crested a steep, slippery hill, they heard a dog barking and voices ahead and below their position. It was time to set up a new observation hide for the night and wait until the sounds had died away before catching up on much-needed sleep.

Curious of what lay ahead, they later decided to move down the track and see if this was just another clearing with huts. They both would sleep better knowing than not knowing.

As they got within about 100 yards, they could smell camp fire smoke and hear people talking and moving about, including the sound of several motor scooters. This was now smelling and sounding more like a more populated village than the others they had observed, but there were no plantations this far south.

Very interesting, Spider knew he wouldn't be able to sleep until he got a lot closer for a better look during daylight. He went back to where Brute had settled under his poncho to stay in some semblance of dry, and Spider told him what he'd encountered. Brute was also intrigued and wanted to see more and close up right now. This reconnoitring in the dark was going to be a bit tricky as wandering about in unfamiliar surroundings is fraught with problems, which include getting hurt, bitten, falling or – even worse – getting spotted and caught.

With their initial enthusiasm dampened, it was agreed that they would move down at dawn while the occupants were still asleep. The dogs would be a problem if they were clumsy and made too much noise. Spider sat down and sent off a text message on the satellite phone to the patrol boat captain and copied DIO as a progress report. It basically said:

Landed north on Sulu Island
Travelled centrally to new point 5km off south coast
So far target not sighted
Intend to move further south tomorrow

It's hard to sleep when in a jungle and wet through. Odd noises are all around and, to cap it off, the midges like to eat human flesh and bigger things are slithering and crawling about. Spider sat watch for the first two hours and then gave sleeping Brute a nudge to do the next shift, and so on until Brute finally whispered 'Time to go mate'.

They pulled their ponchos over their heads and rolled them up, then squashed them roughly into their backpacks while thinking of the best course of action to approach the habitation below them. They ate some cold rations to conserve energy as it might be the next evening before they ate again. It was decided to split up; Brute went to the east and Spider to the west side of whatever was to be observed below.

They decided to meet back at this same location at dusk to discuss what they had observed and decided that they would trek to a new location way back behind from where they had traversed if this one was a bust.

Spider moved forward until he was in a position from which he was able to pick out huts and smoke from fires. This involved a lot of tiger crawling on his belly in among the undergrowth. Wet and muddy all over, it probably made for great camouflage and some sort of expensive full-body beauty treatment, but he was thinking he would have preferred sitting by a resort swimming pool with a beer. Fortunately, there were a few ruts, crevices, fallen palm trees and washaways on the ground that made for good hide positions. At last Spider could sit up and peer through the foliage at his side of what was a small village.

Brute had a similar experience but for him the floor of the jungle was more open with less cover, sandy soil under foot with stagnant water pools to skirt around or wade through and bigger trees that forced him to stand up and crouch behind. Then he had to duck down and dodge creeping ferns with vicious spikes protruding and gripping at his clothes and backpack. Finally, he arrived in a spot further south than planned but a good vantage point from which to see the compound and watch the comings and goings on the entrance track.

Brute had ended up getting to a hide that was a rotted and partly hollowed out tree. All he needed to do was pull some palm fronds in front of the opening and he was basically out of the rain and out of sight within 50 yards of one of the huts. Although the dogs had not heard them moving about, there were several pigs that were better than dogs at smelling and spotting intruders.

Pirates' Lair Identified

As observed at the previous plantations with huts in a clearing, this clearing was large and was almost a village with wider tracks all around. People were beginning to stir from the huts. This time, they both saw firearms being carried by men, women and teenage boys. Their prayer leader began his call to prayer. It was their Moslem morning prayer time and everyone headed toward a flat area with their rattan prayer mats. After about half an hour of praying and being spoken to by their leader, they disbanded and went about their daily activities, still with weapons in hand or shouldered. There had to be hostages here or this was a paramilitary camp of some sort – or both.

Attention was being paid to the two huts in the centre of the compound. Food and water were being carried over and white faces were pressed up against their prison window bars and skinny arms were extended to exchange buckets. Spider quickly pulled out the satellite phone from his backpack and typed a text message to the captain on the patrol boat with a copy to DIO:

Hostages spotted – caged
Locals all well armed
Monitoring for extraction plan and timing
Will advise.

Brute and Spider held their observation positions all day, counting how many pirates and associates there were, sketching where they were billeted, noting the types of weapons and recording the locations of guards, pigs and dogs. At sunset once most of the pirates had prayed, eaten then settled in for the night, Spider slid close in against one of the huts to get a better look at the layout of the compound and get a glimpse of the hostages. They looked pretty forlorn and skinny but otherwise all eleven were present and alive. There were at least two guards sitting on a bench in front of the huts currently talking to each other and not taking much notice of the hostages or their plight.

Brute slipped back to his observation point and oriented himself so that he could see how to leave and return to the same spot at dawn tomorrow. Then, back on his belly in the sand and smelly water, he headed up to the muddy track where Spider was now waiting.

Rain was now falling as a mist and made their return further up the hill easier as their movements would be shrouded, tracks washed away and noise muffled.

They headed north away from the compound and back into the original hide where they had slept the previous night. Both warriors and the hit team all carried Sig Sauer silenced automatic weapons. Currently they were not in a position to retake the hostages on their own. Even if all ten of the SAS warriors surrounded the compound and attacked the pirates, a number of the hostages might also be killed.

Chapter 15

Black Operation Extraction Planned

Spider and Brute discussed the operation scenarios for several hours until they came up with the only plausible and safe way to extract the hostages alive. The extraction plan was to slip in and silently take out each and every pirate – no matter man, woman or teenager – as they were all well-armed and would put up a fight. Spider used the back of one of the island maps and sketched the layout boundary of the compound, wrote down the GPS position and drew where the two hostage huts were, showing the general location of where the dogs and pigs hung out (their security alarm system) and where the night shift guards sat.

Spider's next satellite message read:

Main team required this midnight at the south cove beach.
One of us will meet you there.
Use satellite phone when a mile out for final GPS landing instructions.
All pirates armed and to be taken out – repeat ALL – will brief onshore.
On arrival team will split up at compound to terminate as follows:

1. Two-night guards
2. Two dogs & two pigs
3. All occupants in every hut

Treat all contacts on way to and from beach as hostile.
Require two navy coxswains to operate Zodiacs and standby on beach for hostages and team arrival and extraction.

Spider figured that this message would get a few people out of bed tonight, short notice and all. The SAS team waiting out on the Royal Navy patrol boat would be chafing at the bit to get this operation under way and over. It's what they all have been trained to do and were very good at it.

Spider hoped that some smart guy in the hierarchy of the DIO or the Government didn't get hold of what they planned to do later that night and want more clarification or the mission would definitely be a bust. Timing was everything and they would only get one shot at it.

Brute and Spider began moving stealthy down the track, moving wide east to pass the compound entrance and in the direction of the south beach and fishing boat harbour. They needed to ensure that it was secured before the Zodiac parties arrived.

The track was wider but empty as they came closer to the beach area. A few people were moving about in the huts, so they stayed in the shadows of the water's edge palm trees with several fishing boats beached and others bobbing about at anchor in the cove. The five boats that took the hostages were among them. They had not checked these fishing village people out for weapons and would have to deal with them when the time came. The plan was to get in and get out so fast that they wouldn't be able to react.

Extraction Plan Implemented – With Extreme Prejudice

Almost midnight. The Zodiacs would be on their way as no satellite phone message had countered their plan. Brute waded out to where a shadowy unlit fishing boat was anchored but grounded on the outgoing tide. Spider stayed back on the beach and monitored the satellite phone for the expected message. Right on midnight a beep tone from the satellite phone came in. He hunched over the screen to read the message:

All set – Inbound – 1 Mile Off

He tapped in the GPS co-ordinates of this reasonably isolated part of the beach and 'GO'. Soon Spider could hear the low burble of the 130hp Zodiac outboard motor. Brute flashed his pen light torch twice on the blind side of the fishing boat hull so the Zodiac could come on station alongside the boat. As requested, the captain had sent the two coxswains to stand by the Zodiacs for a fast getaway.

So far so good. Nobody had taken notice of the incoming boats.

Now all of Spider's chosen team of experienced SAS soldiers slid silently into the shallow water until all were ashore, moving low and fast behind Brute. Spider then led them up to the track and at about 100 yards from the beach the team formed a huddle and focused on his torch-lit sketch of the compound. Each man was given a specific target to silently take out and in what order. Spider set the precise time when to execute each action. The team cocked their weapons. They were not there to start a shootout so everyone felt the pressure of a precision hit coming up.

Stealthily, the team of SAS warriors, each now equipped with night vision equipment, moved up the track and then spread out to take each target as cleanly as possible. Brute, utilising his sniper skills through his night vision scope, took out the pigs with only a short squeal herd. The two guards didn't notice as the pigs had not moved. The dogs went down without a whimper as both took head shots.

Time to move in on the pirates; guards first, then each accommodation hut.

After eliminating the animals used for security, Brute moved ahead with two of the team to take out the two guards while the other men slipped into the nearest hut, pop-pop-pop (three in the mouth), the next hut, then the next hut. The men with Spider moved up and began the same action, him in the lead, pop-pop-pop. All done, then silence.

Spider had two of his men begin torching all of the huts using the wood still burning in one of the hut stoves. The huts were made of rattan and woven palm fronds and would quickly light up.

The hostages began to stir once the team had finished their work on the armed pirates. It was now time to work out how to break open their jail doors and release them. There was no time for explanations or introductions. Brute and Spider motioned to the men now standing in front of the hostage huts to just get the doors open no matter how. The doors were held closed with lengths of chain and padlocks, so the men each in turn shot off the locks and yanked the doors wide open.

Hostages Extracted

Spider called out softly but firmly to the hostages 'Vite, vite (hurry, hurry). We are Australian soldiers. Go, go, go. We must hurry.'

It took about five minutes to get the eleven hostages assembled out in the open in front of their huts and they pointed them at the track leading to the beach. Each warrior half carried the hostages between them down to the beach. So far, no stirring from the fishermen's huts below, even though the flames at the compound were now beginning to light up the night sky. Ammunition in the huts would start to burn soon.

The rush down toward the beach and the Zodiacs was not entirely silent but it was too late to stop and rest or discuss what the hostages had to do or not do. Everyone rushed to the Zodiacs and piled on roughly in pairs of hostage and soldier.

The navy coxswains had already turned the Zodiacs around facing out to sea to save having to reverse out, which would slow up the extraction. Time to rev up the 130hp engines and skat out of there before the locals worked out what the heck just happened and were distracted by the fire up the hill and ammunition beginning to burst, a good distraction away from the water.

It was pitch dark out there on the water except for the dim glow of the GPS used by the coxswains at the helm of each Zodiac. They also had hand-held VHF radios and were in contact with the patrol boat, which had now turned on its running lights some 10km off shore. The Zodiacs were racing at top speed and occasionally lifted over a wave and became airborne, crashing down hard on the next wave and rolling from side to side. These guys really could drive a boat. The patrol boat's spotlight beam hit the water between the Zodiacs and guided them to the stern, where net ladders had been lowered.

A number of deck crew were leaning over the side to grab anyone who climbed up to the gunnels and dragged everyone up onto the now throbbing deck as the main engines fired up. Spider guessed the captain was pretty excited to have this mission come out so well but wanted to get under way pronto as they were in Philippine waters and didn't want its military to become involved.

The hostages were immediately taken below, identified, fed and given crew clothing and bunks to finally rest on after their ordeal in cages on bare ground. They kept to themselves during the three-day trip down the south-east coast of Borneo to Brunei. The team also kept to themselves and, as per SAS protocol, they did not spend time with the Navy crew. They had received orders from DIO not to divulge any details of this operation to anyone except the DIO, which included the captain and crew of the patrol boat.

The captain wondered what exactly happened out there in the dark and apart from what his coxswains told him he knew nothing specifically except for 'We took the soldiers to the beach, waited for them, then a bunch of people were delivered on board by the Zodiacs and we checked and fed them'.

On arrival at the Brunei naval base, the hostages were immediately taken over by the French authorities and, after a brief medical check on the wharf, bussed to Brunei airport. The SAS team returned to the jungle training session in Temburong and took up where they had left off. Spider was summoned to Darwin, where he met with the DIO representatives headed by Commander Coen from his Vietnam War days. The entire episode regarding this mission was to be kept under wraps (that means 'tell no one').

Apparently, the Philippine Government had issued an official complaint to the British Garrison in Brunei, whose patrol boat had apparently conducted a hostage extraction operation in their territory, and demanded a full explanation with possible reparations due to the nature of what went down in Mindanao on Sulu Island.

Spider never heard how the Brits handled that one but he and the team never heard a murmur from the Australian Government. There was no publicity or reports from the French side as they quietly repatriated their people back to France having paid no ransom.

With no significant injuries among the team of SAS professionals, they once more disbanded and went back to what they were doing the day they were called away to action.

The Battle Goes on

The offensive against Abu Sayyaf continues as the Philippine military engage in fierce jungle firefights with losses on both sides. Reports of piracy in the Sulu Sea continue, with fishermen being killed and kidnapping for ransom continuing, with reports of Abu Sayyaf pocketing millions of dollars.

In recent years a peace and development plan for Mindanao with a timeframe from 2011 to 2030 has been implemented and although it has many hurdles to cross it is hoped it will serve as a basis for peace and harmony.

Hold on for one more day, things will change, things will go your way.

Chapter 16

When the Power of Love Overcomes the Love of Power, Only then Will there be a Chance for True Peace

Middle East

Many nations of the world were in turmoil, and Middle East countries had turned on themselves. Iraq and Iran had been shooting at each other for years. One of the problems was related to the different Muslim sects, Sunni and Shiite. They had been at each other's throats since the beginning of time. Now the wacky Iraqi dictator Saddam Hussein had invaded his neighbour, Kuwait.

Eye of the Storm Iraq War Operations

Kuwait's most prominent geographic feature is Kuwait Bay (Jun al Kuwayt), which indents the shoreline and provides natural protection for the port of Kuwait. It accounts for nearly half the country's shoreline. Oil and gas terminals are located in this bay, making it a strategic asset for Kuwait, and for Saddam.

To the east along the Euphrates River lay the Iranian border, with the remnants of a recent war with Iraq. To the south-west, Kuwait shared a long border of 250km with Saudi Arabia. The oil from onshore and offshore fields continued to be shared equally between these two countries. To date there had been no conflict between Saudi Arabia and Iraq, except for there being a US military presence in Saudi, a cause of Iraqi concern about a possible invasion from that direction.

The third side of the triangle-shaped nation was the 240km of historically contested border between Kuwait and Iraq. Hence, this border was patrolled regularly by both sides and minefields had been placed at strategic points on the Iraqi side.

Although the Iraqi government, which had first asserted a claim to rule Kuwait in 1938, recognised the borders with Kuwait in 1963 based on agreements made earlier in the century, it continued to press Kuwait for control over Bubiyan and Warbah islands through the 1960s and 70s.

In mid-August 1990, the stage was set on the Kuwait border in the Persian Gulf, which comprised 195km of coast. Within its territory were nine islands, two of which, Bubiyan (the largest) and Warbah, were largely uninhabited but strategically important. Due to the Iraq–Kuwait war, many inhabitants left their homes on the islands and did not return.

In August 1990, Iraq invaded Kuwait and, shortly thereafter, formally incorporated the entire country into Iraq. Under United Nations (UN) Security Council Resolution 687, after the restoration of Kuwaiti sovereignty in 1991, a UN commission undertook formal demarcation of the borders on the basis of those agreed to in 1963. The boundary was demarcated in 1992, but Iraq refused to accept the commission's findings.

Australia was a member of the international coalition that contributed military forces to the 1991 Gulf War Desert Storm operations. More than 1,800 Australian Defence Forces personnel were deployed to the Persian Gulf from August 1990 to September 1991.

The conflict had taken place between Iraq and thirty-four other coalition countries led by the United States. It all started with the invasion of Kuwait by Iraq on 2 August 1990 and ended the following spring when Iraq's army was defeated and was preparing to withdraw from Kuwait.

Iran–Iraq War

During the Iran–Iraq War the United States, Soviet Union and France provided support for Iraq, while Iran was largely isolated. After eight years, war-weariness, economic problems, decreased morale, repeated Iranian military failures, recent Iraqi successes, Iraqi use of USA and UK manufactured and supplied 'chemical weapons of mass destruction, WOMD' (Saddam never manufactured any of his own WOMD) lack of international sympathy for the war and increased US–Iran military tension all led to a ceasefire brokered by the United Nations.

The conflict had been compared to the First World War in terms of the tactics used, including large-scale trench warfare with barbed wire stretched across fortified defensive lines, manned machine guns, artillery barrages, bayonet charges, Iranian human wave attacks, land mines from a variety of sources, marine mines placed in the Arabian Gulf waters, extensive use of US and UK supplied chemical weapons fired into Iran by Iraq, and, later, deliberate attacks on civilian targets such as the Kurds in the north.

An estimated 500,000 Iraqi and Iranian soldiers died, in addition to a similar number of civilians. The end of the Iran–Iraq War resulted in neither reparations nor border changes. In order to recoup losses from the war, Iraq invaded Kuwait in 1990, only to be repulsed by the US-led coalition in the Persian Gulf War called Desert Storm.

The Gulf War

As a precursor to any invasion, good military sense needs to prevail in order to reduce the collateral damage to coalition forces. This meant that more on the ground intelligence was needed to cover the posture of unknown Iraqi forces. In late July–early August 1990, a side meeting at the UN in New York between the USA and Australian representatives covered the possibility of Australia providing an intelligence incursion into Iraq. This proposal was taken in confidence to the Australian Federal Government Minister of Defence (MOD) for discussion with the Defence Chief, with the objective of providing the coalition with intelligence-gathering support during Desert Shield for the likely Desert Storm invasion.

The US CIA Director would co-ordinate with the US military chiefs and provide all available intelligence data and point out the gaps that required coverage, including support for any attacks on Iraqi army fixed positions that currently did not show up on satellite imagery. The CIA had not informed Australia that they had already requested British Commandos carry out a similar operation targeting Basra City.

Australia agreed in principle to co-ordinate with the US military operations in the Persian Gulf and provide the specialist resources to support intelligence operations ahead of any forecast military intervention whether by land, sea or in the air.

Other coalition partners would assist the US and Australian intelligence agencies, and their service organisations would have some input to a planning study on a need-to-know basis, but would not take an active role in the establishment or activation of individual covert military operations except for ensuring there was merit in the operation, no overlap or conflicting interests.

The 1991 Gulf War Operation Desert Shield, a precursor to Desert Storm, was to be the focus of the Australian SAS covert incursion and intelligence-gathering mission.

The mission overlapped into the Operation Desert Storm invasion of Iraq and certain recovery actions in Kuwait thereafter. To the west, British Commandos were being mobilised by helicopter north-east into Iraq near Basra City from the Saudi Arabia border and there was a gap of intelligence over at the south-eastern borders of Iraq, Iran and Kuwait.

Approval of Intelligence Gathering Operations

On 8 September 1990, the US CIA Director visited Australia and through the US Embassy co-ordinated meetings with the Australian Minister of Defence, the Defence Chief, Australian Intelligence and Security Service (ASIS) Head and the Defence Intelligence Organisation Head (DIO).

In order that complete security and unanimity of the DIO operation and its operatives was maintained, no cross-bench Federal Government Defence Intelligence Committee would be notified or appraised of the study or indeed the ministerial approval to proceed with it.

The Eye of the Shield Study utilised the most current US and coalition intelligence reports regarding:

- UN advisories on weapons of mass destruction, as insisted upon by the USA and UN Inspectors.
- Iraq's responses and co-operation.
- Iraq's state of war readiness and current posture regarding defensive positions and strengths.
- Mobile scud missile launches into Israel and technical reach radius into other target areas.
- Current US satellite and aerial photography.
- Risk assessment of the mission success or failure options for:
  - o Timing for mobilisation stages (team selection – single point DIO co-ordination of activities – transfers – interfaces – supply – transport options etc).
  - o Ingress and egress of the proposed four-to-six-man specialist intelligence team, including attributes such as which military arm where the best resources and skill sets were located and immediately available.
  - o Political deniability and budget off record.
  - o Operational equipment and proposed endurance duration.
  - o Interfaces with coalition partners.
  - o Reporting and communications protocols.
  - o Selection of several key mission objectives on the ground.
  - o Ramifications in the case of capture or death.

Newly appointed Naval attaché Commander Cowey (RAN) had been delegated to co-ordinate a study paper and report back to the military chief, who in turn would review and obtain approval from the Federal Government Minister for Defence and the CIA chief. Within one week, on 15 September 1990, the CIA chief returned with a response that the operation was a 'go' and to immediately make preparations, set a specific timeline and clearly define what US resources would be needed for field reporting, mobilisation, ingress and egress.

The Minister of Defence officially signed off on the CIA, MOD and DIO supported study on 16 September and appointed Naval attaché Commander Cowey as the interface between the various services and government (MOD).

Commander Cowey was then tasked to place the words 'Top Secret and Priority' on the cover and only three hard copies of the signed document were made. He then arranged to have removed and destroyed all other working papers and computer files from all departments involved in the drafting.

This left only one original for the CIA chief, and one original copy each for the MOD, Minister and the DIO Head.

The MOD had earlier that day been in contact with the DIO head regarding the study approval and discussed details of operation feasibility and resource functionality for sending a small compact intelligence-gathering team into Iraq and Kuwait via submarine as outlined in the study. Indeed, there were some hurdles to jump regarding US and Australian co-operation, with each country having complex inter-service workings, but this operation was not untried in the past and with good communications either way it should succeed. If it failed due to discovery by the Iraqis then there would be a news blackout due to the covert nature of the operation. Hence, there would only be operatives deployed who understood the possibility of the one-way nature of this sort of operation.

In the following narrative, the logistical planning by the DIO and operations undertaken by a select, small elite team of such specialists is portrayed. For security reasons there are no real names used of persons or vessels encountered during this operation. The locations, war theatre and timing are accurate to the best knowledge of the author, who was advised by an operative who was there.

Chapter 17

DIO Specialist Team Selection – Desert Shield Operation

Within the DIO function, there were imbedded specialist intelligence resources and operatives, drawn from existing Australian military organisations, or for plausible deniability purposes, at times the DIO called upon external retired or reserve military personnel or civilians with special skills.

Mobilisation

Immediate mobilisation planning had been initiated, with Commander Cowey delegated as the sole liaison officer between CIA, MOD, DIO and the Minister for Defence on a need-to-know basis from then on. The CIA would be kept informed of satellite radio sat-com sit-rep on the ground by daily situational reports from the inserted intelligence team using the closest US Navy assets in the Arabian Gulf as the base of operations.

Given the limited time for mobilisation due to the high probability of the USA and coalition forces co-ordinated attack on Iraq, code-named Desert Storm, this operation would have to be kept within the timeline of the Desert Shield phase, where limited or no adverse coalition forces attacks on Iraq were made and during the ongoing Iraqi invasion of Kuwait, which had already begun several days earlier.

The task of team selection was generally in line with Commander Cowey's Eye of the Shield Study guidelines and CIA intelligence reports but with enhanced DIO knowledge of its own repertoire of desert operation equipment needed, plus inter-service full-time operatives or on-call contractor resources that had specialist skills and most importantly had immediate availability and deniability.

Team size had been a concern due to the flat desert type of terrain and lack of cover. The team size was cut down from six to four, requiring very fit, hard-nosed and highly experienced professionals who had past DIO operations history on other missions, had no baggage (family), worked effectively together no matter what the outcome, always finished what they had started, displayed ingenuity and adaptability in very trying desert conditions, and understood the rules in case of capture or death. A call off team of currently off-duty freelance (contractor) specialists had been decided upon due to there being mobilisation preparations for the full-time military personnel needed for Desert Storm.

Finding and making contact with each of the freelance team members was somewhat complex as none of them were just sitting at home waiting by the phone. Some were at work in a civilian company that was unaware of their hidden lives. As with most operatives, each did have a land line phone number and possibly computer with internet connection just in case they were called on some day.

All those selected were formally reserve military forces officers and were periodically monitored by the Australian Security and Intelligence Organisation (ASIO), ASIS, MOD or DIO for security clearances and kept up to date with new equipment changes and training, and maintained top physical fitness.

The first selection was for the team leader, followed by supporting personnel that each had multi-tasking skills in order to keep the team size down to four men, able to survive in the desert, able to avoid detection in the vast open terrain and reduce the political fallout if caught, tortured and killed.

- Major Pete (Spider) A hardened professional, active in periodic covert duties for the DIO during previous years. Never failed to complete a mission and known to have left badly wounded colleagues behind when necessary. Comfortable out on the hot, vast open desert of a 10,000-acre wheat farm hunting and shooting rabbits as a kid. As a soldier, trained in the jungles of Canungra, Australia, in the 1960s. Active service in Cambodia during the Vietnam War (1968 to 1972). After that, trained soldiers in the Malaysian and Bruneian jungles with former communist Chinese rebel Major Chin of the Singapore Army and the English Gurkhas based at Collins Lines Garrison in Brunei. Never married but has the occasional liaison. No emotional attachments. Security classification – Very high.
- Sergeant Tony (Brute) A twenty-year SAS soldier beginning with the Vietnam War with follow-on covert operations experience in Nigeria, South Africa, Lebanon and Libyan desert terrains. Capable of long endurance in desert terrain, good second in command, very handy with the M60 machine gun or sniper rifle. A born-and-raised country boy from the wheat fields of Queensland. Divorced with grown children, very limited contact or attachment. No current attachment. Security classification – Very High
- Lance Corporal Alex (Doc) A twenty-year British Commando with desert terrain experience in Lebanon, Libya and Morocco desert

terrains. Excellent as an infield paramedic and expert in electronic warfare and communications equipment. Handy with a 7.63mm SLR rifle. Served with Spider and Brute on several covert missions for the DIO. Has a 'bring 'em back alive' attitude. Divorced with no children, no emotional attachments. Security classification – High

- Corporal Aims (Rat) Former Vietnam War veteran alongside Spider and followed him in several covert DIO missions as sniper spotter. Rat is a short stocky and wiry figure capable of long endurance in jungle and desert terrain. Well versed in the use of Semtex explosive and various forms of detonation applications. Very useful as a motor mechanic. Able to carry the extra ammunition for the M60 and stay closest to the machine gun as loader and spotter, plus very handy with a bayonet at close quarters. No marital attachments but has the occasional liaison. Security classification – High

Mobilisation – Day One

Once the initial DIO officer (code-named Mr Champion) contacted each of the four-man team, arrangements were made to transport each of them separately to a Sydney office location and they were told to bring enough baggage for a two-week assignment.

Commander Cowey met the team and provided a very cut-down briefing of the operation duration, issued open return air tickets to Qatar and told them their next contact would be an individual named Ahmed, who would be their transport driver. The team was then taken down to the basement, boarded a taxi minibus and headed directly to Sydney international airport, arriving two hours before the flight direct to Qatar.

They had a couple of beers – all except for Brute; he had seen the light and put the plug in the jug, as he had promised himself many moons ago back in his home town. They heard their boarding call and found they were seated separately in tourist 'cattle class'. After the in-flight meal, they were able to settle down to the in-flight movies and sleep.

Mobilisation – Day Two

The four-man covert team arrived in Qatar via Amsterdam very early in the morning. Posing as civilians working for a construction project in Ras Laffan, they passed through customs and immigration using their fake passports and assumed names. They were picked up at the arrivals section by an informal and somewhat unkempt driver reeking of body odour by the name of Ahmed, who was holding up a sign with their new names chalked on it.

He briskly ushered all four of them to a construction company minibus and drove erratically in heavy traffic to a building on the edge of the city. They walked up several flights of stairs carrying their duffel bags and were guided to an upstairs apartment containing two bedrooms, each containing two single beds, and two bathrooms.

The instructions were for everyone not to go outside as this was a Muslim area, so they were told to rest, eat and await further instructions. Ahmed said they should definitely not leave the building for any reason and should only open the door to him if he was on his own. If he was not alone, that would mean big trouble as their covers would have been blown.

Dumping their bags on their preferred beds, they took to the showers, and then crashed, snoring and farting for the next eight hours as it had been a long, boring flight. Spider was the first to rise and found a fridge loaded with food, so he decided to cook them all a hearty breakfast of beef sausages and three eggs a piece, with toast and percolated coffee. As Qatar was a Muslim country, pork products were forbidden, so there was no bacon.

Spider unceremoniously woke all of the team from their slumber by pulling off their covers and yanking their pillows out from under their sleeping heads.

'Wakey, wakey ladies. Get your arses up and showered as breakfast waits for no man.'

Each man was used to hearing the early morning reveille trumpet sound or a raging sergeant blasting into their barracks and shocking them awake, so Spider's nicer approach was accepted as quite mellow in comparison.

Mobilisation – Day Three

It was now midnight, fifteen hours after their arrival into Qatar, and they were picked up by the same stinky-arse driver and transported across town. They drove around the Corniche Road at the edge of the water, where crowds of locals were enjoying the cool of the evening. They arrived at the back of Doha airport, where the US had a section used by their military.

They were kitted out with desert uniforms with no labels or tags and directed to board a carrier personnel transport aircraft. The one-hour flight took them to a designated point in the middle of the Persian Gulf and they landed aboard a US aircraft carrier in the dark except for the temporary illumination of on-board landing lights.

With very little discussion, they were offloaded and escorted to a conference room several levels below the main deck. Without any introductions, they were briefed by senior Australian and US military personnel on:

- The objectives of this mission into Kuwait and Iraq.
- Intel that the zone of contact was active and – to complicate things – close to the Iraqi border and occupied Kuwait.

Each warrior was provided with:

- Camouflaged uniforms long sleeve and leg
- No flak jackets (too heavy)
- GPS communications device
- Tactical Z-Tac Throat Mic radio with earpiece and spare batteries
- Desert dust mask and goggles
- Portable sat-com radio equipment
- Area maps and aerial photos
- Weather forecast
- Reporting schedule, formats and details
- Instructions for ingress and egress into Kuwait/Iraq with alternates
- Waterproof kit bag and pony air cylinder for submarine egress/ingress
- Four pairs of ranging binoculars
- Camouflaged back and hip packs complete with:
  o Shade over sheet, camouflage net
  o Food rations
  o Water canteens with evaporative water capture cone kits
  o First aid kits including the usual stuff plus snake and scorpion bite kits
  o Spare pockets for 1lb packs of Semtex explosive, detonators and fuses, plus most importantly the two laser targeting emitters
  o Small coils of wire and string
  o Wire cutting pliers
  o Clothing items
  o Folding spade
- Weapons including:
  o .45 cal Colt shoulder holstered side arm with two extra loaded magazines
  o One M60 machine gun
  o Two 1,000-round cases of 7.62mm fragment link belt ammunition (bullets also useful for the SLRs)
  o One H&K .50 cal sniper rifle with camouflage wrapping and spotter scope
  o One case assorted .50 cal ammunition (fifty armour-piercing, fifty incendiary, 100 solid man killers)

- o Two 7.62mm SLR rifles
- o Four 1lb Semtex explosives packs, very separate time fuses and detonators
- o Four laser targeting emitters
- o Four smoke grenades

As team leader, Spider understood from their briefing that a UK SAS team code-named Bravo Two Zero would be entering Iraq by helicopter from the Saudi Arabian border under similar intelligence reporting orders at approximately the same ingress time as them.

The key maps were distributed to each of them to peruse and ask questions for clarification if needed. The first map provided a general layout of rivers, borders, roads and towns.

The second map provided an indication of Saddam's various armies and zones of concentration. Due to the changes in Iraq's situation after being forced to retreat from Kuwait, these concentrations and numbers may had changed. Their instructions were, whenever possible, to identify which Iraqi military units, equipment and approximate numbers were sighted in their travels.

The third map provided an overview of the Iraq–Kuwait contested border zone (no-man's-land). This cross-hatched zone on the western half would be where they must operate during the mission. They were advised that their commanders had local Iraqis who used to have families in Kuwait providing a series of observation points right across to the Saudi Arabian border.

Operation – Day One

After the briefing ended, with questions answered and orders given, their full kit out and final inspection completed, they were abruptly ushered outside of the air-conditioned coolness of the conference room into the 48°C heat of the open lower cargo deck by a US Navy officer. He had orders for their immediate transfer off the US aircraft carrier by the ship's tender boat over to a surfacing US class 688 nuclear submarine, one of several operating in the Gulf at the time. The only way they knew it was US was the small flag at the top of the fin where the submarine commander was witnessing the action on deck (no one ever got his name). Several no-name officers and observer crew were also monitoring their arrival.

The submarine commander had previously received orders setting out the need for immediate mobilisation once the special observer team boarded. Then, once it had arrived at the specified location submerged, it must have the team egress the vessel immediately.

The commander's orders were to:

1. Monitor the team progress to shore and report back on successful or otherwise shore arrival.
2. Monitor for the team's satellite radio comms check and forward intelligence reports to the Gulf Fleet commander as needed.
3. Stay close and submerged on patrol in the area to keep an eye on the enemy-held shoreline for on-land or marine activities on nearby Bubiyan Island to the west of their drop-off point as well as sailing west to the mouth of Kuwait harbour.
4. Then return ASAP at the teams sat. radio comms signal for pickup at a specified time in about two weeks from now.

That is if the team wasn't caught up somehow!

Spider still didn't trust these Yanks after the Vietnam War operations as they did, without notice, have a habit of not following through with their coalition allies, even with their own people at times. As team leader his only other option would be to radio for extraction by air from the carrier, which would blow their cover and have the enemy move its assets away from known configurations.

The submarine crew assisted them boarding from the aircraft carrier life boat/tender, with the 1m swell making things a bit awkward as the tender banged and scraped against the forward section of the submarine's black steel hull. Only a slack rope used by a sailor for yanking the tender in between surges of waves kept them from going for an unplanned swim, or being pinned between the tender and the submarine. Their waterproof kit bags full of their operations gear were thrown unceremoniously up onto the deck and dragged away on the double by two burly sailors in desert fatigues.

The team could feel the steely glare of the submarine commander above them on the fin (conning tower) on the back of their necks and whispered to each other 'Keep it moving sharpish as we are being watched, no mistakes or we could get a bollixing from the boss once stowed away on board'.

There has always been a rivalry between services, let alone between coalition allies. Spider's mind briefly flashed back to when he did his submarine escape training (SETIF & SERT) and how the Army SAS personnel were treated by the naval personnel. They nearly drowned him for sadistic fun, those swabbie pricks.

With the transfer onto the submarine completed, the tender reversed off, gathered up the slack line and quickly turned directly for the aircraft carrier. The deck sailors anxiously prodded them forward to the gaping open deck hatch. Other sailors below manhandled their baggage until out of sight. The sailors on deck then ordered them to quickly reverse down the ladder and then followed them down, secured the outer hatch, then notified the first officer on the intercom that the package was on board and that the outer hatches were secured.

The team was then directed to grab their baggage and follow the sailors away from the forward deck hatch and bustled further below between rows of missile silos. There they met the submarine's First Officer Jake Wazouski, who in short and sharp tones briefed them on their behaviour aboard as they were the package guests, the amenities available and the safety requirements, which were:

- Follow all orders given by any of the crew.
- No unsolicited crew contact, except through himself personally.
- Silent operations mean:
  o Don't make any fucking mechanical noises
  o Shut up
  o Don't fool with your equipment
- No loaded weapons while on board.
- No switching on, use or testing of the Z-Tac throat mic and tube earphone or sat-com equipment.
- Sat-com signal frequencies needed for sit-rep reporting, receiving incoming message.
- Procedures for egressing and ingressing the submarine:
  o Forward escape hatch and associated immersion lock will be used to egress the submarine once on specified location.
  o Verification that all of the team were trained in Western Australia Navy submarine escape and rescue system (SERT).

The team stood or sat around as quietly as possible as can be expected in the confined space and donned their desert camouflage Lycra dive suits over their cotton uniforms. They cleaned the dive masks and hooked on the snorkels, then checked the air pressure in the mini scuba pony air tanks.

Then they just languished on the inflatable kit bags waiting for the order to line up for egress. From time to time they took a gulp of water or chewed on hard dry ration blocks supplied by the hovering silent, watchful sailors, while impatiently checking their waterproof dive watches. They also read the variety of signs and labels on the submarine's operating equipment around their oh-so-comfortable, all-round steel floor and walled waiting room.

They intermittently whispered loudly to each other over the constant hum of the electrical equipment around them a series of defamatory remarks about the lousy hotel service and how they wanted to get out of this claustrophobic tin can. They never once paused to dwell on the coming heat outside and the unknown risks that may face them all on the surface once on shore out in the wide-open landscape with their heavy packs for the planned two-week sortie into Saddam Land.

That's when Brute asked in a loud whisper 'Hey Major Spider, you notice any strange smell?'

Spider looked at Brute with his eyebrows raised. 'What the hell are you talking about Brute, did you fart?'

With a chuckle Brute responded 'No Spider. Hey Doc, Rat can you blokes smell anything strange about these Swabbies?'

Each warrior looked at each other, shaking their heads from side to side.

'Neither can I but every bar girl I spoke to in Pattaya City, Thailand, when I was there on R&R, told me that when the Yanks come to town to play their war games with the Thai military operation called Cobra Gold, they could always tell which Yank was a submariner by their body odour. So, fucked if I know but just thought I'd ask.'

'Well, I don't know what to tell ya Brute, but sounds like they may have been twisting your melon. But going forward fellas, let's only refer to each other by our nicknames, no saluting, or mention of rank.'

The three warriors spoke in unison 'Got ya boss'.

Chapter 18

Operation – Day Two

After what seemed like an eternity but was only about six hours in all, the fully submerged submarine had become stationary at periscope depth. It had at last ferried the Australian specialist team close inshore, positioned in the middle of the channel between the Kuwaiti island of Warbah, 1,500 yards off the entrance to the Khawr az-Zubayr tidal waterway, and the shore of north-eastern Kuwait directly to the west. Eastern Iraq was sighted directly ahead to the north and on the charts the Iranian border further east about 30 map miles, not far enough away to be ignored entirely due to their naval and land patrols. This was definitely hostile country for this mission to begin in earnest.

The submarine commander had been warned that the Iranians, with their border just to the east of their watery position, were using well-armed naval patrol boats that had sonar and could likely detect submarines, so a good reason for silent running. Periscope depth meant nothing as the periscopes were never raised for long due to the proximity of possible Iranian and Iraqi eyes on land or water.

It was late afternoon on day two when they were advised 'Ten minutes to prepare for egress'.

The sound of ejecting air from the ballast chambers and the hull scraping on the bottom of the Persian Gulf channel could be heard above the movements of sailors and machinery. The submarine listed a little to the left and all movement and noise stopped apart from a slight hum of air circulation fans. The submarine finally came gently to rest on the sandy bottom of the deserted shipping channel opposite the mouth of the Khawr az-Zubayr waterway at the apex of the Iraq and Kuwait borders. While maintaining its periscope depth for briefly observing shore movements, this manoeuvre would allow the team to egress the forward lock and swim up about 15 yards or so from the forward deck hatch to the surface.

Without any warning, they received a sharply whispered 'Heads up'.

A command from their friendly first officer, who introduced himself as Jake, ordered them to follow the no-name hatch-operating crew and move quietly up the gangway to the forward escape hatch lock.

Jake had a wide grin on his weathered face and it appeared he was glad to see them off the boat. Everyone was glad to get moving and on with the job of getting to the beach safely.

Once ashore in the long shadows of dusk, they would be in no-man's-land working their way along the borders of Iraq, Iran and Kuwait.

Grabbing their gear, each of them made a hushed trek up the gangway as ordered and assembled in a single line ready for departing this tin coffin in pairs. Quickly and efficiently, as this was not their first rodeo, they:

- Donned their rubber gloves.
- Pulled the Lycra dive suit hood over their heads to avoid stinging jellyfish tentacles.
- Placed the scuba mask and snorkel around their necks.
- Placed their deflated dry bags in front of them. In preparation, they had removed most of the air in the dry bags by sitting, kneeling on and squashing them hard.
- Tightened their weapon pack slings. The firearms were pre-packed in vacuum-sealed plastic covers and worn on a strap down the front of each man ready for rapid removal, cocking and firing if they were spotted.
- Clipped the pony air tanks onto their chests and cross-checked each other for readiness.
- At Spider's prompt, they set each of their wrist compass's raised bezels for alignment with due north, which was a bit hard inside an all-metal shell.
- Hooked the swim fins over the left arm ready for fitting them over their boots after entering the lock as there would be no time and little breathing air once the claustrophobic lock was flooded.

The sailors in charge of the escape lock prepared the guide rope and inflatable float to be used to guide them up to the surface. A sailor was already outside the submarine, fully suited up in scuba gear and air tank. He had taken the rope and clipped onto a cleat ready for inflating the open-bottomed float.

Each of the team in turn entered the lock, the sailors shut the hatch behind them and they all heard the voice over a speaker inside the chamber 'Ready yourselves for flooding'.

That meant no bugging out and that the water would flood in with the air pressure increasing and make their ears pop, sometimes painfully, until the water had equalised over them with a water pressure of one and a half times the surface air. Each warrior placed the pony air cylinder mouthpiece on and opened the air valve. Then the locked overhead hatch could be released by turning the wheel latch above and allowing it to swing open for lock egress.

As the sun began to set on day three, they each began the exit process from the submarine via the forward escape lock, two of them at a time with their kit. It was imperative to stay calm as the escape lock chamber filled rapidly with water before the outer hatch was opened and then they could swim up to the surface, letting all the air out of their lungs to avoid rupture as the air expanded due to reduction in water pressure. Spider always found this more daunting than parachuting; Brute couldn't care less and squatted in the lock with a smile on his rugged face.

Brute and Spider went out first. Climbing out and swimming clear, they dragged themselves and their dry bags away. With a quick nod from Spider, the navy diver on deck inflated the float buoy by placing his second stage air regulator under the open bottom and ejecting a small amount of air into it. The tethered float was released and shot rapidly toward the surface while expanding as the water pressure reduced on its way up. Spider and Brute hooked their tether guide rope line to the ring at the side of the hatch. Excess air began to bubble out of the buoy and it could be seen all the way to the surface in very clear water.

Looking to the sides of the submarine on the way up to the surface, all they could see was a sandy wet ocean desert floor, not a rock or fish in sight. Nearer the surface, they could expect to encounter stinging jellyfish, which had to be avoided at all costs as the sting could immobilise a person in minutes.

The water current was about 5 knots and close to the turn of incoming tide that would favour them for the swim to shore if an opposing wind didn't pick up to spoil the party.

Each warrior, when reaching the surface, quickly inflated his waterproof backpack with air from the pony scuba air tank. They were all now out of the submarine on the surface and holding onto the buoy line. They marshalled in a monkey hand grip circle, then cross-checked:

- All present
- Waterproof gear bags tethered to their belts
- Weapons lashed onto their backpacks
- Compasses set to a single landing point on shore
- Surface buoy deflated

The guide rope buoy air bag was then deflated by upturning it to release the air and it was allowed to fall back to the submarine deck for recovery by the crew dive master, who was the first man out and the last man into the hatch. He was responsible for confirming the successful departure of the package, retrieving the surface line, re-entering the submarine, closing the deck hatch, securing the lock entry hatch and reporting 'hatch secure' to the first officer.

Operation – Day Three – Landfall Early AM

After leaving the sub came the cautious and arduous 1½-mile swim in line abreast formation so they could keep a visual contact with each other as they moved across the current, aiming in a north-westerly direction.

The swim took them towards the corner borders of Kuwait and Iraq, where a sandy beach was the objective, while towing their floating equipment and stores.

They swam across and around several shallow reefs near the shore, with the tide chopping and surging back and forth over them.

The water was a warm 25°C with a 3ft swell. There was no wind but stinger jellyfish were all around them now and contact had to be avoided or the party would be over before it started.

Spider remembered that during a scuba diving training session over a year ago on the Qatar coast, while preparing for a beach entry dive one of the team had let his first stage air regulator dangle in the water on the way in. Unlucky for him, some cotton thread-sized stingers had stuck to the regulator mouthpiece that he didn't notice and he put it into his mouth. He didn't make it to hospital and died of suffocation due to a swollen mouth and throat. That was the reason to make sure the team wore full-length dive suits, boots, gloves and hood with absolutely no skin showing. Even when they cleared the beach and stripped down, the stingers that were stuck to their outer wear and backpacks must be very carefully wiped off with gloves on and wet sand.

According to the aerial photographs provided to the team at the briefing on board the US aircraft carrier, the target beach landfall exhibited some sandstone outcrops at the water's edge leading inland to a line of undulating sand dunes that featured along the otherwise barren landscape. There was not much other cover for many miles in each coastal direction or inland except for the miles of rusted barbed wire entanglements, the odd destroyed building, burnt-out cars, miles of oil pipelines criss-crossing the landscape or pump jacks, which some call nodding donkeys, and wellhead Christmas trees for controlling oil well flows to the gathering stations.

The Khawr az-Zubayr waterway flowed dead quiet over to their right, offering them some boggy marshland to traverse for cover before arriving on firm dry land some 5 map miles inland. Was this landfall a good choice? It was the only choice; the downside would be for them to head straight for an Iraqi trap or, even worse, a minefield. The risks and chances of success were equally balanced.

So, we dare! But winning a prize was another strategy.

All four warriors negotiated their watery passage with rubber gloves on, Lycra camouflaged wet suits stretched awkwardly over their desert camouflage uniforms, swim fins snugly strapped over their boots; all doing a good job of keeping out the jellyfish that mainly resided near the surface down to about 10 to 15ft in the warm Gulf waters.

If one of the team got badly stung or a dry pack leaked and sank, they would all have to suck it up to share supplies and continue as planned, or two would have to return to the submarine that was still observing their progress at periscope depth until they reached the beach. The submarine crew were not in a position to assist them or in any way notify them of any shore movements, so basically, they were on their own the minute they left the boat. Mission failure was not an option in either case.

Surprisingly, no mishaps so far. They were much nearer to the beach now, observing the water's edge for any Iraqi vehicle tracks or footprints. They chose the nearby shallow marsh for cover as it appeared to be deserted and relayed the decision to each other by simply pointing at it.

They all squatted low in shallow shoulder-deep water depth, still line abreast with only their masks and snorkels visible on the light surf line.

Their weapons were still packed away in the dry bags, so no chance of taking on a fight right now. If there were significant obstructions preventing their landing, they would have to about-turn and abandon the mission at this point.

They were all looking for any sign of movement up and down the beach. No watchtowers, no machine guns, no concrete pill boxes or soldiers on patrol, no searchlights that one reads about in Second World War novels. Just plain old silence apart from them moving quietly and more swiftly forward, the water depth reducing to knee deep among the beach's rocky protrusions, while grasping and removing their stubby swim fins from over their boots, hoisting their floating dry packs out of the water, squeezing some air out and slinging them onto their backs. Not a word had been spoken since they had lined up to enter the submarine escape lock.

At a hand signal from Spider, each of them committed to scurrying low out of the water, dodging between the exposed rocky outcrops and vegetation as natural cover to traverse the beach obstacle. The next obstacle was to enter the marsh water flats that drained into the Khawr az-Zubayr. They hid their boot prints in the semi-stagnant, ankle-deep marsh water, around and among clumps of low vegetation, trudging in each other's sodden boot tracks that quickly filled with water as the tide came in, thus removing all evidence of their trek.

Across a wide sandy beach dotted with short vegetation, they approached the coastal road that skirted the dunes further inland about five clicks. They could now see the lights from occasional vehicle traffic that flickered momentarily as they passed over high spots among the sand dunes and then disappeared into the distance. The Iraqi invaders were still very much in control of Kuwait. It couldn't have been Kuwaiti military or civilians as the Iraqis had overrun them and the country was in lock down.

The vehicles might have been mobile Iraqi patrols or troop truck movements as their speed was too fast to be heavy equipment or tanks. That heavy stuff would likely be well hidden under camouflage nets at strategic points during the day. Good airstrike material for sure, but that's not what they were primarily after on this covert sortie. There were bigger fish out there to catch.

Chapter 19

On Enemy Soil

An hour later, out of the marsh, across more sand, while still staying one behind the other in one set of footprints, they could now hardly see in the coming dark over the potholed bitumen road parallel to the beach and marsh. Then they were into the adjacent sand dunes to the north-west that had some meagre growth of low shrubs and grasses suitable to hide their shadowy outlines. The last warrior in line dragged his dry bag to cover their tracks in the sand near the roadway. Checking each other for stingers, they removed the Lycra wet suits and then opened all the dry packs for distributing contents, donned and tested their Z-Tac throat mic and tube earphone radios, and began saddling up the mission-specific gear issued to them on the carrier. Definitely no personal items were brought along that would identify their originating country, organisation, or operation such as family photos, letters, mobile phones, wedding rings, etc. These could be used against them or the mission during interrogation by an enemy.

They removed the folding spades that were strapped on the outside of their backpacks to bury the pony scuba air cylinders, swim fins, gloves, Lycra suits and empty dry packs. They were all packed flat into one dry pack and they placed the lot in the shallow hole, filled it in and placed a small stump of drift wood on top, hoping that the wind would not uncover the cache. Then each of them checked and noted the GPS position in case they were able to return this way as originally planned in order to head back into the water, swim about a mile or two, and reboard the submarine using the small pony scuba air cylinders before descending a line tethered with a flotation buoy down to the deck hatch on the submarine. Or so they had planned, but they knew from their vast number of cumulative experiences like this that the best-laid plans of mice and men often go astray, and generally do.

It was time to stop moving or be spotted in the waning daylight. If they could see for miles, so could anyone else searching the horizon. They dug in as best they could behind a low sand dune, their camouflaged sheets sheltering them from prying eyes. Time to eat and test the radios, then report to the submarine that they had successfully arrived without enemy contact.

They were officially now on their own.

Brute organised a schedule of two-man, two-hour watches under a starlit bright moon sky, while Spider reviewed the maps and plotted tomorrow's trek as moving out in the dark on their first night may place them in a minefield or they could walk straight into the Iraqi forces. They all quietly and soberly unpacked and loaded the weapons ready for whatever challenges tomorrow would bring.

Their wet uniforms would dry quickly enough once the sun rose fully, but for now they were all feeling heavy, tired and wet, with a smelly marsh deodorant to attack their delicate senses. A light very hot dry wind had picked up that would be good for drying them and obliterating their ongoing boot prints in the sand.

The old-type sat-com radio, about the size of a laptop PC and twice as thick with fold-out foil antenna, was checked and it hissed with nothingness, showing no text message on the screen. They didn't transmit a word and had received none. The bonus of satellite communication is the ability to use voice, text or photo image transmissions. Unfortunately, beaming a message directly up to their satellite system could now be detected and reported to the enemy by other satellite operators.

Spider's only concern was: will the sat-com radio work and if so, for how long? And what if it doesn't?

Also, their GPS's were the old type with no inbuilt maps, just co-ordinates and set points that they used to refer to the maps.

Oh well, it was another gadget to get used to. The backup was a trusty watch, prismatic compass and protractor rule, which was plastic, along with a waterproof map that each of them had. They did not realise that all of that stuff was as useless as tits on a bull.

By early morning the sun was just beginning to show above the horizon in the east over the tops of the sand dunes with their long shadows. The team had now finished gathering their kit together, removing sand from their boots and looking over the map to visualise the way ahead. Now in 50-yard separation ready to set out, with one warrior still on guard at the back with binoculars scanning 360 degrees with his self-loading rifle (SLR) cocked at the ready in his right hand, the rest of the team waited for the hand signal from Spider to move forward in a single line.

Brute spoke 'Fellas, it's time for me to have a jolly swagman's breakfast'.

'What the hell are you talking about?' asked Rat. 'What's a jolly swagman's breakfast?'

'It's an old western Queensland proverb Rat; a piss and look at the sun as he stands by the billabong.'

That roused a few chuckles. Spider, grinning, replied 'You fucker Brute. Maybe that's something we all could use but there's no fucking billabong in this rat hole desert'.

They paused for a few minutes to allow their eyes to refocus on the sun rising, offering them a long-shadowed landscape before them to the north by north-west.

They set their compasses to 310 degrees magnetic on the raised bezel and watches were zeroed to the same time to the second for the first leg of their long march. Their heads were covered from the sun with their tinted eye shades down.

They calculated that in several hours without interruption, this route march would bring them in a direct line for the old town of Markaz Hudud al Abdali, the Kuwait and Iraqi border guard post on the highway from Kuwait City to Baghdad. They were tasked with making observations from the outskirts and providing sit-reps on a daily basis.

They trekked up the partly made road and part track parallel with the Khawr az-Zubayr waterway on the Iraqi side of the unmarked border with Iran to their east as a reference for some 30 map miles but there was still no encounter with anyone. The place seemed eerily deserted and this stressed them more than having spotted enemy movements along the way.

Ever get the feeling that you are being watched?

They route marched rapidly without stopping for a break, taking sips of water from their canteens from time to time, and using minimal terrain cover where possible that took them progressively away from the beach and further into the direction of Saddam land.

Nothing but sand dunes ahead and a river over to the right somewhere. Eventually they were heading towards some old Kuwaiti oilfield facilities within the disputed border zone. They looked mostly unattended except for possibly the occasional mobile maintenance inspections on the ever-rotating nodding donkey pumps, natural gas flares and water separation tanks. The tyre tracks were not fresh so they could assume there wouldn't be any unwanted visitors today.

The terrain gradually changed from undulating sand dunes to flat gravelly ground, with deep vehicle tracks indicating what appeared to be a multitude of recent light and heavy vehicle tracks made alongside rusty rows of raised oil pipelines. They had less cover and harder ground now, some points in their favour and some not.

The M60 pair led by Brute the muscle man and supported by the ever-active Rat would head further out on their left-side flank from time to time, then swing back in line to signal if a target, contacts or obstacles were sighted. In past jungle operations, they used to change positions and duties hourly but there was less cover here to try and see or be seen in this open terrain.

Perhaps the mission objective of gathering intelligence on Iraqi troop and significant equipment movements would bear fruit. By day, the team only used hand signals to avoid being triangulated at a distance by over-using their Z-Tac throat mic and tube radios. If they lost sight of each other, a single click with the press-to-talk button on the radio would be enough to get everyone's attention and close up a bit more for visual line of sight.

Stopping in a shallow wadi to check their position and observe the surroundings, the satellite pictures taken only a week before their arrival had identified vehicle tracks emanating from the Kuwait to Baghdad highway to be around this area but not the vehicles, their cargoes or destinations as they must have travelled after dark with the dust, occasional rains and wind partially covering new tracks from old, or they had returned to hard top roads. They were now intent on tracking these vehicle movements using the deepest and widest marks as they may also indicate recent activity, heavy loads such as military ordnance, troop movements, artillery, tanks or the greatest prize of all: an elusive Scud missile.

Complete with launching system, radar and support vehicles, these missiles had been causing havoc over Israeli and Saudi Arabia territory in recent weeks and the US had not had much success with their new Patriot anti-missile defence systems in bringing them down. Their prime objective was to laser-point a Scud site and call it in for an immediate air strike with text, time sighted, photo, longitude and latitude fix.

All very nice when they said it, but not necessarily all that easy to do.

Twice previously, they thought they might have been spotted by Saddam's small mobile 4×4 vehicle patrols as they had seen dust clouds in the distance when they had stopped and checked the surroundings that they had traversed several hours before. So far, they had made about five clicks an hour, including the now necessary, ten-minute rests every hour for measured, precious water drinks, eating cold rations and doing their foot and kit checks.

During one of these ten-minute rests, and to ease the tension, Brute started humming a tune and then he hit them with the lyrics: 'Two old women sitten in the sand, each one wishing the other was a man.'

They all chuckled and felt a little stress relieved.

Gradually the cover of man-made obstacles began to diminish until they faced open ground ahead.

This would slow them down due to there being no shade or cover from prying eyes. Avoiding the exposure of open ground was cause for considering a plan 'B' as they didn't plan to traverse this terrain until dark. Then they spotted some dust rising in the distance to the south-east behind them. That could only mean trouble for the team if an Iraqi patrol came upon them huddled up in a shallow wadi.

Spider ordered the men to scatter wide and lay low, pull their camouflage netting over themselves for meagre diffusion and only move forward after nightfall. A group of heavily laden soldiers like them moving together would more likely be spotted from several miles away and would be pretty defenceless. Spider decided to travel up front alone out into the open, from time to time laying low in the sand as much as possible with his backpack left with Doc and just his sniper rifle, side pack of ammunition and water canteen for company.

He planned to be in a position to hit the enemy from a different position to his men to distract the enemy line of fire if needed. The 4×4 sped past, raising a cloud of dust between the warriors positioned on their bellies ready to open fire. It wasn't necessary to defend themselves and each warrior sighed in relief. The mission had not been discovered and they were all in one piece.

Spider guessed that with a bit of luck and good planning, they would all join up at their next rendezvous not far up ahead of them, maybe 12 to 15 miles, where there appeared to be an outcrop of what looked like a pile of rock among other piles of rocks that stood out in this monotonous terrain and haze. It was a possible vantage point for keeping a watch on the eastern and western approaches that led along the old highway to Baghdad.

At that time, they had no idea what conditions they were heading into due to their limited on the ground intelligence or whether this location would provide adequate security and cover from the sun and Iraqi patrols.

The dust was constantly getting into their boots, building sweaty clumps under the foot arch, ball or heel and grinding away at the skin. Fortunately, the ground was not so sandy where they were right now, almost like hard gravel, and it didn't leave much of a track. That's why they came over by this indirect route. No point in advertising that they were there.

By day the team would usually march out about a mile apart from each other, just visible but not too close to get caught bunched up or fired upon. Every hour they made sure they could still see the warrior in front and the one behind.

The gravelly rocks under foot were nearly crippling everyone as their boots gripped, slipped and twisted to one side or another. They wondered what was worse: the sand or this muck. No one would be much use if they twisted and sprained an ankle.

They knew from intel briefings that there are some pretty tough soldiers in Saddam's Imperial Guard, but they would be hoping for the dregs of his conscript soldiers driving about without any idea what to do if they did spot one of them popping away at them.

More likely they would speed off out of range and call in some tank jockey to take a pot shot in their direction. The Iraqi air force and navy had already escaped to Iran, so it would not be too long before something big happened here, one way or another.

There were deadly snakes and scorpions among the sand, rock and gravel, and they were easily missed in the sandy patches as they were pretty well camouflaged; better than a land mine that's for sure. That sort of company wasn't needed, nor did they wish to get bitten by it.

The forced march overnight and ultimately into the first light of day sapped most of their strength and they still had a few clicks to go before they paired up in a set ambush pattern at the rendezvous point for hunkering down during the day.

Operation – Day Four

They had still not been spotted and they hadn't spotted anyone or their vehicles either. There would be a couple of hours of rest, rations and changing their socks. They still used the old hexamine tablets as low-flame fuel to cook their food or they ate it cold. The pale white blue flicker of the flame in a hand-dug hollow under their Dixie cooking pan that was barely visible in the daylight gave out enough heat to warm the rations as they cleared an area large enough to either sit or lay down flat without a rock pressing against an already sore spot or creating a new one. Washing the dishes was simple; just scrub with sand and a dash of water. The sun did the drying up.

It was amazing to think that the place really came alive at night as the burning earth cooled rapidly and hunters other than themselves began their sordid work in order to survive long enough for an even more devilish predator to seek them out. They stumbled constantly on the oversized gravel that had been strewn by a millennia of driving winds that had ever so gradually broken down mountains into small hills and the grit into fine sand that made up the moving dunes that they trekked around and over on this job of soldiering.

This region was once a fertile flood plain but the plentiful rains had long gone along with the mountains and hills that attracted the moist clouds and brought regular seasonal rains. Now there were only gullies gouged out by the occasional drizzle overnight and the rare downpour of heavy rain every few years. Water would just be soaked up and lost to the seeds that were blown in the wind.

It had gotten cooler overnight, their best time for marching even closer together as the line of sight to each other was reduced to match what the phases of the moon allowed. Ever present was the thought of being spotted by an encamped patrol with at least one guard awake and vigilant. Never underestimate your enemy as he too can be well trained and ready for a fight. They had made good time overnight and the last of the cool air had invigorated them as it chilled their sweat and dried the dust in small cakes under their armpits and groins.

The thought of having to dig for cover in this hard-packed gravel and powdered sand did nothing for their sense of humour as getting blisters on their hands at this stage of the trek would not be doing anyone a favour. So far, they had done pretty well avoiding any form of laceration, bite or injury. Not all of them could brag about that. Several of the team had the beginnings of heals cracking or faces blistering, no matter how much cream or tape was used or how often the dust was removed from their boots. They moved on regardless.

Operation – Day Five

Almost half of the planned operation phases had been achieved without enemy contact and the team had all settled into their daily hide and nightly route marching routines. Night crept on slowly but inexorably across the harsh oven earth that they were pressed against. Soon the light would dwindle enough to allow all of them to decamp and move out and trek on to the next predefined position that they had been ordered by command to set up as a forward observation post. This was a position from which they could carry out several days of intel surveys before retracing their steps back down to the beach and out to the submarine. Thinking of which, a nice swim in the Persian Gulf waters would be quite a nice treat right now.

The route march overnight had almost reached the target location of the outskirts of Abdali village close to the Iraq border as marked on the map by their commanders at the briefing on the aircraft carrier. And sure enough, there used to be a small border town or village with what looked like a police station and border sign in Arabic here in the middle of nowhere. No one could imagine who could live out here in the gravel and dust.

At least there was a minute amount of breeze to ease off the coming beating sun that was beginning to light the eastern horizon. They chose to sortie several of the bombed out or decaying ruins of houses for establishing cover and checking for human habitation, but they found none. The place was long deserted, one of the remnants of the Iraq–Kuwait conflict over borders from the 1980s until now. However, the highway was intact and open for use.

Spider finally chose a ruined house structure about 200 yards south on the Kuwaiti side of the border to hunker down for several days and nights as there was nothing else in sight high enough to spot for enemy movements and ordnance emplacements. Brute took to the highest point of the structure and although the building was half buried by sand it had the form of a typical Arab house. It had an almost intact flat roof with the stairs collapsed but he could climb up onto the roof without too much effort using an old wooden beam as a makeshift ladder.

There was a water well that looked dried up and half full of sand and an intact ground-floor room under the flat-top roof with gaping holes in the north and south sides and no hard floor.

The remaining perimeter appeared to be the broken-down remnants of a compound ring wall with sand heaped up against it randomly wherever the wind desired to place it.

Once on the roof, the team set up a defensive position by removing sand from two corners and making it more difficult for anyone to climb up by removing the timber beam they had used to initially get up. It had originally separated the roof and clay floor structure, leaving a jagged edge like protruding ribs of some prehistoric beast. The camouflage nettings came in handy against the metre-high wall using some of the shorter pieces of timber bearers lying about to prop it up.

More protection was achieved by assembling each of the canvas sheets below the camouflage netting and then each of them and their gear disappeared under it and out of sight of the sun with one side open slightly to let what breeze there might be filter in. The canvas sheets were also used to capture sparse rain water, saving them from having to forage for water in daylight. This roof top provided a good vantage point in order to keep watch without being watched.

With the sun came the heat, over 48°C, but in the shade there was less glare and it was maybe 10° cooler. The radio was silent and only whispered chatter among each of the men occurred as sleep, although needed, was far from possible. They just needed to conserve their energy, rations, water and stay alert and out of sight here for two or three more days. Hours had passed and with the sun moving almost to the afternoon position overhead, they were perusing satellite photos of this decimated town discussing the next trek and calculating time, distance and rations when Doc, who was on watch, hissed 'Shut up and listen'.

The distant dust cloud and rumble of vehicles gradually became louder and more visible until it gradually stopped – silence descended once more. What the hell was all of that about they wondered. With heads down under the netting they could only wait and watch as the occasional movement of small vehicles from the south Kuwait side of the border of the highway caught their attention. Spider, looking at his map, figured that Iraqis were now within a mile of the border and stationery.

Then sounds from over the border on the Iraqi side indicated some heavy equipment being manoeuvred with accompanying escort vehicles emerging from the gravel-surfaced road from al-Zubayr in the north merging with the highway some several hundred yards away. The 4×4s slowly moved passed their hideout and over the Kuwaiti border to meet up with the larger group, leaving them more freedom to manoeuvre around for observing what all of the racket was about.

Could this be the setting up of field artillery pieces, mobile radar or their special target? Night time would tell as Spider directed a two-man sortie to move out at dark. Doc and Brute with the M60 would take first sortie. Spider and Rat would remain on the roof to cover them if needed. The moon would be in the last quarter and dimmer tonight, so more of the team moving about would be spotted for sure.

Chapter 20

Contact

New rumbling was heard and this time the clanking noise of what sounded like a tank. The Iraqis had some old Russian T-72s in the field and this might be one of them.

As the shadows lengthened in the afternoon, Brute and Doc, the two stealthy observers, moved slowly forward out of the camouflage and down the makeshift wooden beam ladder, which was pulled up when they were clear. They moved north across the border, parallel to the road, to a position several hundred yards closer to the source of the noise. They had taken their personal camouflage netting and kept it draped over them as cover from the sun, blending with the open ground. It would also be useful later that night if spotlights were switched on.

Lying behind the largest pile of old clay bricks and sand about half a metre high, Brute could see a surveyor with a transit level, a soldier placing marker pegs into the ground with a hammer and a bulldozer starting to carve out a pit set out large enough to park a couple of tanks in. This type of dugout formation had been spotted on satellite photos at other locations, but these were either within Kuwait along the coast or closer to Baghdad along the main highway and Tigris River.

It may be that Saddam's generals were expecting a marine invasion from the Persian Gulf – perhaps. Or maybe this was a haphazard dispersal of his limited field hardware across this zone to discourage any potential invaders from approaching from this direction. In any case, this was something to mark on their charts with GPS co-ordinates laid in for a future kill.

The occasional hum of rotary and jet aircraft out there in the distance caused Brute and Doc to prick up their ears so as to ascertain if it was a chopper with that clack-clack sound of its rotary wing, the constant reverberation of a piston-engine fixed-wing aircraft or the whining of alliance jets reconnoitring above them. It could also be the Iranians across their border some 30km to their east. What they didn't want to hear was any of those sounds coming any nearer to their position as they had previously experienced so-called friendly fire in other places and at other times. A chopper downdraft could easily blow their camouflage covers off, the same as one did in Vietnam many moons ago.

Before the sun had finally lowered to the horizon, the bulldozed hole in the ground had got bigger and wider. Dust rose as more vehicles thundered in convoy across the oil field, this time from the Iraqi north-east, the direction of Basra on the main highway between Kuwait and Iraq.

It was impossible for Brute and Doc to move without being spotted. Brute whispered over the short-range Z-Tac throat mic for the team to hold, lay low and wait. The two warriors, Spider and Rat, on the roof could not see what was happening below or ahead of Brute and Doc. They had to trust them with their lives right at this moment.

Neither Brute nor Doc were able to move back to the house structure without being spotted, so they lay motionless for several more hours in that dusty oven. Doc made occasional short bursts on the intercom radio to the house roof top pair, giving them reassurance that they were OK and that there was no immediate threat from the Iraqis, who were intent on their own labours.

The Iraqi workers eventually did quit and slid under their trucks out of the morning sun for a siesta. The two observers gradually reversed painstakingly back to the house roof, never standing upright or taking their eyes off the trucks or the workers, while erasing their tracks in the patches of sand at the same time. Covering their tracks at the house entry, Brute and Doc happily clambered up, slithered under the camouflaged hide and dusted off the M60 machine gun that they had lugged around at ground level. The next sortie would go in light without packs, with only the .45 calibre pistols and SLR rifles to be used at ground level.

The M60 would remain on the roof top for heavy cover fire and the H&K sniper rifle would be used for long-range shots from the roof, particularly to take out vehicles.

If and when a firefight erupted, the cover fire from the roof top might allow the two men on the ground to escape and fight another day or reach the submarine offshore.

They discussed tactics based on what the Iraqis were currently up to and Spider reinforced to all that they were not there to kill Iraqis but to gather intelligence information to forward on to their commanders.

The Iraqi convoy had to divert around some pipe racks full of oil from the nodding donkey pumps to the storage tanks located near the potholed gravel road they had all crossed earlier. The little mud house roof was now closer to being overrun the closer the Iraqis came. A huge semi-trailer and its prime mover ground its way within a hundred yards north-west of their position and stopped immediately adjacent to the bulldozer and support vehicles they had been observing all day.

The Iraqi soldiers from the work crew involved in digging the enormous hole all came out from the shade and sauntered over to the covered semi-trailer and met the driver and passengers.

From Spider's perspective, he knew that they had to find out what was in that large semi-trailer, if not, at least where was it headed. He needed to do an up close and solo personal inspection with the other three men remaining on the roof with the M60 for covering fire and receiving any intel messages from Spider (in case he got caught).

Before setting off, using the sat-com, Spider notified command of their situation and that of their Iraqi friends just down the road.

Spider received a one-sentence response back: 'What do the Iraqis have inside the truck? Report!'

Down at ground level, Spider now had to manoeuvre among the sand dunes, bricks and broken houses in order to get a better line of sight of the back and side openings of the trailer. Given that the Iraqis had no idea that they were present and there had not been any Iranian border attacks for some years, they were off guard and lax in not establishing sentries on their perimeter. As the team's maps were useless in providing any form of topographical layout of the local area, Spider had to improvise and pick out spots where at least one man could hide with a view.

It took two hours of snaking around small undulations and clay bricks from broken and wind-blasted buildings until an observation position had been secured. Surprisingly, Spider saw a cement truck ambling down the gravel track and, without much direction, poured its entire load onto the floor of the pit dug out by the bulldozer.

Another cement truck followed thirty minutes later, and then several more until the pit floor had been covered. Not very elegant, but it was a foundation for something. The Iraqi work crew immediately got busy roughly smoothing out the wet cement before it set in the hot sun.

The trailer, with its 40ft sea container doors exposed, was now flung wide open to display pallets of cement bags and cement building blocks. It appeared that this location was likely going to be a weapons dump and possibly a rest station area for the Iraqis – but not for the four hidden observers. Spider had to get moving as this site, although interesting, was not currently their target objective.

A bit disappointing but he had to let it drop for now and move on further to the west on a compass line bringing him further inside Iraq, a mile north of and parallel with the Kuwaiti border.

The terrain was punctuated by more oil pipelines, Christmas trees on well heads and oil storage tanks including maintenance and accommodation huts for oil workers. At least there was water available there if needed. Spider circled wide of the Iraqi work site and returned later in the day to the roof top sanctuary, where the other three warriors were waiting patiently. He then briefed the team and everyone marked up their maps in case they got separated later. After a short rest and rations, it was time to move position during the night to check out other prospective targets.

The four-man team of warriors left the Abdali house by marching south, then west away from the Iraqi position. The sun was setting in front of them to the west; Doc was tasked to hang back and creep stealthily over to the bulldozer since he was closest to it, and rig up a nice little 5oz surprise package of Semtex C4 under the fuel tank. Triggering the detonator was to be by wiring it to the ignition wires on the engine starter motor. Given the intense daily heat and a possible lack of detailed maintenance, the small charge should merely pop a hole in the bottom of the fuel tank, ignite the diesel fuel and hopefully not alert the Iraqis of sabotage. The delay in construction could be tactically useful on two fronts:

1. Focus Iraqi attention on fire-fighting and work without a bulldozer at this site while they went for a walk in the moonlight across to the next target.
2. Delay the construction here until they had more time to deal with what it was for and do something about, if necessary, on the way back.

They waited for Doc to return and continued their march all night westerly along the disputed border zone between Kuwait and Iraq without seeing or hearing any enemy army or civilians but ever mindful of land mines. This march brought them directly parallel with the border, which was not marked by any signs or fences. Very eerily in this place, there was utter silence. Even a small sound could travel for miles out here.

Operation – Day Six

Early dawn sun began slowly but surely rising over their shoulders. A muffled bang was heard and they supposed that the bulldozer had been started up with fuel igniting and spilling out and under the engine. This would cause a lot of panic and consternation back there for some time. In addition, the delay in construction would be a good outcome for their efforts.

Better that than a live shooting contest and an Iraqi radio call for reinforcements ending their trek and camping holiday out there in the sun. They were warned that capture would mean torture and death, so it would be best to shoot it out until the last man in that eventuality.

This was the pep talk given every time a soldier was volunteered for a new assignment by the DIO.

So far, every time they got back alive, they were well paid and went home to their day jobs, leaving earlier actions behind and compartmentalised until there was a next time. The only thing that would catch in their throats would be having to terminate civilians in an urban environment or leave one of their own behind. The choices would be harder and more poignant as innocence is more difficult to judge in one second compared with hitting an armed uniform. That was better left to the other agencies. For now, as the lines of separation were getting closer and justifications more blurred, they should keep to the shadows and avoid conflict so that everyone went home safe on both sides.

Even this conflict had its quirks for the reasoning man to consider. The justification for this operation was not really the supposed discovery of Weapons of Mass Destruction, it was for Iraqi and Kuwaiti oil, plus selling weapons. It was certainly not for humanitarian aid as was told on scripted TV interviews.

Maybe that's why the command was using contract soldiers and in need of plausible deniability to protect the guilty who sat in the shadows back in the US and Australia.

Right now, reality kicked in as the warriors could vividly see vehicles and fixed-position lights along the Kuwait border to the south-west, indicating that the Kuwaitis and invading Iraqis were also awake that morning. Cover was needed soon so they could set up an observation point and get out of the rising sun during the day. The border – the un-official border marked with cross hatching on their charts – had another set of advantages. According to the satellite photos, there was likely to be lifesaving water at the oil workers' huts scattered around the oilfield, and around them were low shrubs and structures giving shade and cover for them to set up shop unobserved if required.

As dawn heated up to the midday sun, they found themselves in the midst of an Iraqi-laid minefield in this border section. Perhaps they had walked right past other minefields in the dark last evening. The wind and moving sand had exposed literally hundreds of large anti-vehicle mines here in a series of parallel lines going for miles on the border.

Brute had previous mine clearance training and laying experience during the Vietnam War and subsequent covert actions with Spider in Cambodia during the 1960s and '70s. The Khmer Rouge had indiscriminately laid many thousands of anti-personnel mines. Many are still out there today maiming and killing farmers, women and children.

Brute returned to Cambodia after that war and trained the locals on how to detect and dispose of the mines. He married a Cambodian mine clearance technician, who later died clearing a mine as there was one set beneath it as a booby trap. This mode of laying anti-personnel land mines in Kuwait was also practised by the Iraqis. Brute's advice for the team right now was to stay as close as possible to oil pipelines, structures or mature clumps of shrubs as it was more likely that the large anti-vehicle mines had not been placed close to or under them. They were to look for visible evidence, such as partially uncovered mines and regular lumps of sand that the wind had piled against the mine, and assume that the placing was about the same distance apart as the last ones sighted.

A memory flashed across Spider's inner eye as he stood frozen to the spot momentarily and raised an inward smile as an early 1970s picture of a big black US soldier who had stood on an anti-personnel mine back in the jungle came into his head. His yelping and hollering still stuck in Spider's mind and he still carried the trusty coil of Aussie farm fence wire and ball of string used to free him as they did have their uses apart from landmine clearance.

Back to the present afternoon in paradise, they all had to spread out by at least 50 yards in case one of them set off a land mine in this wide-open area with no tree for any of them to stand behind.

Brute called across to his teammates 'When in doubt, retrace your steps and go a new route. Try walking in my footprints as I lead you through this shit.'

This method had to be used as a protective strategy that day until the sun was low enough for all of them to move back to the gravel road, using each of their own footprints for getting into a hide position. Right now, they were in bloody serious shit, having to park themselves in a minefield with no fucking cover and their progress slow going.

The situation reminded Spider of his younger days when, while he was shooting rabbits and having to lay very still downwind in an open wheat field, a bloody snake crawled over his legs thinking he was a lump of wood.

The day in the minefield dragged on slowly, minute by radiating hot minute. The plan for that night was to not enter the oil camp buildings sighted below the next rise as they would be obvious shelters for unwelcome insurgents or local civilians who could spot and report them. Before they arrived at the buildings, they stopped by a rusty raised pipeline, dug in for a rest and observed the area around them.

The only action was for each of them to look, listen, rest, eat today's rations, and sip a little precious water, which was getting scarce in everyone's canteen. They also kept an eye out for the other team members dispersed in a staggered line of shallow dugout positions among the mines, perched under or among oil pipelines and low groups of shrubs with the camouflage netting tucked into the sand and propped up by shrubs and backpacks.

The metal on the pipelines and their weapons was so hot that they would get blisters if they touched them. Spider signalled the team over the Z-Tac throat mic to remove the bullets from their SLR rifles and M60 machine gun breach in case they fired off a round accidentally due to the heat. It would not be wise to make their position known to the resident enemy. They could reload the weapons once the night engulfed them and the firearms had cooled and they were again on the move.

It was evident that one of the team would have to get across to the nearest hut water tank at sundown and check if it was accessible and drinkable. Then he would need to fill up their water canteens and get back up to the gravel road where they were planning to meet up. Spider requested each of the team to look out for the safest way across to the hut and visualise a safe track through the minefield that provided some cover in case they were observed. Their concerns – above the threat of being in a minefield – was enemy patrols on either side of the border, plus running out of food and particularly water as there were no supermarkets or corner stores locally.

As the sun began to settle in the west, they readied for careful and stealthy extraction from this God-awful spot that they had accidentally stumbled into on the previous evening. It was obvious that there was no reliable mapping or satellite imagery that would have identified this sort of obstacle, which now caused them to rethink the night march.

Before they could move out of the minefield and up to the gravel road surface, which was considered a safe route, the sound of heavy vehicles in the distance caused them all to freeze. No need for radio chatter right now. There was no telling which side of the border they were coming from, but at a guess about 5 miles to the west. However, the lack of dust cloud could mean they were further away than they thought, or it was a very slow-moving vehicle or vehicles.

It was wiser just to lay low and observe, as that was their primary task for being out there (apart from amusing themselves by destroying a bulldozer for tactical reasons no less!).

The rumbling of vehicles became progressively louder and closer, along with a now-visible dust cloud; a slight wind drifting the dust across and towards the south side of the convoy. This would be helpful to them in their current positions as the drivers would be blinded on their side of the gravel track being used. It was likely they were aware of this minefield and did not stray off the track.

They finally got to see the entire convoy as it passed by, being led by two Toyota 4 × 4's, one troop carrier half-track truck, followed by a long semi-trailer with an equally long tubular cargo under camouflage netting.

This was not the group they had sighted back at the old relic roof top at the Kuwaiti border village. Was this a Scud missile mobile launcher? If so, where were they headed? Hopefully not just here as that would be most inconvenient for them at this moment.

The convoy travelled on past the minefield and appeared to go further westward, leaving a light cloud of dust to settle over everyone and everything and hopefully making a track for the team to follow. Brute was in the best position to photograph the oncoming convoy and he snapped a number of passing shots as the convoy disappeared out of sight. Brute noted the current GPS position and approximate direction using his prismatic compass, then marked the details on his map for later discussion with Spider for the daily sat-com relay as needed. Notably, there had been no movement over on the Kuwaiti side of the border when the convoy had passed. It was assumed that there was nobody over there or just a few civilians not wanting to engage the Iraqis, and hopefully not them either.

Time to move out once the convoy vehicles were out of sight, and as the sun was now just settling on the western horizon all the shadows were now long and highlighted many protruding mines. It was also helpful for the lifesaving water-gathering exercise that was essential prior to them moving onward.

The four of them regrouped up on the gravel track and briefly discussed the safest track back down to the hut for helping Doc with water gathering. Doc indicated that he had the best view of the line between this track from his last position under the oil pipeline in the minefield and the hut water tank due to the mines being more exposed by wind on a slight rise in the sand dunes. As there was no better information or advice, Doc was the only volunteer for checking out and securing the water. They each topped up one water canteen with all the available water and then about half of another and handed over two empty and one half empty canteens to Doc. Spider advised Doc to use his ball of string to set up a line from his last position then down to the hut as it would be dark on the way back and torchlight was not a go as it could be seen for miles all around.

The remaining team took up guarding cover positions either side of the track while Doc carefully headed back down to his last position with only his rifle, now re-cocked at the ready, ammunition pouch on his hip, ball of string in his pocket and the three water canteens crossed over both shoulders. The first stage to his hide position was carried out quickly using his own boot imprints up to the track, which brought him about halfway to the hut and water tank on its shady side.

The next stage to the hut took about an hour as Doc had to tiger crawl on his belly and knees while trailing the string line across the minefield and use his bayonet to feel around for any buried mines as he moved forward.

Several buried mines were found, lifted to the surface to the side and left fully exposed. If one of these types of mine went off, for one member it would mean instant death, loss of the water for ongoing survival and possible discovery of the entire team. End of mission and them.

Time was now of the essence as daylight was rapidly fading into darkness. The track across to the hut water tank, although not particularly straight, was not too much of an obstacle. Closer to the hut boundary, Doc found fewer or no mines were laid within the area. He continued crawling until up against the hut. Sampling the water from the water tank ball cock, Doc found it hot, clear and tasteless, so he filled all three canteens and turned around to retrace his footsteps in the sand and pulled on the string line in order to reel it in as he carefully paced his way back to where the rest of the team were waiting up on the track.

Goats appeared in the half dark on the opposite side of the huts and pipeline layout, about 150 yards to the right of him. His teeth began to grind and ears were alert for anything else out there that would cause him to shoot and alert the Iraqis. Goats definitely meant civilians were also living in the vicinity. Flat on his belly now, he lay silently and listened for several minutes. A woman's voice was heard apparently calling to the goats and her shadowy figure appeared momentarily at the opposite side of the huts about 150 yards away. She appeared intent on herding the goats away from the minefield and back to safety. Once the woman and the goats were out of sight and sound, Doc stood up, shouldered the now full canteens and turned back along the string line toward the gravel track and his waiting comrades. No time to stand about and chat, they grabbed the canteens and quickly headed away from the mines and people out there.

On the horizon looking toward the west, roughly where the convoy had gone, vehicle lights flickered in the sunset and then gradually came the sound of their engines; they were bloody well getting closer. Doc had instinctively moved back into his daytime minefield position, lying flat behind the pipeline and shrubs that had helped shelter him from the sun during the hot day. The remainder of the team up on the gravel track had also noticed the vehicle movements.

Decision: should they return into the minefield across from them in the dark, get ready for a fire fight or seek new cover? As no mines were spotted on the northern side of the track, Spider called over the headset radio and whispered the order for the team to spread out, drag their camouflage netting across their tracks to partially flatten them and jog due north about 200 yards out from the track. He told them to then lay low and ordered Doc to stay put as there was no point in running across the minefield in the dark with the prospect of avoidably losing a man, at the same time alerting the oncoming vehicles or civilians where they were. Even worse, the Iraqis would call for backup forces once the firing started; end of mission!

Chapter 21

Locating a Scud

Two Toyota 4×4 patrol vehicles rumbled past them heading slowly east back to the Abdali village, apparently oblivious of their existence and staying strictly on the gravel track. This time they had a spotlight facing the track and a machine gun mounted and manned on the back tray. This was probably a regular patrol along this route and the team should expect them to return at some point. This changed the plan for marching along the tracks made by the suspected Scud missile launcher seen earlier in the day.

All hell suddenly broke loose the instant an Iraqi spotlight picked out a shadowy movement about 150 yards south of the track among the huts. Their mounted machine guns immediately swung around, there were shouts heard, the team heard the ratcheting sound of guns being cocked and then sporadic bursts of rapid firing. Then there was silence apart from spent shells tinkling onto the floor of the vehicles and down onto the gravel.

The spotlights swung wildly left to right in the direction of fire, to reveal their inaccurate aiming as the woman Doc had seen earlier was still standing frozen to the spot and watching her goats running off in all directions and the shocking source of the lights and gun fire.

She then screamed some sort of obscenities at the Iraqis on the 4×4s, who began to regain their composure by ceasing fire and focusing the two spotlights onto the woman, who was wearing a traditional head-to-foot Muslim black burqa with only part of her face reflecting the light.

None of the bullets had hit her or any of the goats – a bit of a miracle given the amount of shots fired at close range. The troops began to laugh and chide the woman. They then started their engines and began moving off along the track while still trying to light up the goats, who by now had stopped and turned back to seek out the woman.

From their standoff positions, having witnessed this almost deadly comedy of errors, followed by zero hits and outraged banter between locals, the relief for the team for not being spotted again enabled the tension down their spines to relax, but the sweat running down their arms and necks did nothing to cool the adrenalin. They all began to move further up the track in order to move in the opposite direction to that of the patrol.

Spider gave the all clear to Doc for him to re-join them at the track, where they had begun to marshal once more. Doc eventually reached the track near where he had left it. Brute was waiting for him with the M60, to help catch up and relayed to Doc that the plan was for them to go look for the others further up the track – and don't spill the bloody water.

This minefield and its civilian neighbours was clearly and indelibly marked on all of their maps in case they happened to pass by this nice oil field summer holiday camp setting with goats' milk and water supply in the future. It was obvious that they would run out of rations and water if they simply just plodded about the Kuwaiti–Iraqi desert for much longer, keeping in mind the planned route back to the submarine was way behind them now. They were about halfway through the assignment duration and there had not been much to report until today.

At 20:00 hours, it was time to contact the commander via satellite phone and provide a sit-rep synopsis on their observations after departing the Abdali village, including the bulldozed construction modifications, the suspected Scud missile launcher progress with map co-ordinates, photos taken by Brute and the convoy compass heading. Plus, the location of the minefield, and their current endurance status, fitness and supplies. They also reported their likely contact with Iraqi forces, such as the expected 4×4 patrol coming back that way at night or the following day.

The signal was sent off digitally in text with photos of the convoy, a marked up photo of Brute's map showing the hut and pipeline layout, Iraqi convoy direction, their present position and the minefield. An hour passed while they waited for a response. At about 22:00 hours, while trudging onward in the dark, they heard the beep of a message coming through on the satellite radio. They closed up formation and huddled close in order to hide the LED screen illumination and read the incoming message:

YR MSG RECD – ENDURANCE NOTED
INTEL INDICATES MOVEMENTS ARTILLERY & OR TANK
MOVEMENTS PLACEMENTS
POSSIBLE SCUDS SETTING UP FACING STH GULF DISP
ALONG KUWAIT IRAQ & SAUDI BDRS
REQUIRE YR TEAM RECON IRAQ KUWAIT BDR TO ID
SCUD PLACEMENTS & DEPOTS
WILL ADV IF LASERS TO BE DEPLOYED
END.

Given that they were tasked to go back over their tracks towards where the convoy had gone and the patrol had come from, they began to get the feeling that action would eventuate sooner rather than later. First it was time to move off the now busy track about 1,500 yards into Iraq and further if necessary, depending on available cover.

A cooling breeze had risen from the Gulf waters overnight, giving them some feeling of relief from the recent stress and incessant heat. This was not a find and kill mission, it was an intelligence-gathering mission, so getting into any form of conflict with the natives was out of the question – for now.

Having trudged over countless sand dunes, encountered more oil and gas facilities that they felt it best to widely avoid in case there were more civilians making use of the huts and water, or protective minefields, the flickering of dim lights towards the Abdali village and highway direction indicated they were on target, maybe a mile away.

The commander's message was clear and they would follow it to the letter. Right now, the distance gap must be closed quickly as dawn would be upon them in about an hour or so, when they could be spotted and the sun would parch their skins out in the open.

Arriving within 1,000 yards of the original construction site and the burned-out bulldozer was as close as could be managed based on what limited cover they found. Circling around to the south, they targeted the roof top position they had previously located and used. This time though, there were soldiers wandering close by the ruins intermittently using their flashlights to check out the ruins and have a piss and a smoke. At least their footprints would not be the only ones in the sand. Spider split the team in half, Brute and Rat on point ready with the M60 if Spider and Doc were spotted entering the roof structure.

Spider and Doc carefully tiger crawled over to where the roof top could be reached, listened for Iraqi soldiers nearby, found the convenient ladder beam still lying in the sand, hoisted it into position quietly and shinnied up it onto the roof.

Still being careful, they crawled over the roof top pile of sand that Brute had raised as cover on his last observation post position. Then Spider clicked twice on the headphone radio as a signal for the remaining two to make their way across and up onto the roof. The wooden beam was then retracted onto the roof.

It was unavoidable that all four of the silent warriors should be in one place at the one time as detection would likely expose the entire mission and team if those Iraqi soldiers accidentally stumbled upon any one of them out in the open. Each team member wondered if those on the roof top would open fire as cover or hold back and let the Iraqi soldiers take out the straggler, keeping mission integrity intact.

This was not an unusual decision to make as 'all for one' was not always an option in their business. The mission success came first.

Piper Cub spotter aircraft.

Map of Cambodia.

One of the two US-built jet boats.

C-130 Hercules – the Bird.

One of the two STOL Caribou.

General Arrangement of Organisation and Entities.

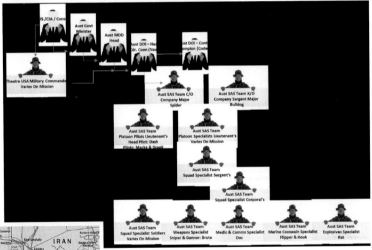

Kuwait.

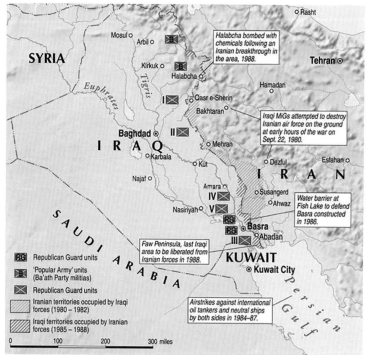

Iraq - Kuwait.

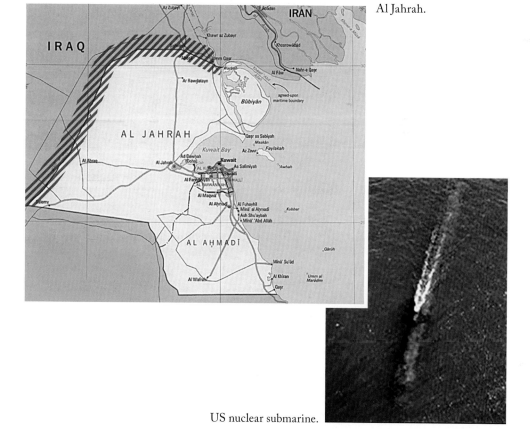

Al Jahrah.

US nuclear submarine.

Iraqi Russian T-72 tank.

Iraqi-laid minefield,
Kuwait.

The route into Iraq.

A typical Kuwaiti–Iraqi desert oilfield installation.

Billowing smoke from burning oil wells shielding the midday sun.

Al Rawgatayn minor road massacre.

Iraqi T-72 tank with its turret blown off.

Iraqi monetary note featuring Saddam (So Damned Insane – the Wacky Iraqi).

Kuwait oil well fires reflecting in lakes of crude oil.

1989 Timor Gap Treaty.

Darwin.

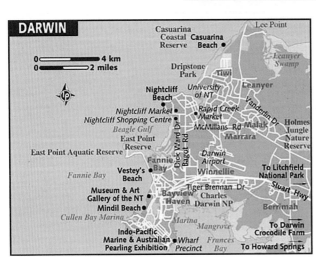

Darwin street demonstration.

Christmas Island.

Somalia.

US aircraft carrier anchored 50km off the Somali coast.

An SAS team prepare prior to a HALO jump at night.

Photo: SAAF

South African Air Force Douglas DC-3.

Operation – Day Seven

Dawn was upon them in no time. They hustled to set up their camouflage nettings and canvas shades, food and water, then the M60 was positioned so they could observe the comings and goings down below. Of course, they took a close-up look at the marvellous job they had done on the bulldozer sitting out starkly on the side of a half-completed walled hole in the ground. It was still unclear what the quickly dug hole was for but it had rapidly taken shape regardless of the loss of the bulldozer. Many hands made fast work, which was impressive.

Right now, there was another semi-trailer, several 4×4 vehicles and two large troop carrier trucks covered with camouflage mesh, with lean-to tarpaulins strung out by ropes and poles from the trucks and semi-trailers. This was a temporary camp for construction and setting up a site for some sort of military defence equipment.

The work carried on without delay and was well photographed from the roof top nest. Nothing to report yet, but time would tell once the construction was completed and the construction crew had moved out. Time was not on the team's side though.

Day became night and gradually the construction crew had progressively packed up and loaded their work equipment onto their semi-trailer container. The wrecked bulldozer was also winched laboriously onto the semi-trailer in order to remove any trace of construction at the site. It was probably dumped off at one of the oil pipeline stations along the way out. A very different uniformed army group moved in and began feverishly working on the site. First they aligned their large semi-trailer with the excavated foundations, then they reversed precariously off the gravel track across the soft sand then down into the hole in the ground.

This took about four slow hours in the cover of darkness except for several 4×4 vehicle headlights indicating the way backwards. Some of the SAS warriors actually got some sleep that night despite the equipment movements and lights flickering down on the dugout site.

Operation – Day Eight

At dawn the camouflage had been reinstalled right over the trailer and foundation walls, completely hiding the shape and contents within. The semi-trailer prime mover was separated from the trailer by now and the troop trucks were loaded up with military men and their materials. They left the site as the sun began to shed long dawn shadows over the broken buildings. Right now, their curiosity was palpable as their guts felt like they would burst if they couldn't see what was hidden under that shroud.

'Patience, patience men,' Spider whispered.

'Whatever is under there must have company and we sure don't want to wake them up, particularly to our presence.'

Sure enough, several heads appeared from under the netting. This exposed the two 4×4 vehicles, but still not the package. Activities were pronounced by mechanical noises under the netting, so something was going on and everyone hoped it was not a mobile laundry or other dreary mobile field mess unit.

Soon enough, the form of a radar dish took shape and several stick-type radio antennae protruded. Was this simply a radar monitoring site? It would be useful to MOD as a mid-level target but not something urgent enough to be hit by the coalition forces on a first strike. It would still need to be taken out if Iraq were to be attacked though. They must establish how many defenders and operators were present, what they were protecting and then what tactical hit was needed to take them and their ordnance all out in one quick action. Maybe the laser emitter pointers would soon need to be dusted off for the occasion and there would be a need for the team to do the mopping up after an airstrike. Time would tell.

However, as the coalition powers or the UN had not even decided upon a sanctioned full-on attack on Iraq, all of their work could come to nothing and they might just have to quietly pack up and go home via submarine cruise boat.

The day arrived and went, and although there was constant movement under the netting, nothing of consequence remained to report. Most of them slept, ate or did their meagre ablutions. The problem with remaining in a confined space like this is the utter lack of privacy while having a crap, just like a kitty cat having to firstly dig a hole where someone else hasn't dug and then cover it up so as not to leave a smell for their own comfort but also not give the men below under the netting something to attract their attention. Squatting for a piss while fully dressed is not all that easy.

It was now time to go and take a little peek under the netting. It appeared that all great minds think alike, as the saying goes, as all four of the team were on the same page and volunteered. There were no established perimeters, mines or patrolling guards down below, and lots of footprints all about the site, so there would be a chance to wander up, on their bellies of course, and take a gander at this new toy of Saddam's.

The light of the full moon would not help any of them to be sneaky and easily get quickly in and out so again only one or two men could have a direct go at it. The M60 was positioned ready on the roof of the ruined house and needed two men, Brute and Rat, to operate and feed it, leaving Spider and

Doc to do the sneaky job this time. They left all gear on the roof except for their side arm .45 calibre pistols with two spare magazines each, plus for good measure two golf ball-sized blobs of Semtex explosive that Rat had set up with separate detonators and a couple of yards of slow-burn det-cord fuse and clip-on igniters. That was just in case the opportunity presented itself and they could pass the explosion off as an accident caused by the Iraqis setting up the equipment, just like the bulldozer scenario.

Apart from an occasional Iraqi sentry sauntering about the perimeter and back into the semi-darkness of the camouflage netting, there was no other movement. Hoping that no new vehicle visitors would light up the site, Spider and Doc slid down from the roof top and moved warily parallel with the road and about 100 yards past the location. They then turned west at right angles so they could cut in and behind the netting to get a look under it. After about an hour, with the sentry having just returned beneath the netting at the front, they moved in at opposite sides and stopped where the netting had been pegged down and tied with ropes.

There was an air gap of about half a metre wide for Spider and Doc to belly crawl in between the netting and the canvas tarpaulin that was propped up by poles and draped over the package. Spider gave a one click signal to Doc, who responded soon after with one click on the radio; both warriors were now in place and observing. Spider stopped and waited to hear any voices before whispering into his Z-Tac throat mic to alert Brute and Rat that both of them were in position.

'We are in at the back door on each side.'

Operation – Day Nine

As there was very little light under the covered site during the night, Spider and Doc planned to burrow into the sand under the edge of the tarpaulin, where they entered and awaited the dawn light. More likely the Iraqis would be too busy to consider if there were unwanted visitors above them in the sand on the outskirts of their picnic area.

As the hours passed, movements began in earnest on unpacking the contents of the 4×4 vehicles and trucks, which appeared to be the components of a portable radar unit. Then by mid-morning, the package on the semi-trailer they were most interested in was started on. Yes, it was a Scud missile launcher complete with camouflage-painted missile.

In addition, an anti-aircraft ground-to-air missile launcher with Chinese lettering on the containers was unpacked and set up, with cables hooked up to the radar unit. This looked like a very ambitious attempt to launch the Scud southward across Kuwait and into the Persian Gulf waters, where the US and coalition fleets were positioned. The anti-aircraft protection set up appeared to indicate that it was to be an important fixed location launch site and that possibly more Scuds would be delivered.

Having taken a number of photos during the day while lying partly buried under the Iraqi tarpaulin covered by the camouflage netting, and writing down the precise GPS position, they were now ready to extract. Dusk was approaching and they could see the Iraqis starting to settle down, the smell of food wafting past their noses and causing their bellies to rumble, which was the same for the observers just above them.

Spider was able to dig a hole by hand and have a piss in the sand under him and cover it up, while Rat had to move slowly out from under the tarpaulin and take a shit in a hole he had scratched out by hand. The joys of camping out in the rough.

Doc let Spider know over the radio that there was no sentry out on patrol as it was dinner time below and so a good time to move back to the roof. There was no argument from Spider about that suggestion as lying in a groove in the sand gave him the cramps and standing up or crawling away would be a nice change from the monotony and his proximity to the spot he had used to piss in.

Covering their tracks as best they could among the patrolling sentries' and workers' tracks, Spider and Doc retraced their original tracks back to the safety of the roof. On Spider's mind was that coalition airstrikes may fail if they tried to attack this site based on the ground-to-air missile launcher placement. Time to consider tactics and whether to:

1. Destroy the mobile Scud launcher, although it could be replaced and they would have a hell of a fight to survive the mission.
2. Destroy the ground-to-air missile launcher in advance of an air strike on the entire site (a possibility, or it could be jammed by attacking aircraft).
3. Note the longitude and latitude of this site and move away immediately to try and identify where all of the vehicles were coming and going in case there was a larger dump of ordnance further west towards the highway between Kuwait and Baghdad.
4. Sit back, call the commanders to confirm a positive package site, wait for orders and, if necessary, set a laser emitter on the target for an air strike (that might be shot down by the radar-guided missile battery).

Well, being lovers of nice long walks, they agreed a compromise plan. A new challenge was to head out and leave this juicy target for another day, reassured that the Iraqis had put a lot of labour into setting it up and hiding it so it should not move for a while yet. That left the issue of how would the Scud launcher be rearmed if it was used, hence the question: where did the Scud come from and did it have any brother and sister Scuds?

More to the point, was this the only launcher site being set up along the disputed border between Kuwait and Iraq? What did Saddam have in mind? Was he at the point where the weapons of mass destruction story had reached an end point and would the US and its coalition attack Iraq from the sea to their south? Spider guessed that this consideration was on his commanders' minds as well.

Doc was given the sat radio and he sent a text message with photos covering their previous night's activities in a sit-rep. He also relayed Spider's recommendation that they move off ASAP and try to find the next high-value target. In the back of Spider's mind was that they were moving a long way from their extraction point for meeting up with the submarine and ingress/egress as originally planned. Doc was sure his DIO commander would pick up on that when he read the sit-rep and Spider's recommendation; they both knew each other too well not to make comment and unsettle the team.

The response came back just one hour after the message was sent:

MSG RECD WITH PICS.
PROCEED AS YR RECOMM.
ENDURANCE NOTED.

The team had already assembled down from the roof and were outbound when the beep from the sat-com was heard. Spider had enough faith in his commander to get the team on the move as it was highly likely he would want more intelligence coming in. Even if they were told to extract, they were on the move anyway so no effort was wasted. The morale remained good with no adverse chatter on discomfort or fatigue. This type of team didn't talk a lot anyway, and particularly didn't grumble when they did talk.

The Iraqis had left sufficient tyre track marks from the semi-trailer carrying the Scud for the intrepid warriors to walk along during the night at a good pace. By the start of dawn, they could hear vehicles (possibly tanks) and from time to time see flickers of lights well ahead of them. This border area was very active and now they were in need of finding an observation point and cover. The team headed towards an oil field gas flare, hoping not to find a new minefield alongside it like the last one. As there were multiple vehicles tracks around here, they had enough confidence to stick to them and cut across from one set to another that provided a better heading for where they needed to go.

The terrain was beginning to become more undulating here, so they gained a little more confidence in finding a hollow or wadi scour to set up shop before dawn for monitoring the comings and goings out on the main tracks.

As the sun rose from behind them in the east, the outline of more oil-gathering tanks and facilities could be seen, and even more workers' huts. Fortunately, or unfortunately for them, civilians were spotted by Rat, who was scouting ahead and moving about among the facilities. Rat called in on his radio with 'Occupied – civilians'. In response, the team ducked down and moved stealthily back a further 100 yards. They set up under a pipe rack where the winds had piled up sand in a semi-vee behind the heavy steel structure giving them visual cover. This would be their home for the coming day or so, with some protective cover in case they were spotted and came under fire. They could observe both the vehicle movements and the civilians moving about at the same time.

Chapter 22

Operation – Day Ten

The Massacre

As the sun came up above their camouflage-netted heads, a 4×4 patrol vehicle passed on the track between their position and the huts. It was lucky they had moved that 100 yards further back. The vehicle halted when the occupants sighted several of the civilians scurrying away towards the huts. The co-driver then started jabbering something into his two-way hand-held radio. Several minutes passed, all quiet, then the sound of another vehicle, a half-track troop carrier, arrived on the scene with up to ten soldiers on board, their AK-47s bristling over the railings towards the huts and oil facilities. Silence again while the two drivers alighted and had a discussion while smoking cigarettes.

The half-track roared into life, diesel smoke gushing from its exhaust, and charged brazenly into the oil facilities, weaving and turning sharply, probably attempting to draw fire if there was going to be any. There was no gun fire, only screaming and yelling from the civilians as they had almost been rounded up into a tighter formation.

Then the 4×4 Toyota started up and joined up in front of the half-track. The civilians were petrified and were standing, by now frozen in place out in the open.

They looked like startled rabbits or sitting ducks, which even a blind man could see. Both vehicles opened fire in unison, using AK-47s and mounted machine guns. The soldiers had simply, without speaking to the civilians; machine gunned them all down until none stood and there was no movement. Poignant silence now contrasted with the weapons fire of a moment ago. The warriors all lay in their hide, aghast and shocked by the unexpectedness and immediacy of this murderous act.

The Iraqi soldiers from both vehicles, having satisfied their heinous need to indiscriminately kill people they didn't know or care about, simply trudged over to the dead, chased and took three goats on board the half-track, then walked past the bloodied, lifeless forms as if this was a normal after-breakfast walk in the park. They all stood around the vehicles chatting and having a relaxing smoke before being rousted aboard their vehicles with the goats. Both vehicles then moved off back towards the westerly direction from which they had come as if nothing had occurred.

Out of sight of those murdering fucking Iraqi camel jockey bastards, and with the dust almost settled, the team cautiously left their hide position, bent low, and scurried over to check each of the bullet-riddled and bloodied bodies. They saw several families of women and children, with no menfolk present. It was a very shocking and sobering scene, particularly looking at the children lying with their mothers, their eyes and mouths wide open as if in a frozen trance. All were clearly dead except for one woman who lay wounded, moaning quietly in pain. Most of these people were white skinned, not with the darker skin pallor of Arabs of this region, although there were several darker-skinned corpses intertwined.

The team all had the same thoughts running through their heads:

- Who were they and where from?
- What should they do with the wounded white woman?
  o Patch her up?
  o Leave her to die?
  o Shoot or knife her?

Brute bent sympathetically and gently approached the wounded woman with Doc the medic alongside for a closer look to ascertain her medical condition, ask who she was, where she was from and how she got to be there. She had taken a bullet through her upper shoulder, which was treatable, but the round that had ripped right through her and shattered her hip was another story and needed immediate hospital attention.

She was in no condition to walk or be moved far from this location and they couldn't do much except pack and strap her hip and shoulder wounds, give her a good shot of morphine and leave her some water and food. They could offer no promises for their return or help. The same would be done for each of them if they were critically wounded, but they had all accepted that a long time ago. Spider stood there sullen for a few moments of contemplation and thought back to the Cambodia operations where he had left five of his soldiers in a shallow grave after they were killed by friendly fire from a US helicopter. Those bodies were never repatriated.

For this woman, it would be different and harder for him to accept.

Gradually through the pain, clenched teeth and occasional groaning, she told them her name was Janice Copley and that her husband Michael worked for an oil contractor in Kuwait. She explained that she and the other women and children had been neighbours in Kuwaiti and expatriate European homes in their local area, with children at the same schools. They had decided to escape after their expatriate husbands and local menfolk had been rounded up by Iraqi soldiers and taken away.

The soldiers had systematically raided their comparatively luxurious homes and taken anything that was not bolted down, including, vehicles, jewellery, money, food, bottled water, alcohol, furniture items and clothing. These women and children were all afraid of having the Iraqi soldiers return to rape them or the young girls and had evacuated their town on foot at night with whatever clothing, food and water was left to them.

Then, without any idea of where to escape to and any good sense of direction, the women had just walked out and away from the invaded and pillaged city with the Iraqis wandering from house to house all around them, breaking into stores and offices. With hostile Iranians over the eastern border, Persian Gulf waters to the south and Saudi Arabia to the west, they had very few options and had just walked, camping out at several disparate locations on the outskirts of Kuwait City over several days before being squeezed towards the north-west due to the movement of soldiers and shooting nearby. They had eventually arrived here during the last week.

At least, for a time, there were no soldiers nearby, there were several huts for hiding in, shelter from the sun, weeds and low shrubs as food for the goats and some rust-tasting water available in old water tanks. However, their greatest fears had come to pass and these dead families would be no more than dust in this unrelenting desert. Some families would remember this loss from far across the world, but not here in this now silent and bloodied place.

Before leaving this scene of death, Brute and Doc lifted Mrs Copley's limp body as gently as possible, eventually moving her over into the shade and inserting her securely under one of the lowest water tanks. They placed some clothing under her head, then they mounded up the sand at her sides and placed some scrap pipe sections to help hide her. She was now groaning loudly in pain, which couldn't be helped. They could do no more for her.

Dispersed, Spider and Rat moved rapidly about the oil facility area, expecting that at any moment the shooters would return for any spoils they might find and they intended to beat them to it. Rat was able to find some of the civilians' meagre personal effects, including some clothing items that were left in place. Then gathered some canned food and water in plastic bottles, which they gathered up to be used by the team. Spider placed the water bottles alongside the injured lady. If she was to survive a bit longer water would be imperative and food would only add to her thirst. They would have to gather their own water later on in their march forward; their canteens were full right now.

One thing that stood out from searching the belongings was that they had no passports or other identification, and it was assumed that the Iraqi soldiers in Kuwait City had taken them for later use when interrogating the women.

However, those vicious rag heads would not find these women and children at their homes in Kuwait. Neither would their spouses, which would be a mystery for them no doubt, but not for the SAS warriors. This event would remain etched in their minds forever.

The team met near where Mrs Copley was secreted and they squatted silently in the desert sand and sipped on some precious water. Brute was the first to speak: 'I ask each of you as soldiers, what kind of miserable lowlife fucking inhumane people could just shoot down in cold blood these unarmed women and those poor little kids? They died with those terrifying death mask faces in their mother's arms.'

Brute's eyes were almost on the verge of overflowing.

Doc responded: 'There has never been a war when atrocities have not occurred, now I know there is no excuse for this massacre Brute, and for you and you other warriors, I have only this to say: You'll never know how strong you are until being strong is the only chance you have.'

Spider spoke trying to settle down their anxiety. 'Tonight, for our next sat-com sit-rep, I will send off the only survivor's details, condition, endurance of maybe two to three days and the GPS location along with individual photos of this massacre of civilians and site local area. We will never know who the rest of the dead are and we have no way of informing anyone except for taking photos of each of them for now. Only one body was moved and hidden, to more likely soon die from exposure and loss of blood over the coming days and nights out here.'

The sun would soon burn and bleach these bodies if left untouched over the next weeks and months. However, they didn't move the bodies from where they fell in case the Iraqis returned and noticed a disturbance and came hunting for them. No one spoke more than a word at a time over the next hours. All were lost in their own thoughts about what they had witnessed and had to leave behind.

They returned to their hide not far away and tried to refocus on what lay ahead for them if they got spotted. Not a pretty picture!

Thank God for the night and a change in attention from past hours to the next hours of reporting and then some action. The sat-com report with text and photos was transmitted. They knew what the response would be:

What are these Iraqis up to?

Are there any big targets – packages out there? If so what and how many?

All of the team were energised to move forward, this time with adrenaline and anger brewing in their guts.

As planned previously on an earlier trek, they moved well off the vehicle tracks after taking several compass plots and marking up their maps. If they were separated, they would make their way back to this hide and wait for the others for at least twelve hours.

If no contact, try the Z-Tac throat mic once. If nothing heard, then shut it off. Make tracks back to the submarine, if possible to do so safely. No other plan was contemplated at that time; they didn't need to be told that going forward towards a lot more Iraqis held certain dangers and would limit their ability to egress in one piece.

The trek took them about 30 miles in the dark, parallel with the vehicle tracks and fairly flat terrain, looking out for mines and sentry trenches; not good if they needed to run for cover at dawn. Cautiously they came within a quarter mile of a very active Iraqi depot that appeared to be used for refuelling vehicles and staging stores, and an ammunition dump no less. This was an excellent package to mark up for an air strike if the coalition forces actually invaded. The depot had the usual canvas covers in a variety of sizes covered further with camouflage nettings spread out over 100 yards in each direction. Brute and Rat moved forward and spotted machine gun emplacements just under the edge of the canvas, which was not unexpected.

Operation – Day Eleven

Just prior to dawn, they had to go to cover and were forced to dig out a series of fox holes about 500 yards from the enemy. Now, as the sun rose, all were covered up with the canvas and camouflage nettings. The displaced sand was used as a barrier to the Iraqis looking directly at their hide due to the flatness of the terrain. It looked like they were stuck there until dusk, cooking and trying to rest in little holes in the sand!

At least they did have some additional water in the canteens and food to extend their endurance a couple more days. Their hearts and thoughts went out to the dead people laying out in the sun behind them, and especially to Mrs Janice Copley, who was almost killed and then almost saved by them, only to be left to lay under a rusty water tank, in pain, drifting in and out of consciousness, wondering where they went, all the while waiting for the Iraqi soldiers to return or to succumb from her wounds and never wake up again.

Some people who know what the SAS warriors do comment about their ruthless tactics, even leaving each other to die if needed to save the rest. They will never have to face what these brave men have done or continue to do. Not many of them reach retirement in this business. The SAS train and know and accept that any one of them might be left behind alone, therefore they rarely take on any social baggage.

They rarely ever socialise with each other as it would likely compromise their decision-making in the field. Each warrior fully expects that the other members of the team have to leave them behind if compromised. Completing the mission successfully comes first.

Well anyway, the Iraqis were on the move and they were on the chase.

There were lots of noises coming from under the canvas over there with vehicles starting up, spotlights turned on inside and silhouetting on the canvas sides. Dozens of kitted up soldiers now began herding out into the open desert.

Then three Russian T-72 tanks moved out on the back of dimly lit semi-trailers. Five artillery pieces were then towed noisily away by half-track vehicles and their associated covered stores trucks. Doc raised himself up enough to take some photos, then slunk down out of sight to review his artwork. 'This will be a good report for the commander,' he whispered through his cracked lips.

All of this heavy equipment being moved at night was to avoid it being picked up by US satellites, no doubt. Their commanders certainly didn't have any intelligence reports or aerial photos of this site, or they would have provided that location to them. Guess what? Another Scud trailer and then a second one emerged from under the cover along with their convoys of radar and troop carrier half-track vehicles. Four things came to mind:

1. Was that all of the contents of this depot?
2. What remained in there after all this lot moved off to parts unknown?
3. Were the machine gun posts still manned? Were there sentries?
4. How could they track the moving parade of vehicles and equipment?

There was going to be a whopper of a sit-rep later today. Plus, the usual inquiring response of:

Now we know WHAT, tell us WHERE and WHEN?

Intuitively they were searching for the answers and scenario solutions. They didn't need or want any armchair jockey telling them how to run this operation, particularly right now as it was close to the end of the mission.

Spider crawled out of his fox hole in the sand behind the low bund mound, trying not to be observed by Iraqi night vision glasses in order to whisper some thoughts with the team. Radio chatter would definitely be tracked by their foes. They agreed on splitting up with each man focusing on ascertaining the daylight direction of each set of equipment tracks.

The priorities were:

1. Two Scud launchers depending on if or when they split up.
2. Three T-72 tanks or single tank depending on if or when they split up.
3. Observe and report on the remaining contents of the depot.
4. Five artillery pieces depending on if or when they split up.

This strategy would split the team up too wide and was impossible to achieve more than one or two objectives on foot and without getting spotted. Doc, the electronics whizz-kid, suggested using their throat mics as permanently on radio transmitters and, if they could, hiding each of them on four trucks, say:

• Two Scuds as the primary packages – Spider and Doc.
• Two out of three T-72 tanks as secondary value packages – Brute and Rat.
• Leave the artillery pieces as tertiary opportunity targets, if they found them later.

It was apparent that getting anywhere close to the artillery pieces would not be advisable due to the close proximity of a half-track loaded with artillery crews and following ammunition trucks. All agreed to tape the throat mics' talk switches in the transmit on position at the last minute and hide them somewhere on the associated transports.

Rat piped up and offered to make a nice baseball-sized Semtex C4 package with detonator inserted, fuse, igniter and timer attached.

All that was needed was to pull the tab on the igniter's timer to set it off. Twisting the timer clockwise shortened the ignition time and the fuse had five seconds to burn after that.

Simple, eh?

They all took him up on the gesture, which he had already prepared for use by him and Brute if needed. No need to waste such precious plastic stuff with a single big bite.

The alternative would have been to bury it with the M60 machine gun as they had to travel light from now onward.

The plan for using the throat mics switched on and leaving the heavy M60 machine gun and excess ammunition buried where they currently lay would be transmitted immediately via sat-com radio to their command, along with the current GPS co-ordinates for the military store depot. This hastily planned action would be a foot race in the dark and hopefully they would get a break with the transports getting bogged down or stopping for the familiar smoko for the Iraqi soldiers in a couple of hours from now.

Their fall-back rendezvous position whether they succeeded or failed would be the previous murder site hide in case this depot was hit by US or coalition forces if Iraq was invaded. They sure would like to be close by if that happened.

There would be no time for counter-discussions after they had all moved out. It was understood that their short-range throat mic radios could be tracked by command radio operators in the Persian Gulf or by satellite if they knew the frequency (and they did because they had issued the co-ordinates) and the radios would be set permanently on. They had assumed that the transports would only travel until just before dawn and then cover up. The risk of losing the radios would be minimal, however, if they were discovered the Iraqis would begin a wide search for them. There would be no stone unturned until they were captured and or killed.

'When the going gets tough, the tough get going.'

Operation – Day Twelve

Dawn was now about five hours away and hopefully the radio batteries, once turned to transmit at the last minute, would last for another six to eight hours. Doc reminded them to tape over the throat mic piece to save battery life in case background noise kept the mic transmitting sounds. It did cross their minds that Iraqi forces radio operators might also pick up the radio signals and think they were sitting on the vehicles getting a free ride, or maybe not! Seriously though, it would take the Iraqis some time to locate the moving transports that might well be on radio silence anyway.

Hopefully a poorly organised Iraqi radio communication and tracking system might not be able to expose the radios for some period of time, and by then they would hopefully be well away from the packages and heading for the submarine.

Given the enormity of this challenge in front of them, their hopes lay in audacity and a good bit of luck as the transports moved away from them in differing directions. The convoys' low speed due to heavy loads, mines and travelling at night would be to their advantage. Dust up front would be in their favour. They shook hands firmly, then moved off one by one into the dark in different but specific directions on their bellies in the sand, then up and jogging into the dust raised by each convoy.

Doc and Spider jogged together for a couple of miles behind the two Scud carriers and wondered if and when an opportunity would present for at least one of them to radio tag a Scud-carrying semi-trailer. They couldn't run like this for much longer, and then it happened: the two convoys stopped momentarily prior to separating down each side of a crossroad track.

Doc was quicker than Spider, as usual, having the lighter stature of the two, and he quickly took the initiative and went off the track about 50 yards where the dust had been drifting and headed down the side of the trailing vehicle. Spider ran up to the target trailing vehicle and climbed up the back using the tyre and wheel hub as steps. The camouflage netting had been tightly roped down, giving him something solid to grip onto as the semi-trailer jolted forward and turned right.

Interestingly, there were not a lot of places to hide the Z-Tac throat mic radio, on which by now he had taped the transmit switch to 'on'. He lay flat on the tray, looked over the side and found a tool box slung on the underside. It didn't look like it was in use due to the rust from stone chips and it being half full of sand. He placed the radio transmitter in the tool box and pulled a half-buried rag over it for camouflage (it should work for the time being). Easy, and he then just rolled off the back of the trailer and stood in the dust cloud watching it carry on ahead of him.

Doc didn't catch up to the front semi-trailer as he went a bit too far wide of the vehicle and only made contact when it was midway around a left turn corner and had slowed down to a walk. He was able to jog alongside, tape up the radio's 'on' switch and out of the corner of his eye pick out the spare tyre chained to the bed of the trailer with a large space in the back of the wheel rim in which to toss it in.

The road dust would camouflage it fairly quickly and hopefully the driver wouldn't have a puncture anytime soon. Spider didn't know why Doc was not spotted out in the open like that; probably the driver and crew had their windows up with the A/C on high. Doc just trotted off to the dust cloud and stopped, waiting for any response. There was none, so he jogged back to meet up with Spider.

'Good job Doc,' Spider said as he slapped him on the back, causing dust to fall off.

Doc grinned and spoke 'A soldier's gotta do what a soldier's gotta do Spider. Same to you.'

Both of them were exhilarated, but exhausted, and in need of vital water to clear their parched and dusted throats.

Time to march at a fast pace back to the hide and away from the direction of those vehicles.

At the same time, both Brute and Rat were also jogging after the two T-72 tank carrier semi-trailers. They had a similar slow road speed to the others due to carrying the over 50-ton tanks plus stores and fuel drums. Both of them had caught up and jumped onto the back of the first trailer. There were plenty of cavities among the crates and fuel drums, not including the tank. A crate of spare parts was selected with the hope that it wouldn't be opened anytime soon. The mic was taped 'on' and snugly stowed out of sight. Then they turned to consider how to get at the front trailer and its cargo.

It was over two hours with a road speed of about 15 to 20mph when the convoy came to a slow stop. The men jumped off the back of the rear trailer, which they had been riding on, and quickly headed for the dust cloud and out wide and parallel to the convoy. It was not an easy task to board the front semi-trailer as the rear driver or accompanying crew could spot them. With both transporters stopped and the dust settling, it was time to watch and wait.

True to Iraqi spirit, they were going to have a smoko and all joined together for a chat and to ease their circulation, having been in a bone-rattling truck cabin for a couple of hours on a very potholed track. Some went and had a piss in the sand, some walked up and down both sides checking the tie-down chains for the tank and some were drinking water from a hose from a drum on the rear trailer.

Time to go around the blind side and pop under the front trailer, plant the radio up underneath somewhere, then get out of there before the trailers started up again.

Rat, being smaller and more likely quicker, decided it was his time to act and picked up the radio, taped the switch to 'on', nodded at Brute – who immediately understood the plan – and watched as Rat scurried low using dust and darkness to circle the convoy from the front, where none of the Iraqis had gone. Rat also found a spare tyre slung under the centre of the trailer. The tool box was on the other side, so he skipped trying for that. It would be unwise to climb up on the trailer deck in case he was in the open and spotted if the rear truck lights were switched on.

The spare tyre was the only place to poke the radio into, and with time running out and the Iraqi drivers becoming impatient going by the harsh notes of their voices, Rat deposited it by wedging it under the tyre-holding chain. He then moved off, backing away low in case one of the crews came around to his side. Several Iraqis did start to head over to his side of the truck cabin for reboarding. Rat pressed his smallish frame to the ground and tiger crawled awkwardly backwards until he was far enough back to lay still and wait for the convoy to move on its merry way broadcasting its positions to the world. Or at the least, for the fleet command radio operators tracking radio signal movements over the next day or two. Even a satellite could be used to track the signals.

Rat made his way back across the track to where he had left Brute.

'Well done matey,' said Brute. 'You'll get a bloody Victory Cross medal for that one. I nearly pissed my pants when the crews began walking over to your side. I couldn't imagine you having to hang under the trailer for the next 20 or 30 miles or so. You could have gotten caught and I would have had to tell your mum you were a bad boy – ha, ha, ha.'

Rat knew Brute from a number of previous missions and was delighted to hear him in a jovial mood as he was usually fairly surly and quiet until he was typically playing at being a sergeant and dressing everyone down short and sharp, so he replied with a wink.

'Thanks mate, I am glad you approve. However, I don't have a mum. We were too poor. I was born under a cabbage leaf, I was told. And did you mean Victoria Cross?'

Both men, feeling that success does not go to one's head but to one's heart, headed off to meet up at the hide and their comrades.

The chatter would be about who did what with their radios and their hopes for some sort of success.

The seriously wounded woman was lying hidden not very far away from their rendezvous and this weighed heavily on their minds. All of them were concerned about what orders their command would give to define their next action. Spider crawled over to the three men to discuss their recent actions and observations to formulate what they would send on the next sat-com sit-rep message, which would include quantification and qualification in very brief terms and requesting radio tracking of the throat mic radios.

The message sent read as follows:

URGENT MSG – ACTION REQ
HAVE SIGHTED SCUDS – TANKS – ARTILLERY ON MOVE
INTERDICTED PACKAGES BY PLACING LIVE Z-TAC
RADIOS ABOARD TWO SCUDS – TWO T-72 TANKS ON
MOBILE TRANSPORTERS – STILL ON MOVE WEST
SUGGEST YR RADIO TRACKING FOR AIR STRIKE – PHOTOS
– MAP ATTCH
STOP
WITNESSED IRAQI MASSACRE OF CIVILIANS FR KUWAIT
ID NIL – MOST DEAD – PHOTOS – GPS – MAP ATTCH
ONE LIVE BRIT FEM CRIT INJURED – EVAC REQ – MS
JANICE COPLEY
STOP
AWAIT INSTR

Each of the team were hoping for a positive tactical response to the radio tracking of the target packages. The plight of the injured lady was now strictly in the hands and resources of the commander and associated coalition forces. They had made their case clear, particularly with the massacre photos and GPS location of one live survivor. Their minds immediately turned to Janice Copley's current status. Doc and Rat slipped across to where she lay silently under the water tank with a first aid kit in hand and a water canteen.

She was conscious but not very communicative, so he injected her with a shot of morphine, assured her that help was on its way and urged her to hang in for a while longer. Spider and Brute sat and waited while Doc and Rat had finished looking after Mrs Copley and came back where they were huddled close.

There may be a window of hope for her to be extracted once the Iraqis had been pushed out of Kuwait completely. Or a chopper could scoot in low and rapidly medevac extract her out of there.

Come on command, let us know what our orders are so we can get into the fray of the fight.

Meantime, Brute and Spider considered what new sorties they could do over the next twenty-four hours prior to heading back toward the beach and submarine for egress. They still had the laser targeting devices and the Semtex C4 packs with detonator, igniter and timer attached all ready to go. Perhaps a timely goodbye and parting gift might brighten up the night skies at the nearest store's depot, either where the fuel, Scud and radar were set up at the Abdali village stores depot or at the other depot where the Scuds, tanks and artillery exited.

There might be other packages or a large store of ammunition in there. They hadn't checked in the flurry to place their live radios onto the outbound convoys. They couldn't personally go in and brazenly hit them both and expect to live to regret it. Perhaps the laser pointers would do the trick at some point later. Within one hour the sat-com beeped and a message arrived promptly:

MSG RECD
SUB NO-GO – HOLD YR CURRENT POSS
BE READY TO SET LASERS ON DEPOTS – WILL SEND CO-ORDS FOR ARTILLERY NEXT
TKS TO YR RADIOS – AIR WILL TAKE ON SCUDS TANKS CONVOYS
EXPECT DESERT STORM FR TONIGHT VIA SAUDI
WAIT FTHR ADV ON LIVE FEMALE EVAC

Each of them froze. These were a series of shocks as they had not been informed at the briefing about Desert Storm, which appeared to mean the invasion of Iraq by US and coalition forces via land through Saudi Arabia.

Saddam really would not be set up for this orientation of the battlefield as his military was postured facing Kuwait for a water-borne invasion.

Chapter 23

The Invasion

Operation – Day Thirteen

Early morning even before daylight, they heard the first battle sounds as fighter jets rushed overhead and in the direction of Baghdad. Others at low altitude attacked the T-72 tanks that they had radio tagged and were by now half buried in bulldozed holes. They were hit with such force that the turrets went flying into the air as their ammunition inside exploded.

The Scuds never got raised to get ready to fire and were taken out by very low-flying A-10 Warthog fighter-bombers. The Iraqi radar only picked up a blip before, boom, they were evaporated in a fireball of rocket fuel. Iraqi ground forces were giving up the fight wholesale within their country and just dropping their weapons and uniforms on the ground. There appeared to be very little intervention required by the coalition allies intent on driving rapidly straight into Baghdad, which was currently copping a beating from the air.

Meanwhile, within their line of sight, they were able to send sit-reps on distant movements of Iraqi troops who had driven south into northern Kuwait and begun setting the oil wells ablaze with explosives. There was work to do here but they were a four-man intelligence team with limited rations and not enough ammunition to do much, particularly faced by dozens of Iraqi troops scattered about and around them.

They could now see across in the direction of the highway between Kuwait and Baghdad and a lot of firing and explosions could be heard, even as far away as they were. The action over there was surely heating up. The sat-com radio beeped and they had voice mode incoming from command; security was obviously not in protocol right now. They were given the general co-ordinates of several buried T-72 tank emplacements that required laser targeting for the A-10 Warthogs to go in and kill. Work at last and supplies would hopefully be dropped by chopper at some point down the track.

They were ordered to briefly stand by to talk in a US carrier-based chopper that would recover Janice Copley within the next hour. They would extract and deliver her onto a US navy cruiser that would be swinging by just outside the Kuwaiti port. The cruiser had the job of checking out the Kuwait harbour for utilising the wharf facilities but had come under Iraqi artillery fire and identified with sonar that there were marine mines that would need deactivating.

Rat heard the chopper before any of them and signalled for them all to shut up and listen.

As the chopper descended through the haze with the sun almost overhead, Spider jumped up and began waiving both arms, while Rat and Doc headed across to Mrs Copley to move her out into the open. The helicopter hovered about 100ft above them for a few seconds with the belly gunner's machine gun trained on them, and after reassuring themselves that they weren't Iraqi soldiers, landed on the gravel road above in a cloud of dust. Two medics followed Doc around the minefield and ran across to Mrs Copley with a small stretcher.

Spider walked over to the chopper as its engine slowed and rotors slowed, raising the dust. The pilot indicated that he wasn't in any mood to stop for an idle chat and watched anxiously as his medics carried Mrs Copley at the run back to the open door.

The waist gunner helped slide the stretcher across the floor, both medics scrambled aboard and the engine began to spin up, causing Spider to turn his back and scurry for cover behind the nearest building. Once airborne, the chopper spun around, began gaining height and retraced its inbound direction for returning to the ship. Spider was a bit surprised that the medics paid no attention to the dead bodies lying strewn about. A one-off fast extraction must have been their orders.

Brute spoke: 'After the massacre that happened here, I hope every fucking Iraqi soldier in this God-forsaken desert gets his just deserves.'

Thumbs up all around.

Spider turned to his men, who were also dusting themselves off, to get everyone refocused as they had a new mission to complete. It was reasonably easy for the team to split up in pairs, with one pair heading back to the Abdali village stores depot to light it up with a laser targeting device and the other team go back to the midway point down the track to the west stores depot where the Scuds had emerged from and laser light that one up waiting for an air strike.

Spider and Doc arrived at the western stores depot package and settled into their previous fox holes before sending a sat-com message providing the GPS positions and a report that in two hours exactly they would turn the laser targeting devices on directed at both of the store's depots. He advised what to expect to be destroyed in the stores before being asked by the commander.

Brute and Rat trudged down the track, recovered the M60 and ammunition case and dusted it off ready to fire. They then trudged off and reached the mud house roof top two hours later. There were no radios for confirming 'in position', so this was a once-only chance to execute the targets at a specified time via the only sat-com radio. The house and roof had not been disturbed and no footprints were seen near the access point, only around the perimeter of the broken-down compound wall.

Right on the specified time they heard overhead jets, but didn't see them in the dusty haze. Verrrrooomph! You could feel everything shudder underfoot. One after the other the stores went up in a fireball. At their end, looking over the parapet of the roof, Brute and Rat saw half a dozen Iraqi soldiers who had been blown into the air and out into the open. They waited for some time before the dust and fragments of the Scud and radar station had settled so they could get a good look at the destruction. It was now just a hole in the ground, which had buggered up the nice concrete job put into place not too many days before. Brute opened fire with the M60 and cut down the Iraqis, then he and Rat ran over and circled the scene of destruction to mop up any survivors. None were found.

Similar destruction happened at the west store. A huge fireball went up high in the sky as the fuel dump exploded. Three of the soldiers that were out in the open when the site was hit were injured and began to move on hands and knees, so Doc picked up his SLR rifle and finished them off, saying 'Take that you murdering fucking excuses for humans'.

Spider and Doc moved cautiously down to inspect the destruction and they took photos for their sit-rep later while the midday sun belted down and even more heat from the fires radiated out for some distance. Burned 4×4 vehicles lay twisted and blackened far from the hole in the ground, and bodies could be seen inside.

Spider planned to wait until Rat and Brute arrived back after sundown and assumed that the laser targeting had achieved the same result. No more stores depots and hopefully the jets had taken out the Scuds and T-72s.

The next sat-com from the commander would likely fill them in on the results of the air strikes.

Rat and Brute had taken a few more photos, and the jets likely took aerial shots from up there as well. All good so far, now for their late afternoon trek back to the west store target area to meet up with Doc and Spider. The track was easy to follow and almost serene in the silence after such an enormous bomb blast with associated destruction.

With the whole team now sitting in their old fox holes, as the sun was going down on the horizon to the west, it was time to relax and collaborate on the next move in the start of the Desert Storm phase of the Iraq War. They had not been briefed on this eventuality, so they were going to be winging it from this moment forward. Their original operation was fundamentally over and a new one ahead of them. The submarine extraction was a no go.

Their thoughts drifted towards leaving Iraq and Kuwait and the horror of witnessing the massacre, but they felt a little satisfied with this revenge air strike and that one poor innocent woman being evacuated. Time to head away from here as Iraqi patrols would be on their way to assess the damage.

They were now trekking abreast of the minefields, retracing the direction of their original beach entry toward the south-east and making quite sure that they stayed well clear of the roads and tracks as far as possible. They were a little more confident about their surroundings as familiar signs and facilities were passed, like where the woman and goats had been challenged by an Iraqi patrol about a week ago.

Crack!

A bullet ripped into Brute with such force he lifted up a bit and immediately fell to his right side. Rat hit the dust, trying anxiously to work out where the shot came from and tugging at Brute's outstretched arm.

'Yah alright mate?' Rat asked.

No answer as Brute lay silent.

Shit, who the fuck is out there. Where are you, you son of a bitch?

Both Spider and Doc lay flat on the gravel road, unable to see where the shot came from or how many shooters were out there. Another shot rang out, which sounded not more than inches above Rat's head as it whizzed past him. The bullet appeared to come from near the oil field hut below them on the other side of the minefield.

'Betcha that was that fucking burqa-covered Iraqi bitch or one of her pals,' Rat thought.

There was no way of him calling for help from the other two, who had bitten the dust about 100 yards behind them, as they had gotten rid of their Z-Tac radios.

'Can't stay here with Brute right now or I will cop it once they get their range. Gotta flick over into the minefield where there is some limited cover and our footprints are still there to follow,' Rat mumbled to himself.

He dumped his backpack and dragged over his SLR rifle and a belt of M60 ammunition that was now dangling from Brute's backpack.

If I appear to have moved, they will look for me and not continue to shoot at Brute. Rat figured.

He raised his SLR and rapid fired in the direction of the hut while scrambling low until he could dive down onto some boot tracks and a hump of growth and sand.

More single shots echoed, with bullets striking nearby and not up further where Brute lay motionless.

Rat mumbled to himself 'They are now after me and firing for effect hoping I will return fire. Me not so silly, pal.'

This was not a good position; a mine could be set off close by and blow Rat to kingdom come. Rat would have to take his time, knowing that the sun was going down and improving his chances to either take off, leaving Brute to the Iraqis, or try to terminate this threat.

He kept his head down, looking left then right for a possible next move. If he stayed there, he would eventually be hit from either side if those doing the shooting had half a brain.

He rolled right to his next hide, which also provided a little more cover and took him a few more yards away from visible mines. More shots rang out and thudded in the sand within a yard of his previous position.

Think man, ya gotta get into or outta this shit.

He noticed that the shooters had not fired at his new spot, so he dared to assume that either they didn't see his move or they had not been quick enough to take the shot. He figured that might mean that he was smarter and quicker at this point, but don't make it repetitive, he thought.

By now they may think he planned to move further right, maybe left, and get fixated. He went straight over the top of this mound and skidded up against the pipe rack that Doc had hidden behind previously.

Spider sighted where Rat was and what Rat was doing and pointed his SLR in that direction. Doc did likewise, but the hut was on the other side of the pipeline and they couldn't spot the shooter.

As expected, several shots rang out from the hut, one, then another.

They must have a bolt action rifle as it's slow to repeat, Rat figured. One more thing in his favour, he figured, and he guessed that with their eye along the sights and the other closed, they might not have spotted exactly where he had landed.

About a yard to his left was an exposed mine.

'A big bugger for vehicles or tanks,' Rat muttered.

Around the steel legs of the pipe rack, he could now see the hut. No window or door on this side, so either they were shooting from the sides or had moved. Time to outwait them and have the SLR aimed at one side.

Think man, where do you think the shots came from?

Left or right side?

He remembered where they had seen the woman days earlier. She came out from the right side of the hut chasing the goats. He guessed the goats were now inside the hut and that meant the doorway may be in that direction, too.

Rat set himself about a yard further back from the steel legs and mounded sand so he could gouge a narrow groove in the sand big enough to slide the rifle barrel forward next to the steel leg and not to be easily seen from below. Doc's boot marks were still visible ahead of him, providing a possible route to attack with the SLR automatic fire targeting the right side. Until dark he couldn't take out this target or go up to the track and help Brute.

If he found Brute was dead, he would grab the M60 and ammunition and if alive he would have to safely carry or drag him back to a safe position.

One is trained to make decisions on the run from the enemy, no matter what operation you are on. The same would be done if it was himself laying there.

An idea dawned on him. Rat reached down and removed the ball of string and roll of wire from the front of the left leg pocket of his cargo pants. Carefully looping the wire big enough to fit over the nearest exposed land mine, he then tied the string to the loop of wire. He tossed the loop over to the mine, missing it several times until the loop settled over the outside of the mine base. Hoping there was no booby trap under the mine, he slowly and carefully began to drag the mine toward him.

He was now in a sweat, the string slipping in his wet fingers, at the same time maintaining regular glances along the rifle barrel of the SLR.

This will make a bloody big hand grenade, he thought to himself.

Meanwhile, the Iraqi woman was still squatting low at the right side of the hut, listening for any sign of Rat.

She couldn't see past the building and the pipeline obstructed more of the ground behind while she squatted. Eventually that enemy of hers among the minefield would have to make a move and she would take him out. She did have a portable army radio in the hut up on a sheet metal shelf. She was a soldier of Saddam and proud of it. Her discord with the Iraqi soldiers on 4×4 patrol who had shot at her and the goats a couple of days ago (and missed) was a prank.

That's why she got pissed off and yelled at them before they drove off. She was on guard duty on this track and used the burqa as a disguise over her uniform.

Her pride was well earned, as she had helped execute several civilians near Baghdad for Saddam's military. That was easier than what faced her now; this guy was able to move and shoot back. The situation made her shudder, realising that he could also kill her if she made a mistake. The first man she shot didn't know she was there, but the second one was still alive and there was only her there to kill him. She got tired of squatting and got up intending to try spotting him again. Where had he moved to? She fired one shot in the direction of the last place. No return fire, maybe he had moved elsewhere as there were several obstacles for cover. Or had she got lucky and already wounded or killed him with one of the shots that she had fired?

Curious, she moved a little forward, ready to pull the trigger at the slightest movement. There was no movement except for Rat pulling his trigger. The bullet clipped the corner of the tin hut, cut right through and fragments struck her shoulder, making her swing around and backwards. Shocked, she fired her rifle into the air, hitting the roof of the hut.

'Gotcha my girl,' Rat whispered after seeing the turned-up bullet hole appear in the hut roof.

But no kill this time, just one for Brute still lying on the track motionless.

This situation needed reinforcements, she thought as she slid against the hut door that opened inwardly. A goat rushed out, shocking her nerves even further. The radio that she must use to call for help was out of reach and standing up would be dangerous. She was now starting to feel a sharp pain in her shoulder and the wetness of warm blood beginning to run down her right arm.

Rat was not aware of what she intended as she was out of sight. He hoped he had stunned her enough to give him two seconds to get up to his feet while grasping the mine. He hurled its 15kg weight as hard as he could at the hut, hoping to at least get her to run for it when the mine exploded. He dove for cover and watched the mine roll on its side down the rise toward the hut.

At the same moment that the mine landed against the wall of the hut with a clank, she was stooped awkwardly and stepping over a goat while desperately grasping with her left hand extended for the microphone on the radio. She hit the press to speak button as the mine scraped against the wall, wobbling until the striker hit the corner and it exploded.

The hut virtually blew over on its side. Half of it was missing as fragments of mine and hut momentarily hung in the air before falling haphazardly among the oil tanks and pipelines. The blast had blown away from the direction of the minefield due to the mine being on its side when it went off. There were bits of guts and other material that masked what was the woman's and what were from the goats.

As soon as the bits of explosion, hut stuff and dust settled, Rat raced up to the track to where Brute lay, his eyes open, semi-conscious, and Brute said 'What the fuck have you been doing? You scared the fucking shit outta me with all of that commotion.'

Rat began checking Brute for a bullet wound. Sure enough one had passed straight through his ribcage and grazed his left arm, ending up in his backpack. The whack in the ribs had knocked the wind out of him as he fell he had hit his head, which had knocked him out for all of this time, forty minutes in all.

Not seeing it as a time or place to joke or even discuss what had just happened out in the minefield, Rat encouraged Brute to sit up and lean forward while he placed a first aid kit antiseptic pad on the rib wound and then taped it to stop the bleeding. Then he wrapped his arm.

Rat said 'That will do for now mate, so get the fuck up before the neighbours wake up and come see this mess you've made'.

Several hours later, Spider, Doc, Rat and Brute made it back to the roof top mud house and provided a summary of the west store's depot demolition.

'Thank Christ you are OK Brute,' Spider told him.

Doc chimed in 'Yea mate, glad you are still in one piece'.

Brute nodded and muttered a 'thank you', to all of them, and a special thanks to Rat for killing that fucking Iraqi split tail bitch that shot him.

The sat-com sit-rep message was drafted, stating:

> PACKAGES EAST WEST ARE DOWN – PHOTOS
> ENEMY ENGAGED EAST WEST
> ONE WALKING INJURED – PATCHED
> ALL AT CURRENT POS ABDALI
> ADV ORDERS FR TOMORROW
> ENDURANCE TWO DAYS

The rest of the evening was uneventful, however, they did expect the Iraqi patrols to come down quickly to check out the carnage. However, none came so far – unusual!

Operation – Day Fourteen

The liberation of Kuwait was a US-led military operation to retake the country from Iraq after a massive air campaign between 24 and 28 February 1991. US troops and the coalition entered to find the Iraqis were surrendering en masse; however, pockets of resistance existed, particularly at Kuwait's international airport where Iraqi troops, seemingly unaware that a retreat order had been issued to them, continued to fight, resulting in a fierce battle over the airport itself.

The majority of the fighting took place in Iraq near where they were, rather than in Kuwait.

Days before the attack, an amphibious force made repeated feint attacks and landings at Kuwait City, attempting to fool the Iraqis into thinking the coalition would attack that way. Instead, the troops were to enter over the border with Saudi Arabia. The coalition forces based there soon became accustomed to the constant Scud missile threats, chemical missile threats and near-constant shelling by Iraqi artillery. When the first troops began the assault, they were warned that casualties could be as many as one in three.

At 4 a.m. on 24 February, after being shelled for months and under the constant threat of a gas attack, the US 1st and 2nd Marine Divisions crossed into Kuwait. They manoeuvred around vast systems of barbed wire, minefields and trenches. Once into Kuwait, they headed towards Kuwait City. The troops themselves encountered little resistance and, apart from several minor tank battles, were met primarily by surrendering soldiers. The general pattern was that coalition troops would encounter Iraqi soldiers who would put up a brief fight before deciding to surrender.

Brute never made a squeak about his close call during a sleepless night – typical of him though as it wasn't the first time he had been hit. His backpack did suffer from the bullets that had passed through his kit, including his ration packs, but luckily most of the impact was taken by the shovel strapped on the backpack. His wound and the loss of some rations could compromise his endurance over the next period of the mission.

They rested for the day and did a complete health check of their bodies, then reset the packs and cleaned the weapons. The GPS and sat radio batteries were changed; there were no more spares.

There must have been a ton of sand in everything including their hair, ears, arse crack, jocks and socks. Their feet were inspected by Doc, then retaped. With their bodies and kit sorted and equipment packed properly, the sun set after a relaxing day in the shade under the roof top home they had used for the last week or so. Now it was time to leave their holiday house and point south-east, remembering that there wasn't much cover but that there appeared to be a lot of smoke in that direction due to the Iraqis' malevolent destruction of Kuwait.

Chapter 24

Operation – Day Fifteen

By early morning they received a sat-com from command:

```
MSG RECD
SUB OUT OF COMM – NO WET EGRESS POSS
DESERT STORM BEGAN EARLY TODAY FROM SAUDI – BY
LAND
YR Z-T RADIOS – LASERS – ALL PACKAGES HIT – WL SEND
A BILL 4 RADIOS
IRAQI FORCES WITHDRAWING KUWAIT – NOW
DESTROYING KUWAITI OIL FIELDS
HEAD FR KUWAIT PORT SOONEST
EXPECT SOME IRAQI RESISTANCE – PACKAGES
SUPPLIES – OR EVAC AT PORT
SIT-REPS REQUD FOR STH ROUTE
AIRPORT UNDER FIRE – NO-GO
PORT FACILITIES MINED – TRAPS – USABLE – AUST NAVY
ON FIX
CONFIRM YR EVAC STH
```

It would have been nice for them to say thanks, they never did though. This invasion news was a big surprise for them as there had been no mention of it during the briefing (no need to know), plus no relief or supplies prior to reaching the Kuwaiti port (bloody typical – always busy). They had to trek about 60 map miles on foot as the crow flies to get to the port. This would take them a day or maybe two to arrive there if there was no conflict with evacuating Iraqis on the way down. They regrouped and audited their supplies. By sharing they figured they could make it – just, with an endurance of two days.

There was no telling what they would encounter on the way down south from where they were. The Iraqis would be either running for their lives north along this, the only highway, towards Baghdad, or resetting their military formations and field pieces to face the US and coalition invasion from the south. That could mean incoming Iraqi covering fire into Kuwait, so they must get moving before the situation of fright and flight by the Iraqis changed to stand and fight. Dozens of coalition military aircraft of all types could be seen and heard in the direction of the highway west and north of them. The battle was on in earnest for the coalition forces and the Iraqis.

And no, this was not the end of the assignment. No packing up and going home, just heaving up their backpacks, licking their wounds and heading south for the Kuwait port. They flicked a short sit-rep to the commander advising that they were on the move, ETA at the port and current endurance. Along the way down south all of them were being bloody cautious not to take it for granted that random hostiles wouldn't still try to take them out on their way to surrender to the US Army.

They also hoped, but did not trust, that any US military in their area would be aware of their existence. Spider had lost five men in Cambodia due to so-called friendly fire from US choppers, even though he had called in the air strike. How does one explain that to the wives and loved ones of the fallen soldiers? It was bad enough when soldiers were sent back badly injured and the Veterans Association (VA) and the Returned Soldiers League (RSL) gave the returning soldiers the cold shoulder, which occurred in Australia after the Vietnam conflict. Fucking ungrateful pricks!

Their objective was the town of Al Jahar on the outskirts of Kuwait City. This meant they would cross the minor road and highway leading from Kuwait to Baghdad, about halfway and one daylight trek down. Hopefully they would not cross paths with any Iraqi combatants. Also, they weren't interested in taking prisoners or helping civilians; they had specific orders and generally did not make diversions.

The best way to navigate around open ground that may have been mined was to work their way from oil pipeline to pipeline. However, within hours of entering Kuwait, they encountered dozens of destroyed oil wells, oil gushing up into the air, acrid smells and taste in their mouths, gas gushing and whistling and alight with high-pressure flames. They could feel the vibration and the heat from 100 yards away or more.

Their route down south-west was still generally parallel to the main highway, some 5 map miles off it to the Persian Gulf side so as to avoid any road traffic. Their next map fix point would be the crossroad above Al Rawgatayn, 15 map miles down their planned route. So far they had met no resistance out in open desert country but Spider loaded his .50 calibre H&K sniper rifle magazine with one hard head in the breach and three armour-piercing bullets in the mag and checked the scope, with Brute and Rat taking up the rear with the M60 locked and loaded.

Doc would be his sniper spotter if they got a contact and was up front of Spider by about 500 yards scouting armed with his SLR and smoke grenades.

They no longer had Z-Tac radios and had reverted to hand signals and occasional whistling to get everyone's attention.

The sky was beginning to turn black from the smoke billowing from the oil well fires shielding out the sun like a shroud. Black and brown crude oil was falling like rain and changing the yellowish sand dunes to brown. They had to use the canvas tarps as ponchos to cover their packs and weapons from the black rain.

They had to use the sharp pointed ends of their bayonets as scrapers to dislodge the oil-soaked sand from their footwear. It just kept building up on the soles of their boots, making them several inches taller until they found it more difficult to walk. The sooner they traversed the oil fields the better, and they diverted their course two clicks towards the main highway as it should provide an improvement in reducing the sand and clumps of the smelly substance clinging to them.

After reaching the Al Rawgatayn minor road, they found it strewn with destroyed Iraqi military vehicles, equipment scattered all about, civilian cars and trucks, and a number of unrecognisable burned male bodies and some twisted, crispy critters burned black by the incendiary bombs. Not pausing to study this sight, they continued on parallel to the main highway, not aware that the US had recently carried out a massive strike on it that led to it becoming known as the Highway of Death. What they had just seen on a minor road paled in comparison to the carnage over there on the main route. This sort of sight was new to them as their past wars had not been out in the open and the fight was more hidden among jungles and buildings.

This hit was very much a one-sided affair by superior forces. By the middle afternoon, they were getting a bit exhausted with their concentration wavering in the heat so they sought some cover behind a shot-out water tanker truck.

The tanker offered some shade and a temporary hide while they rested. Spider climbed on top of the truck and looked through the scope of his rifle at the route ahead for any movement. Seeing nothing, he jumped down and joined the team as they feasted on cold rations (not again!), checked equipment, emptied sand from their boots, scraped the oil-soaked muck off the soles, then got up ready to move on.

Bloody hell, right where Spider had been scanning, Rat spotted one soldier wandering about some 500 yards ahead. The Iraqi soldier had a piss and then disappeared down a hole in the ground. Spider caught up with Rat to take a look, but there was nothing out there now! Rat got a bit agitated thinking Spider was going to reject his sighting as a desert mirage or him going stir crazy. If he was right, they could easily walk into a trap and that was not going to happen to them. Where the soldier had disappeared was a sand dune or mounded sand.

This feature needed to be investigated and either cleared or killed. Being such a small team with limited weapons, taking anything by force would end up in utter disaster for them as one man down would be one too many! Their greatest asset after being sent out here in the first place was remaining covert – invisible, then hit and run.

The action plan involved them leaving their backpacks under the tanker truck, Brute overseeing the area with the M60 mounted on a tripod part-way on the vehicle. The three remaining men began a time-consuming tiger crawl with their camouflage nets covering them in an open Vee formation about 10 yards apart. Spider was on the right flank, Rat on the left and Doc was back a bit in the centre. That way they could observe the feature from several directions at one time and use visual hand signals.

Without warning, a metal hatch clanked opened, a soldier popped his head and torso up and he slowly scanned the horizon all around with binoculars. He didn't look down to where they were, and then nonchalantly climbed up on top to raise an antenna and check the camouflage netting on the side facing away from them. What the fuck is this thing, a bunker, a munitions store, artillery piece? Spider summoned the team with a brisk wave of his hand to continue the move forward so they could get a better look. One problem that Brute could see but they couldn't was that they were all leaving a clear track in the now brown tar speckled surface. This would attract attention soon and heat things up for those on their bellies with no cover for protection.

Good plan, poor situational awareness and no Z-Tac radios to warn anyone.

Thank God for the hot sun, as the soldier slipped back into his hole in the ground and out of sight. Apparently, whoever was below could not see out very well. They needed to see in though and kept moving forward. Having arrived each side of the feature, the two on the flanks could see a large gun barrel protruding from the sand with camouflage netting shrouding its long straight outline. Given that there was a hatch up top, it was a simple deduction for them to signal 'T' with their hands.

Their SLRs and sniper rifle wouldn't do much damage to a T-72 Russian tank. Spider motioned to Rat, who always carried some Semtex and det-cord, and Doc had the smoke grenades. If they could combine an explosive package, they might just be able to slip up and pop it down the hatch and see what damage it could do.

Brute had seen Spider's hand signal about the 'T' and poof bomb. He had scrambled down with the M60 across his muscled arm, dragged out Rat's backpack and emptied it onto the ground. He grasped the entire Semtex kit and scurried on his hands and knees along Rat's track in the sand. With no movement from the tank, and assuming that it faced away from their position,

Brute had taken the initiative of joining the fray and bringing the key item needed to take the tank out in one resounding pop.

Spider watched in startled surprise as Brute met up with Rat. A few nods and some rapid fiddling with the Semtex kit bag and out came a baseball-sized blob wrapped with duct tape, fuse sticking out with an igniter on it. Brute rolled to one side, M60 poised, while Spider changed the .50 calibre hard slug out of the sniper rifle breach and inserted an armour-piercing depleted uranium slug. Doc just froze in place with his SLR rifle on automatic, aimed but not able to add value right now.

Everything had happened so fast in the last thirty seconds. Without looking Spider's way, Rat took off in a run and up onto where the hatch was, hoping it wasn't locked. He found it jammed open, apparently to allow air in. The hatch was very hot, but he didn't pause and raised it fully open, pulled the igniter on the explosive pack and slam dunked it down the hole while letting the hatch lid drop with a loud clank. Rat rolled off and down the sand mound covering the tank as the explosion erupted inside.

There was sort of a dull 'fffhtt' at first and then the heavy ammunition must have ignited and the turret blew off, landing upside down and smouldering several yards away, and a roaring fire and flames spurted out of the tank's belly, which was spewing melting metal. The whole thing eventually collapsed into the hole with only bits of track left in sight. There had been no time for the occupants to react, and the team all felt the heat and shock from the explosion being so close.

Each of them, now shaken, made their way back to the shot-out water tanker truck for shade and cover. They began to cough and splutter from the choking, acrid smoke with cooked blood and guts emanating from the tank, mixed with oil field smoke and crude oil raining down on them. One thing they did take on board was that they had not spotted this feature until one Iraqi soldier had given it away. They might not be so lucky next time. Resting for an hour, the sun starting to set or be further blanked out by the black cloud caused them to rouse onto their feet once more in order to make another 20 map miles before tomorrow, that is if they didn't stumble upon another package of a tank or otherwise.

There were small lakes forming with oozing oil from the multitude of well heads, most of them on fire by now. Ground fires were spreading across the desert, feasting on the spilled oil. The whistling sounds of countless gas wells shooting gas added to the flames, which were bright enough to light up the scene for miles in all directions. This would become the worst environmental man-made disaster on the planet and may take years to shut down and clean up.

Spider sent a sat-com message over the radio giving their current position and a photo of the destroyed tank.

The going had slowed to a snail's pace because they had to circle around the oil pools with flames licking up intermittently as gas bubbled to the surface. A dangerous place for SAS tourists. Rat was out front on point at this time, with the rest of the team bunched up like sheep. He spotted a maintenance camp with similar huts that they had been involved in several days ago, but which felt like a month ago now. Due to the previous oil pipeline hut scenario with a female soldier dressed as a civilian shooting at them and goats wandering around, they spread out and one at a time moved off 10 yards apart covering the man in front. They kept an eager eye on the structures that were initially in front and then on their left as they circled in an anticlockwise pattern.

Their circle tightened into a spiral as minutes passed and nothing appeared to be moving. They would have copped a load of lead if they had taken a shot. Doc spotted a body lying on the ground adjacent to the nearest hut. It was an Iraqi soldier by the look of his uniform and his AK-47. He was covered in crude oil from the black rain, which would preserve him where he lay.

Continuing on and away from this scene, they heard an engine start up about 1,000 yards away. Adjusting their eyes and ears to pick up the direction of the noise, Brute pointed towards its approximate location. It was not right in the direction where they were heading but close enough for whatever it was to give them grief if ignored.

Spreading out in line abreast over 100 yards, they moved forward, shooting irons at the ready while keeping the corner of an eye on the man nearest and focusing on what was ahead. What luck mates, Spider thought as he waved his hand down for everyone to hit the dirt; another T-72 tank but this time it wasn't buried. There were sand bunds in rows to the left and right of the tank, which was stationary with its main gun facing sideways to its hull. Apparently, its crew had spotted something out there and were readying to possibly fire off a round. They did and it hit what they had aimed at, an oil well that hadn't yet been destroyed. The well burst into flames that shot several hundred feet into the air owing to the oil pressure spewing from the blown-apart well head.

Again, the Iraqis paid no attention to their nearby surroundings. Tank crews often think that a simple foot soldier can't hurt them easily. Wrong – there are all sorts of rockets and mines that can cut them open like a can of fish if one can get close enough. They got up close and personal on the last tank, why not this one? Their options and time to chat on strategy was not available to them as they were out in the open and visible.

The issue was that it was not 'if' but 'when' they were spotted, and they were sitting ducks for the turret-mounted .50 calibre heavy machine gun and a hull machine gun below the turret. The only option apart from standing there frozen to the spot was to slowly kneel, slide flat on their bellies, drag the camouflaged netting over them and pretend that they weren't there.

Time was not on their side. Spider hand signalled to the team to manoeuvre slowly across to line up some 50 yards behind the tank's hull as it had viewing slots more to the front and hopefully not in the back. The raining oil had probably reduced forward and peripheral vision, meaning they needed an observer sitting up high on the turret. The SAS men hoped the observer up there was as hot and bleary eyed as they were. They thought their manoeuvre would help them work out how to deal with this tank, but the observer continued to sit up there for nearly an hour.

If the Iraqis weren't moving out of here, then the SAS warriors would have to move in close and disable the tank. Spider signalled for the other three men to slide up to the tank using the sand bund mound at the side as cover. This action brought them within 5 yards and at the bottom of the turret height, which was now several feet above them. The tank's engine shut down as there were probably no more oil wells to shoot at. The turret remained pointing directly away from them across the other side bund mound.

It was time to attack the heavy machine gun rapidly by jumping onto the back of the tank, taking the observer out, and dropping another quarter-pound pack of Semtex explosive charge into its belly.

Unfortunately, Rat now informed the team that he only had enough Semtex for a smaller charge. It could possibly be used by adding two smoke grenades to it, making a type of incendiary bomb. Spider also suggested adding a couple of his armour-piercing .50 calibre bullets to it, making a hot Irish stew. A wry smile came over Rat's grubby face, teeth gleaming and eyes glowing with acceptance as he grabbed the bullets and grenades and began fiddling in his explosive kit bag.

He emerged with an odd-looking concoction all taped up with det-cord sticking out and an igniter firmly fitted on. This action on the tank could go well or go wrong in an instant. Spider held the men back, noting that the observer on the tank was now rotating the heavy machine gun 360 degrees looking for targets from his high vantage point. If he didn't get back inside the tank Spider would have to take him out before two men could mount it to deliver the bomb over the deck, down into the open hatch and then jump off and get clear over this bund wall.

Several minutes passed. The advantage would be lost if they didn't make a move – it was now or never. Spider raised his sniper rifle with one hard shot in the breach – at this 8 to 10-yard range he couldn't miss – and pulled the trigger. At the same time he had raised his rifle, Rat and Doc jumped and rolled down the other side of the bund wall to the back of the tank. Doc then hoisted

Rat, the smaller man, up and onto the deck. Spider's bullet hit the observer, disintegrating the man's head into vapour, momentarily ahead of Rat standing up and rushing forward to pull the igniter and push the headless body aside in order to drop the explosive into the belly of the tank.

There was an explosion, but not anything like with the previous tank. They were not sure where it landed or the damage it had caused. There was a lot of smoke but no flames yet. To their surprise, the forward hatch sprung open and one, two, three Iraqi tank crew clambered out still with their uniforms smoking.

Doc had Rat's rifle as well as his own and they were quickly pointed at the Iraqis. Apparently, the explosive had landed between the crew commander and the headless body of the soldier that Spider had shot, who had fallen into the tank when Rat pushed the body aside and this had muffled the flash effect of the charge. Good try anyway, and it did achieve the objective of the tank crew surrendering to them. The survivors were fear stricken and visibly shaking.

After an hour of the team watching the prisoners, they waited for the smoke to clear in the tank hull before attempting to enter and work out how to disable or destroy what was left of it. The rack of main gun shells was intact with colour-coded bands on each projectile. Not bothering to make sense of the types of shells and not able to communicate with any of the prisoners, Spider called Rat on board to work out a way to blow the tank up using its own ammunition. Rat smiled and immediately went to work. He twisted all of his remaining det-cord tightly around the shells, one shell fuse to the next on the tip of the projectiles, fitted an igniter and said loudly 'Get the hell outta here boss, ya got one minute before she goes'.

Spider didn't stop to chat; he was up and out and over the hull, yelling at the team to move. They knew that Rat would set a charge and anticipated his hasty retreat.

Rat almost fell on top of Spider as he landed on the ground. Spider guessed that their prisoners were mind readers as they came away hot on their heels over the bund wall and kept on running. Just then, the ground shook as an explosion in the belly of the tank erupted, followed by flames coming out of its orifices but no flying turret this time as the main gun barrel slowly drooped down. They figured that having more than one hatch open released the expanding gas from the explosion; it wasn't a dud though. Pity, they were really waiting for a more spectacular boom than that. The unarmed prisoners continued running.

There was no point in rounding them up, so they left them to their own devices as they needed to keep going in case there were other armed Iraqis in the area. Plus, not too far ahead they would be able to bug out of this operation at the port. They set out again with only one precious day's rations and water left and eager to reach the port, or at least the outskirts of Kuwait City, later that night.

The remainder of what was left of the early evening daylight brought them within visual sight of Kuwait City, and they could see the coast road, moving vehicle lights and naval vessels anchored in the outer harbour. It was time to dig in and set up a hide for the remainder of the night. Spider sent a sat-com message regarding their progress:

ENDURANCE REQUIRE URGENT FOOD AND WATER
2 X T-72 TANK EMPLACEMENTS KNOCKED OUT AND POTENTIAL FOR MORE STILL ACTIVE
CURRENT GPS POSITION

Spider set one warrior on guard every two hours while the remainder rested and tried to remove that tar-encrusted sand off their uniforms, boots and packs. No good going to town without tidying up one's appearance!

Chapter 25

Operation – Day Sixteen

Kuwait City

At sunrise, having shaken off yesterday's action, they finished their last rations except for water. Then they checked the sat-com radio for messages and received the following text:

TEAM INTACT – ARVD KUWAIT – NOTED
ENDURANCE – NOTED
POSITION – NOTED – HOLD
WL ADV CITY CONTROL CONTACTS
US ARMY – AUST NAVY – ONSHORE ACTIVE
WAIT INSTR

After several hours out in the sun and black smoke the commander sent the following sat-com:

US ARMY GIVEN YR LOC – AWAIT THEIR FIELD
EXTRACTION DETAILS ON THIS FREQ
YR ORDERS WITH US ARMY CONTACT
YR TEAM RETASKED TO AUST NAVY
OUT

Spider read out the message, then added 'Well mates, this doesn't seem to be good news. More work to do before home time'.

The US Kuwait Forces area officer did a voice call to them over the sat radio open channel, advising that some fighting was under way in the city and that clearance of harbour mines was being carried out by the Australians. Their team was to be temporarily attached to a Kuwaiti military team going through the suburbs house to house clearing out the latent Iraqis. Where they hit a snag, the SAS team were to act as advisers for expeditiously extracting the Iraqis or their sympathisers.

It sounded easy, but they didn't know how many there would be or how armed, how often they would be called on, or how long this task would take.

Being retasked was not new to any of them and there were no complaints, not that it would change anything anyway. A US Humvee came bounding across the open ground as if there was no fighting nearby. Spider hailed them cautiously as he had had a bad experience with US troops in the past. With only a driver and top deck gunner on board, it was easy to accommodate the four-man team with limited baggage. Spider was asked to identify himself and each team member before they were ticked off a list. Then he was handed an envelope with written orders. Basically, the orders said exactly what they had already heard over the radio.

Firstly, on arrival at the port area sheds, they were allowed to clean up, eat and given completely new US desert uniforms with Australian velcro badges attached. Spider figured they would have burned their old kit and uniforms as they were knackered. A US colonel wandered over and sat down by Spider at their table and asked them what they had been doing out there in the field.

He got a no comment response as they didn't report to him or any of the US commanders. He smiled and accepted that response like he had heard it all before and liked their spunk. Their orders were read out again by the US colonel just so everyone was on the same page right now.

There was a Kuwaiti officer standing in the large doorway of the cargo shed waiting to be introduced. The only way they knew he was an army officer was by introduction as he was in civilian clothes. Apparently, the Iraqis had been searching for the Kuwaiti military personnel to execute during their occupation. Some Kuwaiti military had been able to hide and carry out some sabotage actions while the Iraqis were in town.

More Kuwaiti soldiers in civilian clothes arrived and the US issued them with the same desert uniforms that the SAS warriors were given, this time with no badges. Everyone was issued with AK-47s and ammunition jackets with large pockets for storing ammunition magazines.

Spider retained his H&K Sniper Rifle and requisitioned a case of mixed ammunition, of which the US had plenty. Helmets were offered but all this new mixed nationality team declined as being too heavy and too hot. They were issued with new tactical Z-Tac throat mic radios with ear piece and spare batteries and set on a specific channel for this team only to use. Monitoring would be done at a command post on board one of the navy vessels anchored offshore.

Most of the Kuwaitis did not speak English, so the team was solely reliant on their officer and a couple of his men for communication. Four Humvees were called for over a US two-way radio and they were promptly driven into the store area by US Marines.

The US colonel officially handed over the vehicles to the Kuwaiti officer, who introduced himself as Ali. He made no gesture of introducing his men to the team and, taking a que from their officer (whose proper name and rank the team never did get), his men literally jumped into the driver's seats like they had done it all before.

Spider said to his team quietly 'Looks like we are the hangers on for this gig, so heads up and trim your tails' (meaning 'Watch out for these guys').

Apparently, these Kuwaiti guys knew where they were going ahead of time so there was no radio chatter yet. The team, not waiting to be invited, jumped in the back of the tail end vehicle.

Spider said under his breath 'No rest for the wicked, eh!'.

All four Humvee vehicles moved at high speed out of the port shed and stayed in tight convoy, top turret machine guns cocked and trained on the streets ahead. These guys had done this before, and more than likely had been trained by the US before the war. The convoy met up in the main street down by a private boat harbour near a large hotel, where more soldiers in civvies were standing around brandishing a variety of US M16s, Iraqi AKs and hunting rifles. The different types of ammunition could cause run outs as they would not be able to share bullets.

'Hey guys,' Spider said to his team, 'Looks like we have a gang of homeys forming here'.

He got a sideways look from the driver but no comment. Apparently, this convoy was to split up, go Iraqi hunting virtually door to door and work their way throughout the city. A big job, and laborious as well.

Spider alighted from the Humvee, casually walked over to Ali and asked him what the plan was. He just shrugged and said 'hunting'. Spider offered a suggestion; maybe they should seek out building occupants who had experienced the Iraqi presence and gather intel on a block-by-block assessment to see if there were reports of Iraqis holding out in the buildings, Ali thought that would be a great idea and shouted orders to his troops. They spent the day ferrying his troops around town dropping them off at strategic corners from where they could go door knocking.

By the end of the day, most of the vehicles returned to the front of the hotel that they had started out from. Ali took several soldiers into the lobby of the hotel and grilled them about their day's work.

Ali was on the throat mic radio jabbering away in Arabic for about thirty minutes when the last of the vehicles arrived back with some prisoners in the back. The prisoners were in civvies, making it hard to tell if they were Iraqis or Kuwaiti collaborators. Ali and half a dozen men took the prisoners away somewhere at the back of the hotel complex.

One of the soldiers approached the SAS team and asked them to follow him, which they did as it was better than just standing around scratching their arses. Within five minutes, they were ushered into the hotel, up one flight of stairs and handed keys to four rooms for the night.

The time to meet up was dawn, when they had to be downstairs. As the rooms had two queen size beds each, they chose to stay in two adjoining rooms so they could act as a team and cover for each other, particularly under these odd circumstances.

Lying flat on a soft bed didn't take a lot of getting used to for this brave SAS team, and for the first time in a couple of weeks they showered, shampooed, shaved and took a shit like normal human beings for a change. Spider co-ordinated the men to take guard shifts in their rooms of two hours a piece until morning, including himself taking the first shift. Not that they didn't trust these homeys!

As sit-reps were no longer required, the sat-com radio was not switched on but remained in Doc's pack, just in case. Each man slept with his Z-Tac radio under his pillow right next to the Colt .45 issued to them at the outset of the mission on the aircraft carrier. None of them slept fully and unaccustomed noises would wake them. They would wait and listen, then slip back to sleep. They weren't sure of these Kuwaitis and that form of trust took time, communication and interaction. They hadn't had more than a day to absorb who and what was going down.

At dawn, Spider got a prod from Brute. 'It's time to move boss,' he whispered. It took them five minutes to get ready and march single file down the stairs and into the lobby, where half of the Kuwaiti soldiers from yesterday were milling around eating from a buffet table. They joined in as there was no assurance they would eat again until the evening. The Kuwaitis seemed pleased to see the SAS team there, and apparently Ali had now briefed them on their presence and reassured his men they were along to support and not to command them.

Throughout this region tribal connections were very important and it was assumed that these guys were all related, as could be seen from their close affection for each other (holding hands and kissing cheeks). However, it was later learned that this kind of greeting is common throughout the Arab Middle East and is accepted as normal as the common handshake.

Ali and the half dozen associates who took the prisoners away last night entered the room and silence fell as he announced what information they had given up overnight. He said in English 'All is good now, we have some specific places to go today so please lock and load'. He complimented Spider on suggesting he spread his soldiers out across the city, going block by block. This had yielded the prisoners, who were identified by terrified residents in several houses and surrendered to his men without a fight.

Ali said there was more to come today that would be harder to dislodge as the prisoners said there were some fanatics ready for a fight out there. Ali never hinted at what had become of the prisoners and Spider thought it polite not to ask as he was a guest in Ali's war-torn country.

Ali leant over and told him that there would be a series of raids today and some tonight. He also told him that he and his soldiers took afternoon siestas in the heat and that they should do the same. Spider agreed; the bloody afternoon heat was unbearable. The reason for daylight raids was to break-bash-bang some hostage takers as at night they could accidently kill some innocent hostages. The first building was only two streets away and was approached on foot from front and back at the same time.

Ali's men took the lead and acted like crazy men, just barging in with guns blazing and yelling something indiscernible. Miraculously, none of them were hit and the four Iraqi hostage takers were unceremoniously dragged out the door by both arms, pulled down the stairs backwards and dumped out on the roadway.

Ali squatted down beside one man with a bayonet in his hand. He appeared to interrogate him but got nothing or not what he wanted to hear, so he stabbed the prisoner in the left eye. This caused the man to writhe and scream in excruciating pain. The other three prisoners got up to the sitting position in shock. Ali's soldier's rifle butted them back down, where they sobbed and begged shamelessly.

All ten hostages were brought down to face the Iraqis lying on the ground. To me this was turning into a kangaroo court and the Geneva Convention was out the window. Most of the hostages bore some form of wounds from being taken and held for several days at least. Ali told Spider not to watch if he was squeamish or objected to rough justice.

He handed a pistol to one woman and asked her to identify the prisoner who had hurt and raped her. She slowly walked over to the prostrate men on the ground and pointed at each in turn. She then shot one of them in the lower stomach, then again and again until the magazine was empty. Ali's men then tied up the three remaining prisoners, including the one with his left eye wounded who had blood pouring down his face. They were dumped in the back of a Humvee with the dead man on top and taken away.

The word 'sniper' was heard over the Z-Tac and everyone still standing there in front of the former hostages stepped back into the stairwell. Ali looked over to Spider and indicated by hand for him to follow him out to the back of the compound behind the house. The team followed silently. One of Ali's men was waiting crouched with a bullet wound to the shoulder. He pointed at a tall but narrow three-storey building further down the back laneway.

'OK, this is our territory,' Spider told Ali.

Ali smiled and shrugged before taking his man away.

Spider set up the team in pairs, with Brute and Rat staying in the courtyard to try and draw the sniper into firing at intervals. Doc and Spider went upstairs in the next building to spot a position for a kill shot.

The H&K .50 calibre hard shot can go through brick walls if needed, so Spider was confident as long as they could pinpoint his nest.

At Spider's call, Brute and Rat let off a couple of AK-47 rounds each. No response this time. Spider asked them to change position and target. Ten seconds later they let off a couple of short automatic bursts of their AKs. This time the sniper planted a shot very close to Brute's head. Spider didn't see the flash but a curtain did move.

Time to draw him closer to the windowsill. Spider asked Rat to fire a burst closer down the lane and under the sniper's line of fire that he had on Brute right now. Within two minutes, Rat, with his skinny body, had slipped through a gap in the compound wall into the next-door property.

He fired a burst and pulled back. The sniper fired a round that was not even close to Rat, but the bottom of the curtain moved again. The sniper had to move position closer to the window to take an accurate shot at Rat. Spider was already waiting for him. He told Rat to just raise his AK as if getting ready to step out for a burst so he could ping this guy. Rat did as requested, the sniper leant forward to fire and Spider fired first with a hard shot just through the wall below the windowsill, probably hitting the sniper in the chest.

Spider advised Ali where to look for the sniper to clear his nest out.

The team re-joined Ali's soldiers and waited for the sniper's body to be taken out in front of the hostage house, where they got smiles, slaps on the back and high fives from their Kuwaiti friends. Then it was back to serious business as several soldiers came out of the back lane dragging a dead sniper and brandishing his trophy rifle, an old Second World War .303 Enfield Mk2 with scope (the type Spider cut his teeth on as an army cadet at college and carried with him in Cambodia).

Operation – Day Seventeen

After four days of sporadic fighting across the city and outskirts, all Iraqi troops were expelled from Kuwait, ending a nearly seven-month occupation. A little over 1,100 casualties were suffered by the coalition. Estimates of Iraqi casualties range from 30,000 to 150,000. Iraq lost thousands of vehicles, tanks and artillery pieces, while the advancing coalition lost relatively few. Iraq's obsolete Soviet T-72 tanks proved no match for the American M1 Abrams and British Challengers. All Scud missiles and ground-to-air missiles were destroyed.

There was no accounting of Kuwaiti citizens and soldiers killed or wounded, nor what happened to any of the dozens of Ali's prisoners. As for the SAS team, they had played a small part in the bigger picture and were extracted to Saudi Arabia as soon as the navy were able to bring in a supply ship for mine clearance activities and the airport was secured.

On the morning of their departure for Saudi Arabia the US colonel who had first met the team at the port sheds in Kuwait City approached Spider requesting that he and the team join him for lunch at Ahamadi House, which was located in the city of Al Ahmadi some 25 miles south of Kuwait City, in recognition and appreciation by the United States military for their covert service and contribution to operation Desert Storm. Spider readily agreed.

Al Ahmadi was a virtual ghost town. Before the invasion it had been the centre for vital support services to the oil sector and home for approximately 5,000 oil field workers, mostly Palestinians with a mixture of Pakistanis, Indians and a few Filipinos, all of whom had been dispersed to God knows where during the conflict.

Smoke billowed across the rooftops of the buildings around Ahmadi House, which was nothing more than a large rectangular mess hall that could seat around a hundred guests. It was surrounded by long military-style barrack buildings. The billowing smoke carried with it the black crude oil that had escaped the raging oil well fires, and black droplets rained down on anything and everything. As they pulled up in front of the building, they could see men loitering around in their team-coloured firefighting coveralls with company logos on the back. The SAS warriors read a couple of them: Boots & Coots, white coveralls; Joe Bowden, yellow coveralls; and, of course, the legends, Red Adair, with red coveralls.

The lunch was hosted by General Kelly of the United States Army and it was a white tablecloth affair. The guests were Desert Storm participants from the different coalition forces. The three-course meal was served by women dressed in starched blue uniforms. Their nationalities were Filipino, Indian, Sri Lankan and several other God knows what countries, all of whom had been domestic help to the wealthy Kuwaiti families that had deserted them, leaving them to their fate at the hands of the Iraqi invaders.

After arrival in Saudi Arabia, Spider enquired at the US Embassy about Mrs Copley. After several hours' wait, he was informed that she was in the local hospital, had received needed surgery and was recovering. With that news, he contacted the team members by phone at their hotel and they all agreed to meet up at the hospital so they could, if possible, visit her.

There was some resistance against them (men) visiting a woman but after meeting with an American resident doctor they were given approval for a short visit. She didn't recognise them at first but did express her gratitude. Her wounds were healing but the trauma she experienced might never heal. Her husband had been taken into Baghdad by the Iraqis as a hostage and there was no news of his current status or condition. Desert Storm was in mopping up mode and the team of SAS warriors had finished what they had been mobilised for.

Next day, they took the first plane out of Saudi Arabia, where they were stood down, given civilian passports and clothes, fed, rested and then took separate flights back to Australia. There they all awaited the next call from the DIO while returning to their day jobs in civvy street.

Brute had some infection complications with his grazed ribs and received medical attention for a week or so in a Brisbane hospital, then was given the all clear. Rat suffered from PTSD due to his witnessing of the massacre of the civilian women and kids in Kuwait by the Iraqis and was attending counselling and recovering slowly.

Doc took a job with Mèdicins Sans Frontières in Africa. As for Spider, he headed off overseas following his engineering career that had been left hanging for some time.

Iraq 2003 – the Second Gulf War

US President George W. Bush, his Vice President Richard (Dick) Cheney and UK Prime Minister Tony Blair lied to the world with statements that Saddam Hussein had weapons of mass destruction that included nuclear, chemical and biological agents. Cheney also claimed Saddam had links to Al-Qaeda and supported the terrorist attack on the World Trade Center Towers in New York in 2001.

The Central Intelligence Agency (CIA) later stated that there was no credible evidence indicating that Saddam had any relationship with Al-Qaeda. Bush, Cheney and Blair continued spreading propaganda, even after becoming aware there was no evidence of WMDs, so they cranked up the war machine with statements that Saddam was using terrorist attacks against the Iraqi people and they needed to be freed so a regime change was required.

In March 2003 the US dispatched some 130,000 troops into Iraq, the UK 45,000, Australia 2,000 and Poland a couple of hundred. On 13 December 2006, Saddam was captured in an underground hole where he had been hiding without a shot being fired. Later that month, on 30 December, he was put to death in Baghdad by hanging for crimes against humanity.

In the run-up to the 2003 Iraqi war the US company Halliburton was awarded a contract exceeding $7 billion and only this business was allowed to bid. Before it was over in 2011 Halliburton had gained more than $39 billion in federal contracts related to the Iraq war.

Cheney was Secretary of Defence leading up to and during Desert Storm in 1991. In 1995 he was the CEO of Halliburton, and then in 2001 he became Vice President.

There was a huge pot of black gold at the end of the Iraqi rainbow; was this profit motivation the reason for the Bush–Cheney administration to invade Iraq?

Chapter 26

Timor Sea Fretilin Terrorists

Major Pete (Spider) Recalled

In December 1975, Indonesia invaded East Timor immediately after the Portuguese Government had abandoned it after more than 400 years of colonisation. This sparked a violent occupation that lasted twenty-five years. The day before the invasion, Gerald Ford, who had become US President after the resignation of Richard Nixon, and US Sectary of State Henry Kissinger met President Suharto in Jakarta and gave him the green light for the invasion.

New advanced weapons were procured from the US, Israel and several other countries, which included US-supplied M16 rifles, ammunition, mortars, grenades, food, helicopters and destroyer escorts, which shelled the capital city, Dili. Indonesian marines disembarked from US-supplied landing craft, while US-supplied C-47 and C-130 aircraft dropped Indonesian paratroopers and strafed Dili with .50 calibre machine guns.

Military assistance from the US accelerated during President Carter's administration, peaking in 1978 at $250 million. During the period 1975–79, Indonesia was 90 per cent armed with US weapons. A senior CIA officer in Indonesia stated that East Timorese people were herded into school buildings that were set on fire, while others were herded into fields and machine gunned. The US gave the Indonesian generals everything they requested to fight a major war against an opponent who had no guns.

In September 2000 the Australian Department of Foreign Affairs and Trade released previously held secret documents clearly identifying that the governments of Prime Ministers Whitlam, Fraser, Hawke and Keating allegedly co-operated with the Indonesian military and President Suharto.

A team of journalists for the Australian television networks Channels 7 and 9 were killed during the period leading up to the Indonesian invasion of East Timor. They were based in the small township of Balibo, East Timor. After their deaths in October 1975, they became known as the Balibo 5. An investigative journalist from Australia travelled to Balibo where the five had been murdered and he was also executed by the Indonesian military. The Indonesian Government claimed they were all killed in crossfire.

The Australian Government has never challenged the Indonesian version to avoid damaging its relationship with the country. It is believed a special forces captain with the Indonesian military not only ordered but took part in the killings.

In 2007 the then newly elected Prime Minister of Australia Kevin Ruud stated 'Those responsible should be held accountable for their actions,' adding that the, 'incident should not be swept under the carpet'.

No meaningful action was ever taken and this same newly elected prime minister refused to visit the gravesite of the murdered Australian journalists at the Kebayoran Lama Cemetery in Jakarta in 2008.

A civil insurrection for self-determination led by the political party calling itself the Revolutionary Front for an Independent East Timor, abbreviated to 'Fretilin' objected to the invasion by Indonesian forces from West Timor. The Indonesian Government set about suppressing the local population's dissent by taking punitive action against the Fretilin, a centre-left political party who endorsed the universal ideology of Marxism-Leninism and was in control of virtually all of East Timor. The general consensus of the United States along with its allies, including Australia and Indonesia, was that East Timor was becoming a communist state.

The context of this saga aligns with the then internal West Timor issues and Indonesia's expectation that they also had the historical rights to the Timor Sea oil and gas resources.

Approximately sixteen years prior to the East Timor invasion, an Australian oil company had drilled some wildcat wells and located oil-and gas-bearing results in the Timor Sea.

The petroleum results were in international waters over 200 miles off the Indonesian Timor and Australian sovereign coast lines. The Indonesian and Australian Governments then almost came to blows over who owned the rights to the hydrocarbons below the seabed. All exploitation stopped and in order to avoid gun boat diplomacy getting out of control, while at the same time mutually exploiting the buried resources, a treaty was negotiated and signed by both countries.

Technical and Defence Security Officer Roles

Major Spider didn't have long to wait before he received the call; the shit was happening in the Timor Sea and he was off to the races again.

For Spider, who was working with the Shell oil company in Brunei Darussalam as an engineer, it was a normal day at the office. He had previously been released from DIO duties and under this particular government act the letter he had received stated there was no further requirement for him to report for operational duties with the DIO. In other words, he had been furloughed.

However, unbeknownst to him, he had been secretly selected and co-opted through the DIO by the then Minister for Defence to officially take on a dual civilian Technical Officer role and to act covertly as Defence Liaison Officer between the Australian and Indonesian security agencies (ABBRI).

Two Australian embassy officials arrived at the Brunei Shell Seria head office where he was working. Apparently, they had been in contact with the Shell CEO and had notified him that Spider's services were required (which was not negotiable) and that he would be taken back to Australia to perform unspecified duties for the Government.

The two officials met briefly with the CEO, who called in Spider's HR manager and outlined the need to pack up his office desk and belongings from his apartment and freight them to his home address in Australia, as he was required to return immediately and indefinitely.

The Shell HR manager was requested to direct the two officials to where Spider was located in the office and leave them to explain to him what they required and when. There would be no staff announcement and his direct report boss would be informed of his departure by the CEO after he had left the country.

This was all very nice and efficient, but Spider had no idea and no warning before the two plain-clothes gentlemen arrived at his desk, showed him their embassy credentials and asked him quietly to follow them to the car park downstairs. There he was, he had not yet had his morning coffee and he was out in the car park on a steaming tropical day wondering what the fuck these guys wanted of him.

He recalled how the letter from the DIO had clearly stated that under this particular government act, there was no further requirement for Major Spider. Well, looks like I am fucked again, he thought.

All he got out of these embassy pricks was that he would be driven directly to the Bandar Seri Begawan airport in the Brunei capital and flown to Darwin for a confidential briefing.

Bloody wonderful, he thought to himself, but he also knew that the Australian Government wouldn't send these guys to chat up his bosses and drag him to the airport for no reason. There must be some sort of operation needing his skills.

Ah shit, he was just getting into this civilian life all over again. This was déjà vu as it had happened like this almost every time the DIO called on him and his men for some operational assignment.

He kept his tongue in his mouth as it was clear that these guys were not forthcoming with any details, and more likely they were in the dark as much as he was.

Spider was escorted through the Brunei airport terminal, where he met two Australian military police officers in civilian attire. The two embassy men then disappeared out of the building. The military cops showed him a warrant and said that he must accompany them onto the Qantas flight to Darwin or be arrested. The uneventful flight was in first class, right up in the front row on the port side with one MP on each side. Bloody wonderful; he had to ask if he could go to the toilet, which was only a few feet away. Also, no booze was allowed, which was a fucking waste of first class, where one can have some of the finest food and wines.

About four hours later, with the sun not far off setting, the aircraft touched down, heralding their arrival at Darwin in Australia. Spider was escorted off the plane, priority first, as soon as the front door opened and then whisked out of the terminal without going through the usual customs and immigration checks. It crossed his mind that he had no baggage.

A large white Toyota 4×4 wagon with darkened windows and its engine running was waiting at the kerb. He was ushered briskly aboard into the back seat, and again forced to sit between the two MPs. The driver didn't look back at them and without a word exchanged just simply gunned the engine and drove rapidly off and away from the airport precinct. Spider had run covert operations from this airport in the past and just stared out of the tinted windows at traffic and buildings, trying to gauge where they were heading.

Twenty minutes later it all came clear. The navy base on the coast was just ahead and when the 4×4 pulled up at the gate, the driver showed his pass and they were silently motioned to head up to the main office block car park.

His former DIO, Commander Coen, was standing back in the shadow of a doorway with a broad smile on his face. Spider wasn't smiling and must have looked pretty tired and pissed off by then as he had not seen the funny side of his extrication from Brunei. Commander Coen didn't move as he was ushered toward the doorway. He then nodded and opened the door as Spider passed by. He then led them into a conference room, where the two MPs were dismissed at a wave of his hand.

As Spider stood there looking around the room, he noticed a large marine map of the Timor Sea on the wall and some documents on the long table. Seated were some familiar faces, including Air force Commander Pace, whom he had interfaces with during the Vietnam War operations, and an unnamed Federal Government Department of Defence Secretary. Spider was dying for a coffee by now so he gestured to the bench at the end of the room to indicate what he wanted. Commander Coen nodded and then got up and made him a strong coffee and one for himself, then sat down beside him as if in support.

The following briefing was laid out by the unnamed Federal Government Department of Defence Secretary:

1. Spider would on a day-to-day basis be reporting to the Joint Authority Directors of the Timor Gap Joint Authority Treaty between Australia and Indonesia as Technical Officer and civilian tender board secretary during tendering phases (circa US$500 million). He would also be responsible for setting up and supporting the Authority management systems and providing translations from Indonesian/English language as required.

2. Covertly he was authorised to act as Timor Sea Operations defence liaison officer with the Indonesian Authorities while maintaining his rank of army major and Government Level of First Secretary for security and intelligence matters.

3. Where necessary he should identify threats and carry out interdiction of all Fretilin forces that presented themselves as a real and imminent threat to the lawful operations being undertaken in the Timor Gap Zone of Co-operation. There were East Timorese refugees in Darwin of which he should also be aware.

His direct reporting would be to Commander Coen of the DIO, and it seemed that the Spider was back in the web of intrigue once more. This operation would be code-named 'Red Back' after one of Australia's most deadly spiders

Spider was in effect the conduit between the DIO, military organisations, local emergency services, security agencies and the Indonesian ABBRI (intelligence agency in Jakarta), with specific regard to solely monitoring East Timorese Fretilin Terrorist Organisation threats in the area of both onshore Northern Territory, Darwin, and offshore in the Timor Sea, where various oil and gas survey operations were planned.

It was anticipated that since the Timor Gap Treaty had been signed by both countries there would be threats made against oil and gas operators in the Zone of Co-operation out in the Timor Sea. Currently there were Fretilin separatist activities being experienced by the Indonesians in West Timor and some separatist activities were noted in Darwin, where a community of Timorese refugees lived. The underbelly of the undercover Fretilin movement was located in Portugal, where resources and the planning of attacks were managed.

First Stage – Establishment

An office for the Timor Gap Joint Authority was established in two parts, with first a temporary office set-up in the lower end of town where a 50–50 Indonesian–Australian back-to-back mix of office workers were settled in prior to the formal selection of directors to run the Darwin and Jakarta offices with their mirror-image mix of staff.

Then the official offices were arranged in a more secure building at the high end of town in both countries similar to a consulate set-up with magnetic-coded keys, safes, door locks, a sound-proof conference room and CCTV installed.

Second Stage – Operational Status

While Spider was working as Technical Officer from within the Australia and Indonesia Joint Authority offices in Darwin, he carried out his role as tender board secretary, plus more hands-on technical advisor duties that included the inspection of oilfield seismic survey contractor's vessels offshore safety and security reviews. This position allowed him the access to covertly manage setting up his cover for maintaining closer logistical overviews of all survey aircraft, marine vessels and facilities operating in the Timor Sea.

As a qualified engineer he provided technical advice on contractor operational safety processes and their implementation in order to check on their communications equipment, reporting routines, personnel passports and planned survey activities just in case he had to protect them from the armed and mobile Fretilin during offshore oil and gas field survey operations. This required liaison with the major oil companies' head offices, national security agencies, SAS Regiment and other government authorities.

Spider's Defensive Posture

From his past association with Darwin during the Vietnam War operations into Cambodia, Spider was very familiar with the layout of Darwin and its harbour and airport facilities, particularly the airport runways and air force hangars, which enabled him to quickly synthesise a plan of action ahead of any Fretilin action against offshore oil and gas exploration operations.

The briefing at the naval base had provided details of Fretilin activities and pictures of suspected fishing vessels out in the Zone. This aspect would be a prime focus for him and the resources he might need to interdict active shooters out in the international waters of the Timor Sea.

His secondary focus would be keeping his eyes and ears open around Darwin and the outer suburbs as he had sighted graffiti supporting the Fretilin cause and a likelihood of street demonstrations around Timor Gap Joint Authority office and the Indonesian Consulate at the edge of town. He could deal with the onshore civil disobedience issues by informing and calling upon the Federal Police and ASIO resources. They could also secure the Joint Authority building tower entrance in case of unauthorised access by Fretilin-sympathising demonstrators. These services could not act unless there was, or was a likelihood of, material damage, or people being injured. Being proactive, Spider liked to get ahead of the game using active assessments of risk rather than wait for an emergency call to come in, which is purely reactive.

The first surveillance sortie for him personally was to set up a weekly circuit of key observation points in and around Darwin to obtain a first-hand view of the Fretilin graffiti on buildings and around known Timorese communities where any meetings or gatherings were being held.

Spider set up a joint meeting of Federal Police, Territory Police and ASIO accompanied by his director in order to introduce himself and his security role and the need for joint co-operation to avoid any form of local incident that could escalate into an international one. None of those present at the meeting provided any usable intelligence, so it appeared he was on his own.

His director was astounded by the audacity Spider had shown by calling such a meeting and forbade him from any further actions as he, himself, had not been briefed on what Spider was there for. Oops, well fuck him, Spider had figured that at least the local director would have been informed but he guessed the prick hadn't been. Plus he had no security clearance, so fuck him again. Spider never briefed the director from that point forward.

This was the beginning of a stand-off between the director and Spider as he was the Federal Government prudence man and Major Spider was the soldier on a mission.

Spider met separately with Customs and Immigration officials to share intelligence information regarding the comings and goings of people and marine vessels crossing through the Zone, the Timor Gap, which was also out in international waters. The DIO had left Spider on a loose leash so to speak as Customs and Immigration had limited experience with Treaty arrangements. Spider had less but he made up the rules on the run. He only contacted Commander Coen if he needed his moral support and the DIO contact officer – code-named Mr Champion – for SAS and air force support.

Chapter 27

Intelligence Gaps

Through joint services meetings and discussions, Spider found that there was an intelligence void regarding the movements of marine vessels of all types outside of the international 200-mile border limit where the Zone was located. The Coast Watch Customs surveillance aircraft only patrolled out as far as 35 miles offshore. This was of no value to his role, therefore he needed to extend his military support out to the 200-mile range. This surveillance was also of use to the Customs office, so he gained some allies.

Spider could deal with the onshore civil disobedience issues by informing and calling upon Civil and Federal police along with ASIO resources. The weakness in communications was with the Federal Government, which appeared to play a very separate role and was somewhat averse to him taking any action that may embarrass them. Hence, his inclusion of government or the local director had to be on a need-to-know basis. This was a bit awkward, as he was working and based in the Directorate office right under their noses.

SAS Link

Fortunately, Commander Coen did provide him with an informed contact within the SAS Regiment in northern Queensland with whom he could quietly obtain resources as and when needed for covert operations. His past history with that regiment from 1968 to 1972 would also bring forth bonuses such as former team members from past operations that he trusted implicitly.

Authority Office Routine

There was nothing out on the water, no island or coastline to sight either to the north or to the south of the centre of the Timor Gap Zone of Co-operation for over 200 miles. His job was made even more difficult by the use of GPS co-ordinates but no specific visual compass point nor place to moor a boat or land an aircraft. If an event occurred out there, he would have to react from Darwin by air only. The navy had no patrols out there and the closest patrol boats were at Scot Reef several hundred miles away.

Intelligence organisations were aware but mostly oblivious of the turmoil going on in East Timor under the Indonesian administration. For him, the underground Fretilin activities in Portugal would be out of reach but the root cause of concern now facing him as a potential conflict on the water or in Darwin itself would likely be co-ordinated in Portugal and acted out here in the city or out on the water.

His job as tender board secretary allowed an insight into which oil companies would be operating out in the Timor Sea using aerial magnetometer, seaborne seismic surveys and jack up drilling rigs sampling the seabed for likely reservoirs of oil or gas. He could also use these air and sea platforms as his eyes and ears.

As time passed, the air and sea survey craft were based in Darwin for supplies and crew changes under his watchful steely blue eyes and he had on occasion accompanied these craft on daylight surveys in order to gauge the type of exposure they may be faced with. Every craft type heading out to the Zone had to report to him with their planned activities, crews, courses and duration, giving him a calibrated watching brief. This is when he took the opportunity to link their radar and GPS positioning to a facsimile machine in his office for daily reporting as well as his personal satellite phone for voice calls when needed.

His office staff appeared to be uninterested in his erratic comings and goings and were oblivious of his interaction. For instance, he would receive a fax from radar and course observations from the survey vessels showing large marine cargo vessels transiting in the Zone area and notifications by satellite phone regarding the sightings of small fishing boats coming close to the survey vessels. He then simply walked across the city mall to the Customs office to cross-check any unidentified vessel movements with them. This developed into a good relationship as they were aware of the regular shipping lanes and not aware of the small boat movements, which could be drug or people smugglers or simply Indonesian fishing boats legally operating in international waters – a good exchange of intelligence was in effect.

His interest area was filtering out the innocent and the likely threat to the civilian offshore survey operations while at the same time ensuring the Darwin Airport area was secure from over-the-boundary fence threats against the civilian survey aircraft parked out in the open there. He knew these radical fuckers would and could climb over the fence and damage these aircraft.

Heightened Security Onshore

Spider was aware of heightened activities in and around Darwin as he made his weekly patrols, which were prefaced with more graffiti being daubed on building walls closer to the city centre and the Indonesian Consulate. He informed ASIO, the Indonesian Consul and his office building security as he suspected that demonstrations would follow. He also phoned the air force commander to inform him that there was a survey aircraft located on his airport and it needed closer security.

The commander was not impressed with Spider's intrusion on his turf but, fuck him, he had a job to do. However, the commander did add foot security with dogs up close to the strange-looking modified Fokker F27 aerial fluor-sensor aircraft that was being chartered by one of the oil companies to survey the sea surface emissions out on the Timor Sea.

The Port Harbour Master was called and he immediately had security barriers installed around the dock where the seismic survey vessels moored. At this point in time, although concerned and ever vigilant, Spider had no reason to lock and load any SAS resources.

First Fretilin Attack Offshore – SAS Summoned

Almost as if on cue, he received a fax from one of the seismic vessels out on the Zone with a copy of their radar plot and a text message. Several wooden fishing vessels had been visually sighted within 3 miles of them as long-range radar had not picked them up. The wooden vessels were coming very close to the seismic survey traces (multiple cable sets within a plastic outer tube for measuring 10,000psi air pressure blasts) that were up to 7,000 yards long. The attacking vessels were not responding to radio calls.

The second fax message he received stated that the larger of the fishing boats had driven directly on top of one of the traces and caused sufficient damage that all seismic operations had to be halted. Some 7,000 yards of trace cables had to be retracted aboard until inspections and repairs were carried out.

For Spider this was the first attack within the Zone by these arsehole Fretilin and likely not the last one. He immediately phoned his SAS contact in Queensland requesting:

- Two M60 waist gun-armed Black Hawk helicopters with SAS aircrews for 400+ sea miles flight endurance over offshore operations. This required extra fuel bladders fitted and dischargeable life rafts.
- Two six-man SAS hit teams, fully armed with short automatic weapons and grenades for rope egress onto small fishing boats.
- He would contact the navy for recovering the SAS boarding teams using their patrol boats located at Scot Reef, which is about 200 miles west of Darwin on the north coast of the Northern Territory.

- The helicopters, crews and teams must remain covert and within the commandeered air force hangar on the airport near the end of runway 36.
- Darwin airport had both military and civilian aircraft operations with dedicated military operators on one level in the control tower as different radio frequencies and security protocols were used. Spider required their support regarding their movements not being broadcast on civilian frequencies.
- The US also had B-52 bombers transiting through this base from time to time. Australian military aircraft movements were also under the secrecy blanket.
- Offsite accommodation for the SAS helicopter crews and hit teams would be set up as civilians well away from the general public. That meant no uniforms off base and tight lips.

He guessed the SAS squad was pretty bored doing helicopter egress and fitness training every day in Queensland and virtually jumped at the opportunity to get into a scrum with these Fretilin turds.

Within twenty-four hours the two Black Hawks loaded with men and equipment arrived from northern Queensland base at midnight and by morning they reported they were set and ready for the hunt. The only drawback raised by the chopper crews was that they only had fuel for a 500-mile return flight including extra fuel tanks, which limited the time to locate the Fretilin-manned boat and have the soldiers rappel down onto it.

The two pilots, the co-pilot/waist gunner and six SAS boarding team weight limited the endurance time, and carrying spare resources placed an extra limitation on any offshore operation.

Spider's job turned to getting very accurate intelligence reporting from the survey vessels regarding their course, speed and direction and that of the target Fretilin boats for a more direct interception. This was a live situation and aborting such a mission would be poor judgement and a waste of resources.

Spider's hairy arse was on the line to get it right the first time and for ongoing missions. He urgently sent off a fax from the Joint Authority office to the seismic vessel that had reported the attack on its trace and requested very specific details for him to follow up on. It was also in their interest to do so as delays would cost them money and time.

His full-of-his-own-piss-and-importance director came in, saw a fax going out and enquired what it was about. Spider lied and told the fucker that it was a personal family matter that he was dealing with back home. The director gave him a sarcastic look and went back to his office.

Spider waited, standing in front of the fax machine hoping the shit head stayed put. He did and a return fax from the offshore vessel arrived with the precise information required.

He grabbed the phone and mobilised the SAS personnel, who were at the airport going through details for rappelling head first from the helicopters. He then quickly went to the airport hangar where the Black Hawks were parked. They had been towed out of the hangar, given a pre-flight check and now their turbine engines were just firing up, twin rappelling lines secured aboard and weapons loaded aboard the lead helicopter.

The backup helicopter would follow and provide covering fire if necessary while the hit team rappelled onto the boat below. The SAS soldiers stood to attention when Spider entered the hangar with a screech of brakes. He jumped out of the car and immediately ordered them to stand by for boarding. Meantime, he called over the two pilots and their co-pilots to review the flight charts and the position and directions of the Fretilin boats, with the key boat highlighted for boarding. They had no indication as to whether the boat crews were armed and hostile, so it was agreed:

- Black Hawk crews:
  - This will be a daylight surprise raid.
  - Given that the average cruise speed over the water will be 150 knots, then from take-off to return landing cannot exceed four and a half hours' duration.
  - Today's take-off time is ten minutes from now at 13:00 local time with return at 17:30 hours latest.
  - Spider will remain at the hanger to maintain radio or satellite phone contact with the seismic vessel captain for any course changes of the ship or the wooden boats and progressively update the pilots.
  - A fast and low approach must be made when 30 nautical miles out from the target.
  - The second chopper will fly cover and focus its waist M60 machine gun on the other boats in case they joined in support of the boarded boat.
  - Both choppers must drop the inflatable life rafts into the sea for the SAS teams to board after their operation aboard the one or two Fretilin boats.
  - The lead chopper must notify Spider regarding the status of the boarding by HF radio once they have offloaded the SAS teams and reached a cruising height of 6,000ft.

- ° As the navy are closer for extraction, contact the navy patrol boat at Scot Reef for recovery of the SAS teams.
- ° Return to Darwin and stand down.
- SAS hit teams:
  - ° Board the choppers for take-off immediately.
  - ° The first SAS hit team will be on the lead chopper and are to carry out a head-down rappel down the line with weapons cocked at the ready in case of them being fired upon from the boat below.
  - ° The second SAS hit team have the option of boarding the first boat as backup or board a second boat if necessary, such as shots fired or heavy interference from a second boat with the first team boarding.
  - ° Irrespective of the outcome, both boarding teams must leave the choppers and board the first boat or a second one as the choppers do not have sufficient fuel endurance for a loaded safe return to Darwin airport.
  - ° Worst case scenario: if no boarding by either team, they are to be dropped into the sea, board the life rafts and await navy patrol boat recovery.
  - ° If there are no shots fired by the Fretilin crew and no weapons found aboard, hold the crew for the navy to pick them up for piracy on the high seas. Collect the life rafts and bring them aboard.
  - ° If there are shots fired by the Fretilin crew then it will be necessary to take out all of them and then move the boat as far west as possible outside of the Zone and survey vessel line of sight. Then destroy the boat with crew below and leave no evidence of the operation. Board the life boats and await navy patrol boat recovery.

First Operation – Fretilin Boat Interdiction

Right on time, the two mean-looking grey Black Hawk choppers had ascended low over the water and entered the Zone with their bellies almost cresting the waves of the 1.5m sea, well under the detection ability of the survey vessel's radar, to intersect the location and course of the Fretilin fishing boat that had vandalised the expensive seismic traces on the previous day. The pilots and waist gunners strained their eyes for the timber-built boat as it would not come up on their radar.

The SAS soldiers began their preparations for their head-down rappelling descent onto the boat with weapons locked and loaded. Ten minutes later the waist gunner on the lead helicopter shouted that a bogie was sighted to the right front ten o'clock direction of the chopper at about 3 miles away.

The lead chopper pointed its nose directly at the boat with the second chopper veering to the right about 100 yards to provide cover fire if needed and have their SAS hit team ready to rappel aboard the boat behind the first team, who would be securing the boat crew, dead or alive depending on the crew's reaction to the boarding. The deadly scenario was a 'go' and the predetermined plan of action was unfolding.

Within less than a minute both choppers were slowing into a hover 20 yards above the Timor Sea and the largest Fretilin fishing boat. The roar of the engines and rotors was almost deafening as the soldiers in the lead chopper hurled themselves out and slid down the ropes with their stubby Sig Sauer machine guns aimed at the deck of the boat.

The boat crew stood frozen in place and did not appear to be armed. With the first SAS hit team now on deck, the lead chopper pulled up and to the left about 100 yards away and climbing to 500ft to provide cover fire, allowing the second chopper to discharge its soldiers onto the boat deck. The remaining fishing boats had scattered to the wind when they sighted the helicopters. There was no point or value in chasing them and splitting up the teams.

The first hit team headed to the bridge of the boat and had shoved several crew members face down onto the deck. Lucky for this crew, they were not armed and did not put up any resistance. The skipper of the boat was on his knees with his hands on his head before the soldiers entered the bridge. He was pale, shaking and stuttering something in Portuguese that was of no interest to the SAS men, who went about their business with tough thoroughness until all of the crew were accounted for.

The second hit team went about searching the boat for weapons, maps, satellite radios, GPS units, log books, communication records, cell phones, ID or passports, cameras, registration papers and any other intelligence material on board. Due to the rapidity of the boarding, the crew had no time to destroy or toss overboard any of the material.

The two Black Hawk helicopters were out of time over the target and must return to Darwin. The lead chopper pilot radioed to the lead SAS hit team, which had a VHF hand-held marine radio, and requested 'status'. The team leader came back with 'all clear'. Everyone knew what the game plan was so no need to chat further. The choppers peeled off side by side at 500ft, tilted forward as their rotors bit into the air and hurtled off towards Darwin. The lead chopper pilot then radioed the navy patrol boat at Scot Reef on a predetermined military frequency with the co-ordinates of the Fretilin boat and advised them that the SAS soldiers had secured and taken the crew prisoner and now required a taxi home.

Meanwhile, the hit team had to recover all of the four life rafts that were bobbing about on the turbulent seas tugging at their sea anchors (they look like small parachutes but are under the water). The wooden fishing boat was turned downwind and then came about into the wind in order to bring the two life rafts alongside to be hauled over the gunnels and onto the deck for deflating and packing. All the Fretilin crew were cable tied hand and foot and were lying face down on the forward deck of this 80ft fishing boat, which had no nets or fishing gear on board.

While awaiting the navy patrol boat to arrive, the two SAS teams thoroughly sorted through all the intelligence material now located on the bridge map table. It was a treasure trove of information that didn't need much translation:

- Marine charts were marked up showing where the boat had come from, which was a fishing port in Sulawesi, Indonesia.
- The boat registration was Indonesian.
- The crew ID and passports were Portuguese, while the skipper was Indonesian.
- Marine charts were marked up recently showing the position and course of another vessel (possibly the seismic vessel of which they had attacked the traces).
- Cell phones and cameras had photos and videos of the seismic vessel and the actual cutting across of the traces by the fishing boat. A trophy no doubt.
- Other papers and documents were in Portuguese, so they would have to wait for translation.
- Used airline tickets were among the crew luggage indicating their flights from Portugal into Jakarta and on to Sulawesi several months ago.

It took about twelve hours for the navy patrol boat to arrive and for the prisoners this was a very harrowing time lying on the heaving deck. They had to be toileted and given drinks of water from time to time. Having gotten all of the intelligence material bundled up into their backpacks, the SAS soldiers handed over the crew of the boat to the navy crew. Charges were set in the belly of the fishing boat and under the fuel tank, fused and set alight. The two hit teams then boarded the navy patrol boat and requested the captain to stand off about 500 yards and wait for the explosion and fire. It only took ten minutes for the burning vessel to disappear below the waves into the deep trench just outside of the Zone.

Spider received a satellite phone call from the bridge of the patrol boat from the hit team leader, who confirmed 'boat down', crew secured and heading back into Darwin within twenty-four hours. Now it was his job to send the Black Hawk helicopters to Scot Reef airstrip to pick up the SAS soldiers, then decide what to do with the pirate boat crew as it might create an international incident if they were publicly landed ashore in Darwin port with Customs and Immigration getting involved. He would have a lot of explaining to do if the local authorities or media caught onto the piracy on the high seas incident.

Spider immediately walked over to the outer door of his office and let the secretary know he was 'going for a walk', by which she well knew he was up to his usual mischief and that the shit-for-brains director would be kept in the dark.

He arrived at the Indonesian Consulate within fifteen minutes and asked to speak urgently with the Consul, whom he had met socially at Joint Authority 50/50 staff functions. He was also aware that the Consulate had direct contacts with the Indonesian Intelligence Agency (ABBRI).

Spider briefed him on the outcome of the raid on the Indonesian-registered fishing boat that was captained by an Indonesian and crewed by Portuguese nationals who were formerly from Timor and were therefore Fretilin sympathisers and active operatives who had acted aggressively in the Zone. The SAS hit team had destroyed the boat at sea and within the next twenty-four hours the skipper and crew of the boat would arrive in Darwin harbour on a navy patrol boat.

The consul had to contact his embassy in Canberra as this was above his pay grade to make decisions on. They sat drinking lemon tea and chewed on sweet biscuits for about an hour. Then the direct line phone rang, the consul spoke for a few minutes and then went to the fax machine to retrieve an incoming message.

He spoke: 'Our Government requires that all of the boat crew and all of the intelligence material gathered be handed over to Indonesia, as this piracy action began on their soil, using their resources and people.'

He continued 'We will investigate the sources and support framework and provide you personally with any relevant intelligence we gather regarding any future activities in the Timor Sea. There is a military base at Kupang in West Timor where an aircraft is being dispatched to Darwin airport as we speak. It will arrive in Darwin later this evening to pick up those prisoners and materials.

'Can you please assist us in arranging a silent transfer from the navy patrol boat to the airport, then for a pickup and departure of a diplomatic package? No doubt you will communicate whatever is necessary to your government agency contacts after this transaction is completed.'

Spider agreed reluctantly and left the office, going straight home to wash up and change and then headed out to the airport.

At the secure airport hangar where the Black Hawk helicopters were parked, he picked up the phone and briefed Commander Coen on the offshore operation, its outcome and the link-up with the navy patrol boat, which was now on its way towards Darwin for discharging its new cargo of Indonesian and Portuguese boat crew. The SAS hit team would assist if they were needed during the prisoner handover.

Commander Coen was a bit taken aback but having Spider with awareness of the situation and the Indonesian Embassy in Canberra having endorsed the transfer of people and material, there was no point in waking up the Minister for Defence or others at the moment. Spider took it on himself to call the air force commander in charge of Darwin's air force base to ask his security people to assist in moving the package from the harbour to the secure area at the airport, including clearing the Indonesian military aircraft for an off-the-books short stop, and go landing and take-off. Spider then:

- Contacted the navy commander and advised him of the situation involving his patrol boat. He was aware of it picking up the SAS hit team and dropping them off at Scot Reef before transporting the fishing boat crew to Darwin but was not sure of what to do about the situation on arrival. Spider filled him in on the plan for there being an air force bus to do the pickup at the navy base, with no paperwork to be involved. The commander agreed reluctantly and said he would use the excuse of the patrol boat returning because it needed urgent maintenance.
- The special forces soldiers escorted the fishing boat crew with hands still cable tied onto the bus and they stayed on board with the prisoners all the way to the airport, where the bus entered the secure hangar.

Spider was handed all the intelligence material and with a bit of help from the hit team warriors they were able to copy most of it before it was handed over and loaded onto the Indonesian military aircraft that was due any minute (this copied material would be handed over to Commander Coen).

Spider sat in the cockpit of a Black Hawk helicopter with the radio on Darwin tower frequency and listened into the aircraft departures and arrivals calls. He ultimately heard an Indonesian accent come over the radio requesting inbound approach clearance for an aircraft 60 miles out at 18,000ft. From his own flying time, this sounded much like his inbound radio calls flying a C-130 Hercules during the Vietnam War.

Spider maintained his interest in this particular aircraft as it didn't have a commercial aircraft call sign. The pilot requested a direct approach on runway 18, which would bring it in close to his secured air force hangar – perfect, the pilot had done his homework. Spider dropped down from the chopper cockpit and hurried over to the hangar side door where an air force security officer was standing. He requested that the aircraft that was about to line up to land on runway 18 be directed by ground control to taxi across to the hangar on its starboard side. He then went back to the chopper and listened in on that aircraft's landing clearance and ETA calls.

Thirty minutes later the Indonesian C-130 was taxiing across towards the hangar with an air force truck with flashing lights guiding him over and getting him to about-turn ready for take-off later. With the four turbine engines winding down to idle, the rear ramp was lowered and an aircrew member waved for them to load the fishing boat crew and material as were his orders. The transfer only took ten minutes and from where Spider was standing next to the chopper he heard the C-130 pilot request taxi clearance from Darwin ground control. As there was almost no wind, the pilot elected to use runway 36 at the opposite end of 18 so he would not fly over the city or suburbs of Darwin – a very careful and smart manoeuvre Spider, thought to himself.

The C-130 engines wound up and the ramp closed. Then, with landing lights glaring, the pilot requested taxi clearance for runway 36 and received permission to proceed to holding point runway 18. The transport rolled noisily forward the 100 yards to the holding point, and the radio call from the pilot to Darwin tower given was 'Cargo C-130'. Ready at holding point runway 36 several minutes later, the tower said 'Cargo C-130, clear for take-off – runway 36'. The pilot repeated the command and taxied out onto the runway apron and turned left to line up. With brakes on, he revved up all four engines, released the brakes and rolled forward faster and faster until it lifted off.

The pilot advised the tower that he was airborne and turning on heading 350, not above 18,000ft. Then there was silence for a few seconds and then normality began to set in as the air force men headed back to barracks and the SAS soldiers began packing away their weapons and kit, then headed for the showers and civilian clothes.

Spider got the bus to wait for them and then drop them off at their lodgings. As for tomorrow, it would be debriefing time after a good meal and rest at 06:00 sharp. Spider felt elated in a way because this mission had come off pretty cleanly but he was also concerned as this was not the end of the saga.

For the time being, he stood the SAS soldiers and helicopters down and the warriors returned to their north Queensland base. They would be ready on call for the next operation and, if there was a next time, he would be using the same hit team as no detailed briefing would be required except for the target and position. They all took a commercial flight back to Townsville.

Chapter 28

Darwin Street Demonstrations

Spider had been carrying out his normal duties in the Joint Authority offices along with circuits around town and suburbs on observer mode. He was continuing to monitor the Fretilin sympathiser graffiti dubbings on building walls and had noticed that there were now more than usual, and they were becoming wider spread. He visited the ASIO office and discussed the increase and his concern with them but, as it was a civil matter, he could do no more than that.

However, he did speak with his office building security manager and the Indonesian Consul as forewarned is better than forced entry of demonstrators. So far so good, all was quiet around town. One would feel a bit stupid and overreactive if it were not for his analytical mind and his focus on going out and gathering intelligence rather than sitting back and simply reacting to an incident after it poured out onto the streets.

The Indonesian Consulate in Darwin was attacked by demonstrators on a Saturday night using rocks and red paint representing the blood of East Timorese fighters. The consulate staff were blocked from entering the building for several days. Police and other services attended to quell the demonstration. Consulate staff were being followed home, and a staff family BBQ in a park was disrupted by Timor sympathisers with police being involved in scuffles. This shit was now getting out of hand.

At last, the police protective services division began the task of guarding the Consulate building and its staff and, at Spider's request, began shadowing the Joint Authority directors and their families from a discreet distance whenever they were out on the street or shopping.

The atmosphere in Darwin became heated as the general public were taken by surprise at the number of people arriving in town in support of the East Timorese independence movement. However, not only Darwin was seeing protests; they were occurring around the country and Australian nationals had travelled to East Timor to participate in the resistance movement.

Spider had to see through this haze and try to work out if there was a real or imaginary threat unfolding.

All he could do now was stand among the groups who were demonstrating and hope that this hype would soon subside. One thing he did learn was that he was out of place in a civilian environment and would have to leave these incidents to the police services.

Second Operation – Fretilin Shootout

Six months later another fishing boat arrived in the Timor Gap Zone. This time it was a large long liner-type steel hull fishing boat. It was sighted by the airborne fluro-sensor aircraft and routinely reported to Spider as were all vessel sightings in the area; friendly and foes alike. This time they had advance notification of a vessel that was not a freighter or passenger liner passing through the area.

Spider chartered a Cessna 182 from the local flying school and headed to the position, flying at 8,000ft so as not to attract adverse attention to the position where the vessel was last sighted. Although it had moved, he was able to locate it, mark the new position on his chart and take several photos using a telephoto lens for later examination. After passing within half a mile of the vessel, he continued his course for another 50 miles and then turned around in a wide loop back to Darwin so as not to alert the boat crew that they had been under surveillance.

Spider met up with the Customs Director Bret Harrison with the film and a marked-up marine chart in hand. He asked if he and his team managing the Coast Watch aircraft would kindly develop the film and enlarge any shots that might identify the vessel and where it originated from. The next day he received an excited call from one of the Coast Watch pilots who had been called in to help in assessing the prints.

He popped down during his usual walks along the Darwin mall with a slight skip in his step. The Customs Director met him on arrival and introduced him to several staff members who were waiting in the meeting room. They had a series of photos in various levels of enlargement ready for discussion.

Spider was not the best photographer in the world but these shots came out pretty good. Either that or there had been a lot of enhancements made by the customs folk.

Their observations were that:

- This was a large long liner fishing boat.
- It was in an area where this type of fishing was not carried out.
- The equipment used for long line fishing had no fishing line on the spools.
- There appeared to be a number of people out on the deck, which was unusual as the fishing crews generally lazed about below decks when not working.
- The course provided on the chart indicated the vessel was heading for the middle of the Zone.

Spider sat back and thought for several minutes, considering whether he should wait and see or react to this possible intruder as there wasn't any law against innocent vessel movements in international waters. There was a drilling ship out in the Zone in a stationary position obtaining core samples and he asked for the area chart to be laid out on the table showing the two course plots and drew a line between them. In addition, he added the station position of the drilling ship that was faxed to him the previous evening as per reporting routine. The fishing vessel course was parallel to the drilling ship and if they continued there would be no threat. If they turned toward the drilling ship then a threat was highly likely.

He thanked the Customs team and returned to his office with the marked up chart tucked under his arm. He then picked up the satellite phone, looked up the emergency response contacts register and dialled up the number of the captain of the drilling ship. Within a minute they were in contact. He advised the captain of a possible hostile vessel on a parallel east–west course, about 40 miles to his south, that might either continue onward or turn towards his location.

The captain was on the bridge and asked him to hold while he checked his radar scope, which swept a 40-mile radius. He came back on line and advised that the fishing boat course plot indicated that it had gradually turned in a wide curve that if it continued would pass in front of the drilling ship by about 20 miles or less.

Spider thanked the captain and requested him to send a four-hourly radar screen shot by fax to the Customs office in Darwin – attention himself. Spider then contacted the Customs Director and advised him of the course change and asked if he could phone when each of the four-hour radar shots arrived as it was very important. The director understood and agreed without asking a lot of questions. Spider then picked up the satellite phone and called the SAS base in Queensland and requisitioned the same Black Hawk helicopters and SAS soldier teams for immediate transit to Darwin.

Commander Coen was the next call on his list and he informed him of the possible hostile heading near the stationary drilling ship, the meeting with Customs over the photos and his call-up of the SAS squads and assets needed for a similar sortie into the Zone as the last one.

This time Commander Coen was more pensive and wanted to be kept informed each and every time the four-hour faxes from the drilling ship came in and about the situation observations on the supposed fishing boat course changes. Spider agreed and put down the phone but in the back of his mind was the thought that the commander had taken some heat over the last offshore operation irrespective of how successful and how carefully it was covered up discreetly between them and the Indonesians.

Either his naval friends here at the base or an air force officer had opened their mouths as none of the SAS hit team would have. At this point Spider set up a meeting with the Indonesian Consul and discussed the likelihood of another offshore intervention similar to the last one. The Consul rang his Embassy in Canberra, who put an ABBRI agency representative on the speaker phone. As everyone was aware of the last episode and had more information on the earlier fishing boat crew by now, the discussion was open and discreet.

Spider's operation would proceed as before and the rules of engagement if hostile were well understood. He handed over several copies of photos and radar screen shots to the Consul. The call ended with, 'Good hunting major', from the ABBRI agent.

Before sun up in the early morning of the following day, two Black Hawk helicopters thundered along the coast of the Northern Territory heading for Darwin and directly in line with runway 18, finally setting gently down in front of the secure air force hangar. Their radio communications were on military band through air force personnel in the tower, so they weren't audible on civil aviation frequencies. At 06:00 Spider turned up at the hangar and set up a briefing meeting with the pilots and SAS hit teams to lay out the charts and photos and then show the radar screen shots progressively showing that the single target fishing vessel was in fact still in a circling pattern about 20 miles off the drilling ship.

It was now time to act on this intelligence and follow the same rules as previously set out. There also appeared to be more people on board this larger steel-constructed vessel according to the photos. So, if they are not all crew members then what are they there for?

The flight endurance remained as before and the same drill of rappelling down onto the vessel had not changed. However, the location of the drilling ship and the fishing vessel was further east than the last boarding, which meant that it would take longer for the naval patrol boat to arrive. As this was ostensibly a covert operation, there would be no involvement or communication with the drilling ship.

In front of the airport hangar, the Black Hawks had been towed out, refuelled, pre-flight checked and were ready to be started up. The twin rappelling lines had already been secured and the weapons loaded aboard. The SAS soldiers again stood to attention when Spider entered the hangar and were ordered to stand by for boarding. This time they knew precisely what they were in for and some of them even smiled as they boarded. This should kill their boredom.

Spider gave a final briefing and copies of overnight radar shot faxes with GPS positions marked to the pilots. The two pilots and their co-pilots again reviewed the flight charts on board showing the position and directions of the

Fretilin vessel and the drilling ship. They had no indication as to whether the boat crew and other people on board were armed and if they would be hostile toward a boarding, so the original plan would be followed to the letter. The two Black Hawk choppers lined up on runway 36 and lifted off while heading along and climbing ever higher above the runway.

Spider stood by the hangar and watched them until they disappeared out of sight, heading north-east direct to the target area in the Zone.

The two choppers entered the Zone fast and low, staying parallel but well out of the drilling ship's 40-mile radar range. Then they descended to 50ft above a fairly calm Timor Sea and turned directly north to intersect at the course of the target Fretilin fishing vessel, which they had now picked up on their radar, approaching it from the rear. Again, the pilots and waist gunners strained their eyes for the larger steel-built fishing vessel as it came up clearer on their radar. When within 30 miles ahead, the pilots shouted a warning to the soldiers. Target ahead – five minutes.

These well-trained and fearless special forces soldiers once again began their cross-check preparations for their head-down rappelling descent onto the vessel with weapons locked and loaded.

Two minutes later the waist gunner shouted that the vessel was right in front of the chopper at about a mile away and now turning sharply to face north.

The lead chopper pointed its nose directly at the boat's stern with the second chopper veering to the right about 100 yards away to provide cover fire if needed and have their second hit team ready to rappel aboard the boat behind the first team, who would initially be securing the boat and its crew after boarding. This now well-practised deadly scenario was a 'go', and the predetermined plan of action was now under way.

Both choppers went into a hover at about 20 yards above the Timor Sea and the Fretilin fishing vessel. The warrior soldiers in the lead chopper hurled themselves out and down the ropes with their stubby Sig Sauer machine guns aimed at the deck of the vessel. The boat crew and others aboard scattered and this time appeared to be armed.

A burst of AK-47 fire from the bridge sidewalk came up from the vessel. The first SAS hit team were halfway down the rappelling rope over the deck and the lead two soldiers returned fire at the bridge. The following soldiers began opening fire, as did the helicopter waist gunner on the second Black Hawk with his M60 machine gun.

The second chopper waist gunner maintained cover fire at the people up at the bow of the vessel as soon as they had raised their weapons. Bullets were now penetrating and ricocheting over the bridge structure and deck.

A number of bullets from the boat had hit the lead helicopter. The first hit team had released from the rope and boarded the boat under cover fire and had tossed several grenades onto the bridge walkway, silencing the AK-47 fire. They then went about clearing the upper cabins with stun grenades and entering with a stream of bullets ripping through the smoke into any bodies still standing.

The second team and chopper had silenced the shooters on the bow and were rappelling down onto the forward deck area. They took on opening the forward hatches and dropping grenades down, then waited for the blast before entering with covering fire.

The hit team went about their business with tough as steel thoroughness until all of the crew were accounted for as dead or dying. The second hit team went about searching the vessel for weapons, maps, GPS units, log books, satellite phones, communication records, cell phones, ID or passports, cameras, registration papers and any other intelligence material on board. Some of the material had been destroyed by the grenades and following fires.

With the two Black Hawk helicopters out of time over the target, they dropped the yellow-coloured life rafts onto the Timor Sea and turned toward Darwin. The lead chopper pilot radioed to the SAS hit team lead and requested 'status'. The team leader came back with 'all clear to burn'.

The choppers peeled off side by side at 500ft, tilted forward as their rotors bit into the air and hurtled off out of sight. The lead chopper pilot radioed the navy patrol boat at Scot Reef with the co-ordinates of the hostile Fretilin fishing vessel. The SAS soldiers had secured it and required recovery from rafts on the water with their emergency beacons switched on.

There would be no fishing boat or crew to encounter, only the soldiers bobbing about on the sea. As the encounter with this fishing boat was carried out some 40 nautical miles from the drilling ship, there were no witnesses to the rapid and decisive kill operation executed on board. The drilling ship was not advised and they continued work oblivious to the carnage on board the blip on their radar that suddenly disappeared off scope.

On board the fishing boat, the SAS team took photos and then unceremoniously dumped the bodies of the crew down below. The vessel controls were kaput due to several fragmentation grenades being tossed into the bridge and there was still a fire burning in the wheel house. The hit team set charges along the keel and engine room with a one-hour fuse ignited. 'Time to go for a swim methinks,' said the team leader as he rolled over the gunnels and into the warm water.

This rust bucket would split in half and drop like a rock to the bottom of Davy Jones' Locker – with all hands on board.

The four life rafts had been dropped near the vessel but were now scattered about 100 yards away due to the boat attempting to move away from the helicopters' approach. The SAS warriors tossed their weapons and non-essential kit overboard before inflating their life vests and jumping into the sea for a swim to the rafts and the long wait for the navy patrol boat. Behind them, as they drifted away, the explosives did their job; a shock force erupted and a dull thud was felt in the sea. Water gushed out of the open hatches on deck, then the steel fishing boat lifted up about a yard at the bow, fell back and with a gurgling sound from below, it sank stern first below the surface of the Timor Sea.

It was twenty-six hours before the patrol boat located the rafts using emergency beacon radio pulse signal. The rafts were the self-inflating type and contained survival rations, so the SAS teams just had to paddle and tether themselves together and wait for the water taxi to arrive. The navy crew hauled the teams over the gunnels of the patrol boat and onto the deck. This time the rafts were deflated and sunk with a couple of well-aimed shots for good measure by the crew.

On board the patrol boat, the warrior teams sorted thoroughly through all of the intelligence material taken from the fishing boat that wasn't fishing for fish. This time the registration of the vessel was Portuguese and so were all of the people on board. There would be no stories to tell on arrival at the navy base, just a group of SAS soldiers whose boat had sunk and were recovered in life rafts by the Australian Navy.

Spider met the SAS teams at the navy wharf. They boarded a waiting bus, which dropped them all off at the airport hangar to store their kit and change into civilian clothes, then deliver them to their accommodation. A debrief would be in four hours and the bus would return and bring them back from their accommodation to the airport hangar, where this entire affair had started.

This time Commander Coen was present for the debriefing. He was not introduced but sat silently while each of the men made their action and observation statement for the record. Over thirty hostiles were taken down by either gun fire or grenades, while the vessel was sunk using C4 packages on the keel and engine room. There were no survivors and there was no evidence on the surface. No further radar shots of the mysterious vessel that had shadowed the drilling ship. No explanation about helicopter flights over the Timor Sea.

The debrief over, the SAS soldiers once more boarded the Black Hawk helicopters for the journey back to their base in Queensland.

There they would wait for the next call out from Major Pete – the Spider.

Third Operation – Car Carrier Ferry from Portugal

Seven peaceful months had rolled by with only a whimper from the demonstrators in the Darwin streets, who appeared to have had their fun and many of them, including the press from the southern states, had left town looking for something more exciting to raise hell about. Underneath the somewhat quieter times was an ongoing wrath and fervour of the hard core Fretilin sympathisers who lived within the Darwin community.

Spider wondered what next from this corner of discontent. He guessed, one would say, careful what you wish for, and then it happened.

The Indonesian intelligence agency (ABBRI) phoned him one evening at his condo and informed him that a small ship of about 10,000 tons had sailed direct from Portugal heading for the Timor Gap and East Timor.

According to their sources in Portugal, the ship was armed and about to arrive on the Darwin horizon within a couple of weeks with a bunch of people on board intending to land in East Timor in support of the local Fretilin separatists. It had stopped over in Madagascar for supplies and fuel and it may come into Darwin for provisions and refuelling.

His thoughts raced; a shootout in Darwin harbour was to be averted at all costs. At this moment, he had no idea of the ship's precise whereabouts but assumed it was crossing the Indian Ocean to the west of the Australian coast. He needed to muster some extra intelligence capability, perhaps from satellite photos. He called Commander Coen and apprised him of the situation and asked if he could get some off the record help from the:

- Americans using their satellites to locate and track the ship.
- Port authorities where the ship may have docked on its voyage from Portugal.
- Portuguese intelligence agency with knowledge of the voyage.

Obviously (to him at least) the Australian Navy and or air force might need to be involved in patrolling more than 200 miles out from the west coast, spotting and shadowing the ship when it was closer to Australian waters. This time the commander became unsettled as this was getting too big to not involve the government. He did, however, agree to do some checks with a few of his personal contacts and come back to Spider. Meantime, Spider would continue to liaise with ABBRI via the Indonesian Consul in Darwin for any information regarding the ship's course and speed, its intentions, types of armament and its crew and non-crew.

The wider plot underlying this ship was, who was financing and establishing such a brazen attempt, and what was the end game? Timor is not a wealthy or minerals-rich island and never has been, that is why the Portuguese left it to the Indonesians to take back. Perhaps there was a strategic value in the mind of some country such as China?

Inception of a Boarding Plan

Commander Coen arrived in Darwin ostensibly on a social visit, but Spider could see through his smile that his eyes were intense. DIO chiefs don't make house calls without a good reason. He confided in Spider over a beer at the pub in the city mall that the South Africans were able to identify the ship when it passed the Cape and tracked it until it arrived in Madagascar for bunkering fuel. It had possibly taken on more weapons, ammunition and food provisions, but he wasn't sure.

It is likely that the ship would not be stopping off anywhere else along the way and sailing north by west, which would be very smart of them if they did. They could now sail below Java and somewhere near the Cocos (Keeling) Islands and Christmas Island, which were Australian territories. That is where the Americans may come in handy as they had military satellite coverage over that area, particularly monitoring the Northwest Cape communications base on Western Australia's north-west coast.

'Just a thought,' Commander Coen murmured. 'If one were to be interested in taking some friends holidaying in, say, Christmas Island for a week or two, never know what one might see if they had a plane to fly south by east from Darwin over the Indian Ocean.'

Spider took the hint. He knew what the wily old fucker was saying, so he nodded straight faced, finished his beer, thanked the commander for the lunch that they actually didn't have and headed back to his office.

Thinking things through, an idea came to him that worked on the principle 'better stop things before they start'. Given the wink and nod by Commander Coen to at least do something before the ship arrived into Australian waters, he decided to take the action westward and out on the open Indian Ocean somewhere between the Cocos, Keeling and Christmas Islands via Tindal Air Force base.

Getting the navy involved would take the covert cover off the plot as there had been a leak previously. So, he figured that using the tried-and-true Black Hawk helicopter strategy that had been used successfully in the Timor Sea might just work. The only drawback was the distance and remote islands.

Spider visited the Darwin air force base commander and requested the loan of a J series long-bodied C-130 with extended-range fuel tanks. This aircraft was a lot more modern than those he had flown during the Vietnam War and would easily take two Black Hawks in its belly, plus the two teams of SAS soldiers with their specialist kit of tools for the job.

The air force commander tentatively agreed if:

1. Commander Coen of DIO would sign for it.

Spider called his commander and the deal was done.

2. An air force crew must fly the plane. To that Spider had to say no as this was a covert army operation. Anyway, it would be more likely that he and his army pilots had more flying hours with this type of aircraft than the air force people did.

However, the specific aircraft was based in Mackay in Queensland. No worries, he would take a commercial flight across the top of Australia and borrow the bird from there, plus load up the soldiers and choppers at the same time. The helicopter air crew consisting of co-pilot and loadmaster came from the same team he had used in Cambodia, so he requisitioned them through his commander.

Chapter 29

Mobilisation of SAS Soldiers and Aircraft

No time to waste, he packed his overnight bag and flying kit, then purchased the latest aerial charts out at the airport and marine charts at the marine port offices. Then he got a one-way ticket from Darwin to Mackay, where he was hoping to meet up with a fully kitted out SAS team plus flight crew. The guys were a day late in arriving as not all of them were on base and the civilian contract soldiers had to be called in from Sydney. He wasn't too unhappy with the delay as placing new SAS members into the experienced team right now could cause problems later.

There was some spare time available to brief and refresh training methods before heading for the Darwin base of operations.

The two Black Hawk helicopters fluttered into Mackay airport, landing over in the military aircraft parking area and within 100 yards of the C-130. They had brought along four mechanics to swing the flight rotors back, the same as was done for storage on navy ships. Each chopper was towed across and then pushed up the rear ramp, tail first, and set on an angle in order to take up less room as well as move the centre of gravity balance point forward.

With flying machines, warriors and kit stowed and lashed down for a noisy flight with no movies, in flight dinners, pretty hostesses or nice music, Spider flight checked the C-130 and inspected the maintenance log. The co-pilot finished his walk around visual inspection and signed off the fuel load. In the cockpit Spider settled into the left seat, selected ATIS (air traffic information service) radio to listen to the latest weather forecast and cross-checked it with the weather fax data.

Flight charts were mounted onto the clipboards, heading, track, fuel and endurance records completed, pre-start checks cross-checked again, one turbine engine started, then the next until all four were turning and burning and running smoothly with the propellers in feathered neutral position. The co-pilot dialled up the control tower frequency and requested 'taxi clearance for runway 25, C-130 for Tindal, not above 18,000'. The loadmaster called out to the passengers to buckle up their seat belts and make sure their kit bags were stowed, and then the bird began to roll.

As a precaution, Spider planned the flight of the C-130 from Mackay direct to the Tindal air force base located 8 nautical miles east-south-east of the town of Katherine, Northern Territory, for refuelling and give the guys a bit of a rest before the next leg of the operation. He could also spend a bit more time briefing the SAS soldiers on what was anticipated ahead of them all.

At the holding point before the runway, he called the tower and said 'Cargo C-130 ready runway 25'. The tower held them back until a commercial flight had landed on the same runway and when it had entered the upwind taxiway leading off to the passenger terminal, they were given the 'line up' call. The bird shuddered sluggishly forward onto the white stripes they call the piano keys out on the threshold of the runway and Spider pressed his heels on the brakes as the nose wheels aligned with the centre line. Two minutes later, they were given the 'clear to take-off'. Spider pushed the four throttles forward, the co-pilot moved the prop pitch angle to max and they both released the brakes allowing the bird to lurch forward and rumble ever faster down the runway. At T2 take-off speed the nose lifted high and the awkward bird began to fly like an eagle.

The flight west across country to Tindal was bumpy at times but uneventful. Some of the soldiers took the time to lay down on their packs and try to sleep or rest. The approach to Tindal had a NOTAM (notice to airmen) regarding the arrestor wires being deployed at the threshold of the runway due to fighter jets practising landings.

Spider put the wheels down about 100 yards past the marker cones showing where the wires were and taxied off the runway upwind toward the military aircraft parking area. It was hot and humid outside as the ramp came down but the soldiers needed to stretch their legs and use the terminal toilets. They were all in civilian clothes so using the facilities was not a security breaker.

Two hours later, after lunching at the terminal café and with aircraft refuelling completed, Spider signalled to the soldiers it was time to mount up. He had checked in with the air force flight controller's office and obtained more up to date weather forecast information regarding their flight path between Tindal and Christmas Island, where he intended to land for the time being.

Also, there was more accommodation and other resources available than at Cocos and Keeling Islands. Commander Coen had them all booked into some holiday chalets for the next few weeks and Spider was to contact Coen on arrival by satellite phone for an update on their current status and intel from him as to what the US satellite observations were yielding regarding the Fretilin ship's course and speed.

Arrival on Christmas Island

Thank God for GPS and how accurate it had become over the years as the old gyro compass and radio direction finder (RDF) would have them missing the island by miles if followed due to variable wind and weather conditions and signal strength changes. Almost magically they were able to not only locate the island but line up with the runway even before sighting it through low tropical clouds.

Spider called the tower at 60 miles out and received the wind strength and direction, plus clearance to continue his direct approach from the north. It was raining when they touched down and rolled to a stop just south of the small terminal area. Spider went over to the terminal and organised land transport to the holiday chalets and this ended up being two minibuses. That would mean a few trips for the team and all their 'holiday' baggage.

With all personnel and their personal bags safely tucked into the chalets for the evening, Spider returned to the plane and arranged for refuelling and a place to park the two Black Hawk helicopters.

With a good night's rest and a couple of hot meals under their belts, the tough SAS soldiers and pilots would manually extract the helicopters from the C-130 belly. After unloading the machines, they would be pushed over to their ready station, near the C-130 for security reasons. There was only open-air parking available for all the aircraft so pre-flight checks were scheduled on a daily basis.

Spider clambered aboard the C-130 and sat in the cockpit. He then phoned Commander Coen on the satellite phone to advise him of their safe arrival and thanked him for arranging the accommodation. Coen in turn briefed Spider on the location and movements of the Fretilin ship to date, advising that he would send a fax on the satellite phone to Spider within thirty minutes. After the phone call, copies were received of the satellite photos and text records calculating the course and speed, with forecast projections ahead of the vessel. It would be up to Spider if and when to intercept the ship on the high seas. He resisted the urge to take the big bird out and have a look as the boat crew down there would see them on their radar and may head somewhere else or abort their mission.

It was imperative that the US provided progressive daily satellite tracking of the ship, whereby they could pick a point of contact position in advance of its current progress that would allow the team of SAS warriors to mobilise the choppers to head out to intercept and board it. Only one shot at this would be possible.

There would be no navy patrol boat available to pick up the teams on this occasion, therefore the closer the intercept point to the island the better. In the meantime, Spider would look around for a local fishing trawler or the like to support the at-sea recovery after the ship boarding. Trying to recover the SAS teams out of the water using the helicopters would use too much fuel, there were no winches installed and it would risk the helicopters needlessly.

This was their new weakness – recovery after the operation, not the operation itself.

Back and Recovery Fishing Boat Charter

A day or two later, with the help of the local tour operator, Spider was able to locate several seagoing fishing boats. The next thing was to go and inspect them to ascertain their capability to sail out about 200 miles, then pinpoint and navigate to locate some very small yellow life rafts that would be bobbing about in the swell carrying the SAS warriors. Out of four boats of varying size, range, speed and instrumentation, one chartered marlin fishing boat fitted all the criteria.

Not wishing to miss the boat, he hired the fucker on the spot for the next two weeks. He also allocated one of the helicopter mechanics to go and check the boat engines and fuel tank distance capabilities. He would be on board when the boat headed out to recover the two teams of soldiers that may be languishing about in rough seas.

The mechanic must stay close by the charter boat and skipper with one of the satellite phones and await recovery instructions. The skipper of the charter boat would only be made aware of the recovery mission once the boarding mission was initiated by the Black Hawks taking off.

As there was only one capable recovery boat available on this island, Spider and his co-pilot set out on the same boat to make enquiries about other charter boats at Cocos Island. There were several to choose from. They returned to Christmas Island and Spider made arrangements for himself, the co-pilot, loadmaster and another mechanic to return to Cocos Island aboard the C-130 and landed on its single airstrip, which was not unlike Christmas Island's strip.

They were met by one of the local Malay charter boat owners, who drove them down to the beach head where several boats were moored – not much of a harbour! Spider let him know that they were serious fishermen and wanted to go out far and deep. All of the charter boats were old but one stood out as not that fast but big and very seaworthy. The skipper lived onshore and they met up with him in a shady cabana for a meal and iced tea.

He was very amiable and agreed to a standby charter arrangement for the next two weeks. The old fucker required that he be paid in advance for being on standby. He had Spider over a barrel so he agreed. Spider left the mechanic there with a satellite phone and a briefing on what he and the charted boat skipper had to do when called upon.

The mechanic would have to make sure that the boat selected was fully ready, with instruments working well and fuelled up for long-distance charter. They hired a small cabana for the mechanic and left him standing by the hut at the airstrip with his mouth wide open; he couldn't believe his luck. Spider knew his mind was conjuring up visions of a beach cabana, lovely brown ladies swaying in the breeze and cold beer. But alas, the island was managed by a Muslim committee, so that fucked up that vision. The only thing left was fishing off the jetty.

Satellite Monitoring of the Ship

Twice daily, the fax machine at the C-130 cockpit on Christmas Island hummed and displayed satellite pictures and notes on course and speed with forecast projections. On every occasion Spider was able to interpret the past and present and then dead reckon the forecast location of the ship, which he carefully transferred to his marine map. Mobilisation of the entire team plus the recovery boats was coming closer by the day and hour. There was enough intelligence gathered for him to brief the helicopter pilots as the forecast looked pretty much like they would move in two to three days' time.

Spider picked up the satellite phone and called Commander Coen to inform him of the timing. He already knew how he intended to execute the mission. Then he phoned both of the mechanics so they could mobilise the charter boats at short notice. Everyone watched the weather forecasts as the countdown brought them closer to 'go' time.

The boats were rechecked to ensure all preparations for going to sea at short notice were made such as fuel, bulk food and water. The skippers were aware and available, the instruments rechecked and both boats were taken out for a short sea trial. The objective for the two boats was so they would have built-in redundancy and could form a pincer movement so that no matter what boat reached where the life rafts and SAS team were located first, the spare boat could support or one boat could do the entire job of recovery alone and unaided. Failure to recover the men and bring them back to one of the islands was not an option.

Preparations for Airborne Assault

The Black Hawk helicopters were now given a test flight around the airfield. The fuel was topped up and instruments checked, then the M60 machine guns were stored aboard but not mounted, so inquisitive eyes couldn't see them. Mounting the guns would only take a couple of minutes on the way out from the island. In addition, Spider ordered the SAS soldiers to load the choppers with all their loose kit including their Sig Sauer MCX machine guns. This target was a big ship, so everyone needed to fit and use their Z-Tac throat mic and tube earphone radios as they would lose sight and hearing of each other above and below decks.

The ship was gradually and inextricably moving into the predicted range that Spider had circled on the marine map. It was equidistantly between the Cocos and Christmas Islands and 150 miles east of the line drawn between them. If they did not change course, they would be just where Spider wanted them to be after all of this preparation and waiting.

Spider sent a short text message to the two mechanics giving them the GPS position that the ship would be boarded at and where the fishing boats must head immediately towards. The lead helicopter pilot would give them the actual latest fix on the ship when he departed the scene to head back to Christmas Island. The next text message was sent to Commander Coen's satellite phone as it was not the time for a chat. If he didn't respond that would be good. If he did respond, it would more than likely be to cancel the attack on the ship and tell them to go home.

This would be the only chance to execute the mission, whichever way it would turn out.

It was now two hours before the 'go' point. Spider assembled the SAS teams in front of each Black Hawk helicopter for the last time before boarding and lift off. Everyone knew their job and the circumstances that dictated opening fire or not. He had decided to go on this mission due to the size of the ship and the risk of things going pear shaped quickly.

The silence over the airfield was almost deafening. Only the occasional gull sounded a call. One hour to ago he had made a satellite phone call to the two mechanics standing by both fishing boats to confirm that they had immediately headed out for the crossover GPS position that he had provided and verified that they had it marked on their marine charts. The chopper pilots could provide any amendments to the position during the ship boarding if needed.

'Go' Time Initiated

The final satellite message arrived confirming that the ship had not deviated course, which meant that they had a 'go', and nothing from Commander Coen meant they were authorised to execute according to plan. Spider ordered all SAS soldiers to board the choppers. This was the signal for the pilots to start their engines and lift off. He was on the lead chopper fully kitted out and ready for a fight if it came to that. The lead chopper flew over the edge of the cliffs of Christmas Island's east coast and climbed up to 8,000ft above the sea.

One hour and 150 nautical miles to go.

In the distance ahead and below, they sighted the Marlin fishing boat heading out from Christmas Island harbour, cutting through the waves of the Indian Ocean, and thought about the other backup boat coming from the Cocos Islands that should now be out of the harbour and heading in a converging course to the same end position exactly where these two choppers were now heading directly towards.

The skies were clear except for random puffs of cumulous clouds at about 20,000ft casting shadows on the ocean below. It would be just under an hour before they sighted the ship and before they were picked up by their radar at around 40 plus miles out the choppers would be wave hopping at 50ft above the water.

The lead chopper pilot called the other chopper when he reached an estimated 50 miles out from the ship's position and both aircraft began a rapid descent toward the water, causing Spider's stomach to churn a bit. Everyone's bellies would have felt the sudden change in altitude as a momentary drop in G-forces and air pressure were experienced. The pilot leant across to Spider and said with a wry smile on his sun-worn, ruddy-complexioned face 'Time to lock 'n' load mate'.

Spider motioned with a thumbs up to the SAS soldiers behind him and the two rappelling lines were readied to be released to dangle about 20 yards below the chopper on arrival over the target. Each man cross-checked the other, including Spider. They were as ready as they ever could be on this, the third time around, but they would be on a larger ship and with many more crew and passengers to deal with this time. The pilots scanned the upper decks for obstacles like radio masts and cables over to their port side. The top of the ship crested up and down in the swell, a bit further north than was predicted, but still on its course nevertheless.

The pilot reacted instinctively and notified the second chopper pilot to follow him in and towards the target as he turned left about 20 degrees and aimed straight for the stern. Spider was hoping that the noise from the ship's engines would drown out some of the approaching helicopters' turbine engines and rotor flutter in order to delay any reaction from the ship's crew.

Airborne Rappel Assault Under Way

There were a few people on the open deck of the ship peering up at the helicopters, but no weapons were sighted – so no weapon fire; so far so good. Spider ordered the lead helicopter pilot to take the front bow of the ship and get him to have the following chopper take the stern so both SAS teams could work their way from each end towards the bridge that stood at the centre section of the hull. The lead chopper came extremely low over the bridge and headed in a direct line to hover over the bow at the same speed and course of the ship, with the waist machine gun pointing down at the people on the deck below.

The second helicopter came in low over the stern section with its waist machine gun pointing at an empty deck below. Simultaneously, the rappelling ropes were tossed out of the choppers' side doors and one by one the SAS soldiers plunged down the ropes with weapons locked and loaded ready for a fight if it came to that. Spider was first out, onto the bow deck of the ship and on his knees steadying the rope. Then he raised his machine gun in the direction of the bridge three levels above.

The two helicopters circled the ship once, hauled in the rappelling lines and dropped the yellow life rafts into the ocean in case they needed to use them. Then they peeled off, began to climb to cruising altitude and headed straight back to Christmas Island. The lead helicopter pilot used the satellite phone to text the two mechanics on the fishing boats with the actual ship location and course as it was still under way.

From this point onward Spider would need to keep things under control or there would be a shootout, which should be avoided as there were too many targets to take down. The forward bow team split up, with himself and two SAS soldiers running helter-skelter for the bridge ladder and upper walkway. The captain of the ship, seeing the helicopters and then the warriors coming toward him, ran out to meet them as they reached the bridge's outer walkway. He was roughly but efficiently forced to the floor by an SAS soldier, who put cable ties on his wrists. The other SAS soldiers continued on and stepped into the bridge. By the time they had placed cable ties on the captain's hands and picked him up off the deck, the bridge had been secured. Within seconds the SAS soldiers had all of the bridge crew lying flat on the deck face down. The ship was now without a helm or engines under control for the moment.

Spider left two SAS soldiers in charge of the bridge and ordered them to have the ship heave to (stopped) with no outgoing radio communications allowed until further orders. He turned with his Sig Sauer machine gun pointing this way and then that way, then headed down the internal gangway shouting to every person he sighted that they should place their hands on their heads and move out onto the open deck forward of the bridge.

He got no arguments.

Crew and Passengers Interrogated

Spider called to the two teams using the Z-Tac throat microphone to bring all people up onto the forward deck. He now waited with about twenty crew and passengers until the entire ship's company were assembled and accounted for.

They had taken this ship without a shot fired, a total of 120 persons on board including the bridge, catering and engine room. He ordered all of them to sit down with their legs crossed in front of them.

He and the team leaders would now interrogate every one of those present regarding their:

1. Name and rank or title
2. Apart from the captain, who was in charge
3. Reason for being on the ship
4. Where had they boarded
5. How long had they been on the ship
6. How long would this voyage be
7. What was the next port of call
8. Who chartered the ship
9. What were the political motives for the voyage
10. What course was the ship going to take from here onwards
11. Which cabin were they in
12. Where were their passports
13. Which country did they actually live in
14. Where was the ship intended to go?
15. Were there any weapons on board and where
16. Where were their two-way radios
17. Were there any other ships or boats linked to this voyage and where from

Commander Coen and Spider had prepared this list of questions prior to the mission, which was the reason they didn't get to have dinner a few days earlier when he visited Darwin. Spider only had the list copied fifty times as he had no idea there were so many people on board.

Each person was interrogated separately in the lounge area and then segregated onto the stern deck under guard. It took all of the remaining day, some eleven hours, to complete the interrogation before Spider was satisfied that the ship was secured and that no weapons were aboard. This was definitely a pro-Fretilin East Timor separatism protest ship intending to enter the Timor Gap and was highly likely to head for the coast of East Timor and into Indonesian-controlled territory, according to the marine maps and responses from the crew and passengers under interrogation.

Spider ordered the team to release the crew in order to bring the ship under their full control but to circle and hold this GPS position until the fishing boats arrived – which should not be too much longer. The water was fairly calm with only a 5-knot wind, so the ship did not heave about much.

At-Sea Recovery of SAS Teams

At 02:15, the first of the fishing boats was spotted as its masthead and running lights showed in the darkness. Spider called the mechanic on the satellite phone and requested that they come alongside to take all the SAS soldiers off that they could, then wait off and away from the ship until the second fishing boat arrived.

Within two hours both of the fishing boats were sharing the valuable load of the finest group of SAS soldiers one could ask for. The fishing boats turned up in Christmas Island harbour later the next day and delivered the warriors ashore.

With the mechanics back at the base, they headed for the two Black Hawk helicopters and had their rotors folded back ready to be pushed up into the waiting C-130. The SAS soldiers left their weapons and kit with the loadmaster on the C-130, then gathered their belongings from the chalets and returned directly to assist in hauling the two helicopters aboard the big bird, happy to have holidayed in the Christmas Island tourist resort.

For all intents and purposes for the locals on the island, this operation was a training exercise. There was no evidence to indicate that they had been on either of the islands. Maybe the skippers of the chartered fishing boats had some stories to tell their grandchildren but nothing more. Good money for a couple of days out fishing, though. The so-called tourists had left and all was quiet again on those islands way out in the Indian Ocean.

The C-130 disappeared over the horizon heading back to the Australia mainland. On arrival at Tindal, Spider's co-pilot took over as senior pilot and one of the helicopter pilots with C-130 hours became the co-pilot.

They ferried the hit team and the two Black Hawk helicopters back to the SAS Regiment in Queensland. They were back where they all had started out from, having completed three risky missions successfully without as much as a scratch (not on them anyway).

Ship Directed to Darwin

Meanwhile, Spider remained on the bridge of the ship with two SAS soldiers in order to ensure that it went from where it was boarded directly into Darwin for health, Customs and immigration checks, prior to departing.

The entire ship's company were eventually cleared in Darwin and the vessel searched once again for good measure.

The captain was warned not to proceed towards Timor but as they were legally entitled to leave the Darwin and Australian waters, technically there was nothing Australia could do further to stop them. Portugal officially denied any involvement or knowledge of this ship, its intentions or the crew and passengers.

All the intelligence material that had been gathered on the ship and the people on board was handed over to Commander Coen for assessment. As usual, Spider never asked what the outcome was as that was DIO territory. However, a second copy was handed over to an Indonesian ABBRI representative who had witnessed the ship enter and leave Darwin harbour. He was pleased to receive the documents and headed directly back to Canberra and his embassy. Within a week after the ship left Darwin, it did head directly for Eastern Timor southern coast waters. It was challenged by an Indonesian naval frigate that threatened to open fire if it didn't change course. Apparently, the ship did change course and headed back to Portugal. There was never a report or complaint about a group of Australian SAS soldiers boarding and harassing the passengers and crew. They did eventually find out the ship had been chartered by the University of Portugal.

Epilogue – East Timor

In August 1999 the United Nations sponsored a referendum on East Timor independence from Indonesia. An overwhelming majority of East Timorese people, 78.5 per cent, voted for their independence. Anti-independent East Timorese militias were supported and organised by the Indonesian military and began a scorched earth campaign that resulted in approximately 1,400 Timorese people being killed and another 300,000 forced into Indonesia's West Timor as refugees.

After the demise of President Suharto in 1998, Indonesia's newly elected President B.J. Habibie was prepared to grant East Timor special autonomy, however, it would remain a province of Indonesia.

Newly published intelligence documents declassified by the United States have exposed that it was the United States and not Australia that was responsible for pressuring the Indonesians to pull back from the brink of disaster and allow a multinational peacekeeping force into East Timor. The United States suspended all military aid and co-operation with the Indonesian military.

Declassified documents published by the National Security Archive, Freedom of Information, dispel the Australian Federal Government's own narrative. Australian Prime Minister John Howard's Government policy was to keep East Timor under Indonesian rule; however, it was to reconsider in the end and back flip with the support of the United States for Australia to mobilise a multinational force.

In September 1999 an International Military Force East Timor, INTERFET, consisting of twenty-two nations was deployed into East Timor and brought the violence to an end. The force was commanded by an Australian military officer, Major General Peter Cosgrove.

Following a United Nations administration transition period of two and a half years, East Timor was internationally recognised as an independent nation in 2002. In the parliamentary election of 2007, the Fretilin political party won twenty-one seats out of sixty-five in the national parliament, getting 29 per cent of the vote, and now serves in the official opposition of East Timor.

Ironically, the United States had given President Suharto the green light to invade East Timor in 1975. In 1999, twenty-four years later, it again used its political power but this time to end the occupation.

All life is based on deception.

Chapter 30

Back Door into Hell – Somalia

Everybody Wants to Rule the World

The United States had been leading a UN mission to end the civil war and famine in Somalia.

When Somalian President Mohamed Siad Barré was overthrown by a coalition of opposing clans, precipitating the Somali Civil War, the Somali National Army concurrently disbanded and some former soldiers reconstituted as irregular regional forces or joined clan militias.

The main rebel group in the capital, Mogadishu, was the United Somali Congress (USC), which later divided into two armed factions: one led by Ali Mahdi Muhammad, who became president, and the other by Mohamed Farrah Aidid.

A fifth group, the Somali National Movement (SNM), declared independence in the north-west portion of Somalia. The SNM renamed this unrecognised territory Somaliland, and selected its leader, Abdirahman Ahmed Ali Tuur, as president.

In September 1991, serious fighting broke out in Mogadishu, which continued in the following months and spread throughout the country. More than 20,000 people were killed or injured by the end of the year. These wars led to the destruction of Somalia's agriculture, which in turn led to starvation in large parts of the country.

The international community began to send food supplies to halt the starvation, but vast amounts of food were hijacked and taken to local clan leaders, who routinely exchanged it with other countries for weapons. An estimated 80 per cent of this food was stolen. These factors led to even more starvation, from which an estimated 300,000 people died and another 1.5 million people suffered between 1991 and 1992. In July 1992, after a ceasefire between the opposing clan factions, the UN sent fifty military observers to oversee the food's distribution.

Somalia intervention – 1991 to 1992

By October 1991, the UN estimated that 4.5 million Somalis were on the brink of starving to death. Under international pressure, the warring factions, including Aidid, agreed to a ceasefire, allowing UN observers to enter the country and organise a humanitarian effort. In April 1992 the UN humanitarian effort, known as Operation Provide Relief, arrived in Somalia. However, the undertaking proved to be extremely difficult as various Somali militias disregarded the ceasefire and engaged in extensive fighting as well as in large-scale hijacking and looting of international food convoys.

US President George H.W. Bush, in his last weeks in office, proposed to the UN that American combat troops be sent to Somalia to protect aid workers. The UN accepted this proposal, adopted as its Resolution 794, and on 9 December 1992 a force of about 25,000 US troops began to arrive in the country.

UN Mission Shift – March 1993

In March 1993, the UN Secretary-General, Boutros Boutros-Ghali, submitted to the UN Security Council his recommendations for effecting the transition from the Unified Task Force (UNITAF) to a more robust role to ensure humanitarian supplies under United Nations Operation In Somalia II (UNOSOM II). He indicated that at the Conference on National Reconciliation in Somalia, held in March 1993, in Addis Ababa, Ethiopia, all fifteen Somali parties had agreed to terms set out to restore peace and democracy.

Yet, by May it had become clear that, although a signatory to the March agreement, Mohamed Farrah Aidid's faction would not co-operate in its implementation.

Operation Restore Hope, Summer 1992–Spring 1995

Operation Restore Hope saw the US assuming the unified command of a more robust UN aid protection mission in accordance with its Resolution 794. The US Marine Corps landed the 15th Marine Expeditionary Company in Mogadishu in December 1992 and, with elements of 1st Battalion, 7th Marines, and 3rd Battalion, 11th Marines, secured nearly a third of the city, the port and airport facilities within two weeks, with the intent to facilitate airlifted humanitarian supplies.

HMLA-369 (Helicopter Marine Light Assault 369) of Marine Aircraft Group 39, 3rd Marine Aircraft Wing, 9th Marines; and the 1st Battalion, 7th Marines, quickly secured routes to Baidoa, Balidogle and Kismayo, then were reinforced by the 3rd Assault Amphibian Battalion and the US Army's 10th Mountain Division.

The military operation was beset with difficulties from the start. The lack of a national Somali leadership, as well as the daily mayhem in the streets of

Mogadishu, bedevilled the attempts to improve security. Unsatisfied with the results, the new US president, Bill Clinton, ordered the number of US troops be reduced.

The US intervention would culminate in the so-called Battle of Mogadishu on 3–4 October 1993 in which eighteen US soldiers and hundreds of Somali militia fighters and civilians were killed.

US Situation Deteriorating – June 1993

By June 1993, only 1,200 American combat soldiers remained in Somalia, aided by troops from twenty-eight other countries including Australia acting under the authority of the UN. The already unstable situation took a turn for the worse that month when twenty-four Pakistani soldiers were ambushed and killed while inspecting a weapons storage facility. The UN unofficially blamed Aidid's militia and passed a resolution calling for the apprehension of those responsible for the massacre.

In support of the US's virtual invasion of Somalia, the Australian Government – which had after the Second World War supported the US in its offshore wars of dominance in Palestine/Israel, Korea, Vietnam, Iraq and Afghanistan – now agreed to provide elite Australian SAS soldier resources for gathering intelligence on Somali irregular clan forces movements. This operation was co-ordinated by US CIA and Australian DIO commanders on board a US Navy aircraft carrier anchored off the coast of Somalia.

For security reasons no real names of any people encountered during this operation are used. The locations and timing are accurate to the best knowledge of the writer, who was advised by a participant who was there.

Approval of Intelligence-Gathering Operations – Somalia

On 8 September 1993, the US Embassy Consul in Canberra visited the Australian Minister of Defence (MOD) at Parliament House and through co-ordinated meetings with the Minister, Defence Chief, Australian Intelligence and Security Service Head (ASIS) and the Defence Intelligence Organisation Head (DIO), an agreement was reached whereby SAS forces could be engaged in the Somalia theatre of operations under the direct command of the US Defence Department.

As in the case of the first Iraq War, covert SAS operations under US command were sanctioned. In order that complete security and unanimity of the DIO operation and its SAS operatives was maintained, no cross-bench Federal Government Defence Intelligence Committee would be notified or apprised of the ministerial approval to proceed with providing the SAS resources.

Risk assessment of the mission success or failure options for:

- Timing for mobilisation stages (team selection – single-point DIO co-ordination of activities – transfers – interfaces – supply – transport options – etc).
- Attributes such as which military arm or contractor resources where the best skill sets are located and available immediately.
- Political deniability and budget off record.
- Operational equipment and proposed duration.
- Interfaces with the US command.
- Reporting and communications protocols.
- Key mission objectives on the ground.
- Ramifications in the case of capture or death.

DIO Commander Coen (RAN) had again been delegated to overall co-ordinate the SAS resource requirements using experienced specialist SAS contractor personnel that were permanently on standby for such missions. The Military Chief would mobilise the regular army SAS personnel. Strategically, the requirements were for well-trained and experienced surveillance personnel with HALO (high altitude, low opening) sky diving training who could ride a rough-terrain motorcycle while defending themselves in a hostile landscape – a very high-risk mission with only a 30 per cent chance of success let alone survival.

The US Consul provided via his Defence Attaché a detailed briefing to the Minister of Defence (MOD), DIO Director and Military Chief on timeline and what resources the US would provide for equipment, reporting, mobilisation, ingress and egress. It became apparent to the MOD that the US were in quite a pickle in Somalia and requested confirmation of this mission as a high priority.

Not that Australia could ever say no to the US Government without being threatened with punitive action such as a trade embargo, sanctions, increases in loans or removal of regional military support, etc.

DIO Specialist Team Selection – 12 September

The DIO, for the purpose of plausible deniability, drew from existing Australian military companies, including several retired but on standby ex-SAS military contractor personnel with special skills. These specialists were Spider, Brute, Doc and Rat.

The missions' two squads were made up of the following personnel:

A. Mission leader in the field and squad Alpha leader – Major Pete (Spider)
  • Second in command of squad Alpha – Sergeant Alex (Doc)
  • Six regular army SAS soldiers
B. Mission second in command in the field and squad Bravo leader – Sergeant Major Tony (Brute)
  • Second in command of squad Bravo – Warrant Officer Aims (Rat)
  • Six regular army SAS soldiers

Somalia SAS Mission Brief Approved to Go Ahead – 13 September

On 13 September, the US Consul returned to Government House with a US Pentagon response that the operation was a 'go' and that Australia must now immediately make preparations. The Minister of Defence officially signed off on a Joint Co-operation Memorandum for executing the mission and informed the DIO and Chief of the Military on 13 September, officially appointing Commander Coen of DIO as the interface between the various services and Government (MOD). Commander Coen was then tasked to place the words 'Top Secret' and 'Priority' on the cover of the Joint Co-operation Memorandum and only three hard copies of the signed document were made.

He then arranged to have removed and destroyed all other working papers and computer files from all departments involved in the drafting. That left one original copy for the CIA Chief, one original copy for the MOD minister and the third original copy for the DIO Head.

The MOD and the DIO Heads discussed the details of operation feasibility and resource functionality for sending a small compact intelligence gathering team into Somalia, as outlined in the US briefing meeting. This type of operation was not new for the SAS and with good communications either way it should succeed. If it failed due to discovery by the Somalis then there would be a news blackout due to the covert nature of the operation – as usual. Hence, there would only be the operatives deployed, who understood the possibility of the one-way nature of this sort of operation:

Risk assessment of the mission success or failure options for:

  • Timing for mobilisation stages (team selection).
  • Single-point DIO co-ordination.
  • Direct US Navy command of infield locations, activities, transfers, supply and transport options, etc).
  • Ingress and egress of the proposed eight-man specialist intelligence teams.

- Attributes such as which military arm or contractor resources where the best skill sets are located and available immediately.
- Political deniability and budget off record.
- Operational equipment supplied by the USA.
- Proposed mission duration being ten days and nights.
- Reporting and communications protocols.
- Key mission objectives on the ground.
- Ramifications in the case of capture or death.

DIO Contact to Mobilise Mission Resources – 14 September

The four contractors were alerted to immediately report by phone message to their DIO contact. Each of them knew that the next call they made to the DIO would be serious business and, as usual, they must tell no one and report in *now*. Air tickets and land transport had already been arranged for them to pick up at their local airport to come to Sydney DIO office for a briefing ASAP. So, no matter where they were or what they were doing at the time, they had to drop everything and *go*.

On arrival at the DIO offices in Sydney, the four contractors were ushered into a secure conference room, where an orderly introduced the four to the civilian-clothed regular army SAS soldiers selected by MOD for the mission. No one had been informed on what the mission was about or where it was located and they were not introduced to each other by name; this was not a social occasion.

Commander Coen arrived after the orderly had confirmed that all personnel were present and correct, and he introduced himself in his usual convivial way to all present. He then asked if there was anything holding any of them from proceeding with a risky mission lasting a couple of weeks or more at the maximum (to Spider, this meant the duration was wide open and unknown to DIO).

The room fell silent while Commander Coen waited for any request for being dismissed. Not one warrior spoke up and the air became electric with anticipation of the mission brief. Commander Coen then called into the conference room the US Defence Attaché, who was not named. He was not introduced to the SAS soldiers in the room but did provide a detailed briefing previously given to the Minister of Defence (MOD), DIO Director and Military Chief, including:

- Timeline for the mission.
- What US resources the US would provide for equipment.

- Mandatory reporting.
- Aerial mobilisation for ingress by HALO jump at high altitude.
- Proposed land egress (TBA).
- Objectives of the mission.
- Confirmation the zone of contact was active and liable to complicate things.

On completion of the briefing by the US Defence Attaché, he promptly closed his file folder, nodded to the commander and left the room without taking any questions or exchanging niceties. Commander Coen then handed the briefing over to the transport administrator, a tall olive-skinned woman with coal black hair, flashing eyes and sharply dressed in a naval lieutenant uniform. As all the soldiers were dressed in civilian casual clothes no saluting was needed.

Apparently, the transport administrator had been given all their names and had temporary passports with their photos already inserted, along with a copy of orders to the air force to fly all of them to Mauritius using an unmarked charter aircraft. The lieutenant crisply read out the following instructions:

I.   On arrival in Mauritius, you are simply tourists.
II. A hotel has been booked and a minibus will pick you up at the airport terminal and deliver you there.
III. On arrival at the hotel a US Embassy representative will meet you in the foyer and hand you the keys to your adjoining, twin-share rooms, where you will receive room service and remain until notified otherwise.
IV. At a time to be determined, you will be notified that you all have been checked out of the hotel by the same US Embassy representative.
V.   There will be transport provided to the airport, where you will be covertly flown out of Mauritius on a US Navy aircraft; destination will be advised once out of Mauritius airspace.
VI. On arrival at your destination, you will be handed over to the US commander, who will provide all kit and equipment for your mission, including the most current status follow-up briefing.
VII. Mobilisation arrangements will be made clear immediately after that.

She then told them to stand, leave nothing behind and beckoned them to follow. She escorted all of them by the stairwell down three floors to the basement car park and curtly handed them off to a transport driver, who motioned for them to get aboard. Then, satisfied her job was done, and without a word, she about-turned and left.

Chapter 31

DIO Contact to Mobilise Mission Resources – 15 September

The bus took them through heavy traffic south of Sydney to the official vehicles parking bay at Kingsford Smith Airport's departure terminal. The driver got out and stood on the pavement at the open door, counted them off the bus and checked that they each had their documentation. An air force officer walked up and took over from the driver and politely asked them to stay close and follow him, which they did as there was nothing else for them to do.

He led them into the departure terminal, through a door that said 'airport staff only', where an X-ray machine and security officers stood waiting for airport workers to pass through. The air force officer appeared to know his way around and just showed his ID card, whereby they were allowed to pass through security without any checks.

They went through a couple more doors, a luggage loading hall and out the side of the building, where a sleek-looking, glossy white, seventy-two-seat private jet was parked. A male air force pilot and female officer stood at the foot of the steps at the front, and Spider felt a bit like royalty with this personal attention. They were greeted with smiles and ushered to their seats, with the rest of the plane left half empty.

When the door closed, they all really felt that this was the point of no return – they were committed.

The aircraft's engines began to whine and then rolled forward while at the same time the female officer acting as the hostess gave them the usual safety demonstration and made sure they were good little boys with seat belt and seat upright checks. This flight would take them all the way over the Indian Ocean for about ten hours.

They were served non-alcoholic refreshments and later in the flight they had a hot dinner. One thing Spider did notice was there was no friendly banter or questions from the air force officer-cum-hostess; she kept to herself and was somewhat formal in her manner. There was no entertainment such as movies or music for passenger distraction.

No one got any sleep, they just chatted quietly or rested looking up at the ceiling of the cabin. That's the worst thing about mobilising for covert operations – the periods of boredom followed by periods of downright chilling fear. Close to the Madagascar coast the weather turned from a smooth flight into a roller coaster ride as they descended through tropical clouds. They were instructed to tighten their seat belts and raise the seat backs and tables.

The aircraft crossed the Australian continent direct from Sydney on the east coast to Perth airport on the west coast, some 3,000 miles, where it refuelled. They were instructed to sit tight and not move about the cabin. The aircrew exited without a word and another crew entered the cabin once the refuelling was completed. The pilots were dressed in civilian airline uniforms and silently took command of the aircraft for the even longer transit directly west across the Indian Ocean to Madagascar. In all, they would be on board the aircraft for around twenty hours.

They all breathed a pensive sigh of relief as the plane touched down and taxied toward the arrivals terminal.

The air force officer-cum-hostess stood up and told them to have their arrival papers ready as they would be going through an immigration checkpoint and then escorted to a waiting bus. Like good little school boys, they followed her instructions to the letter as nobody wanted any hiccups at this point. They were guided to the arrivals door and she said, 'Good luck chaps,' about-turned and headed back to the jet without looking back.

The staff in the terminal handled them the same as any other tourists arriving but didn't question their lack of baggage. Apparently, they were expected and the staff had probably been paid off to let them through unchallenged. Out in the reception area a swarthy Indian gent held a placard with Spider's name on it, which shocked him a bit as he rarely used his real name. He went over to the Indian and pointed at the placard. The Indian looked at him, nodded and smiled broadly, then said that he had a bus waiting outside to take all of them to a hotel. Spider waved his hand at the crew of soldiers, who simply lined up and followed like lambs to the slaughter.

They arrived at the hotel, which was on the edge of town. It was not the poshest joint and the room service meals were on par with a Malay tucker stall out in the boondocks. It didn't kill them but Spider wondered if they would end up with the trots and fuck up the operation right then and there. They left most of the tucker for the cat sitting on the windowsill to eat and get the shits.

Several hours later they were all lazing on the beds fully dressed when a bang on the room door shook them out of their daydreaming about night things in the middle of the afternoon, good tucker and their confinement in these shitty rooms without air conditioning. A well-tanned gent in a safari suit stood outside the door with his fist ready to bang on the door a second time when Brute jerked it open and grunted 'What the fuck do you want pal?'.

With a smirk on his lips, the visitor stepped past Brute as if he owned the place and closed the door behind him with a kick of his foot.

Brute was thinking, ignorant prick.

He looked around the room, walked over to the next adjoining room door and looked in. Satisfied that everyone was there and accounted for, he then asked 'Who's in charge of you Jarheads?'.

Spider was not amused and stepped up to this intruder and said sharply at nose-to-nose distance 'I fucking am mate, and who the fucking hell are you?'.

There was a pregnant pause and a deathly silence as each soldier bristled on alert. The smirk on the man's face changed to a jaw drop and he muttered 'US Consulate Military Attaché here to escort you guys to the airport for mobilisation to Somalia theatre of operations'.

Spider smiled at him, turned his back on the Yankee dick-brain and signalled with his hand for his two teams to round up and move out. All soldiers moved rapidly, grabbed their minimal belongings and marshalled into the same room ready to leave.

It took less than five minutes for the SAS soldiers in civilian clothes to head down the two flights of stairs, across the lobby and out into the street, where a white bus with tinted windows was parked.

The door swung open and without a word they climbed in in single file. They all knew this drill from past operations so nobody spoke until the door shut, leaving the Military Attaché outside on the footpath. The driver was dressed in US Marines dress uniform. He looked around to see if they were all sitting, before he gunned the engine and moved into the crowded streets of cars, trucks, buses, motorbikes and people all meshed together.

Brute looked across the aisle in the bus at his leader and spoke 'You wanna know something Spider, I was ready to punch that fucker's lights out when he called us Jarheads'.

'Sure glad you didn't mate but that silly cunt doesn't know any better. Anyhow, it's just US military slang for a Marine.'

The bus stopped briefly at a side gate into the airport, then drove about a mile inside the security fencing to a remote hangar, where an unmarked white passenger jet was parked with its door and steps open for business. Brute was out of the bus first and walked over to the plane, up the stairs and spoke to one of the pilots.

He came back to the bus and informed them their next holiday location would be Mogadishu Airport in Somalia. They all climbed out of the bus, took one last breath, looked at the arse end of this airport and boarded the aircraft.

The co-pilot ignored them, raised the steps and locked the door, then went back to the cockpit and joined the pilot for pre-flight checks and engine run-up, followed by the brakes coming off and rolling out onto the taxiway. Ten minutes later they were holding at the end of the runway for take-off clearance and then off they went.

After reaching climb altitude, the co-pilot came back and announced that they should stay seated as much as possible. The flight would take four hours, toilets were at the rear and the galley had refreshments. At least there was cold turkey and salad sandwiches with black coffee, but there was no hostess or in-flight movies. Most of them laid the seats back and got a few hours' sleep. Some chatted socially but the air was tense.

The sun was beginning to rise over Mogadishu airport as the aircraft began a direct instrument approach. The female pilot called out to them to belt up as they were about to land and that their helicopter transportation had been arranged for when they disembarked.

Sure enough, the air taxi and welcoming party was there waiting just for them as soon as they descended down the half-dozen steps and an army cordon of soldiers and vehicles surrounded the jet. Apparently, the airport was receiving gun fire from Somali rebels on the perimeter.

Lovely of them to provide a reception volley, Spider thought as he motioned his team to keep their melons down and head for the nearby CH-47 Chinook twin-rotor helicopter that was warmed up and ready to go. They were escorted closely by armed Marines until on board, with a M60 waist gunner now cocking his weapon ready for the precarious ride away from the airfield and over the water.

Brute peered out of the open hatch as they climbed and swung away, concerned that a blast of fire could come from the rebels on the ground at any moment. He was relieved to see several Black Hawk helicopters zooming along the fence line to suppress enemy ground fire.

Australian SAS Briefing Aboard a US Aircraft Carrier – 16 September

Two squads of eight Australian SAS soldiers had been flown offshore and aboard a US aircraft carrier. They were rushed below decks by navy crewmen and kitted out with gear to look like local Somalis, including brown face and hand make-up, turbans and clothing. Then they were briefed on their intelligence-gathering mission on a lower deck space by a US Army colonel with no name, which was as follows:

1. This is a short, ten-day plus covert operations mission.
2. Air drop both teams from high level, unseen, into the north-western region of Somalia.

3. Topographical maps are provided showing intended landing zones and militia tribal areas.
4. Communications will be via satellite phones and solely with your DIO commander on board the carrier.
5. Target observations are to cover size and direction of Somali militia movements heading in the direction of Mogadishu city.
6. Send in photos with GPS positions and add explanatory text.
7. Extraction will be arranged by either road or helicopter depending on US operational requirements on the day.
8. Ten days of rations will be provided along with camouflaged Yamaha motorbikes with long-range fuel tanks.
9. Somalis are dark skinned and wear a variety of robes with head covering. The squads will prepare to mobilise wearing similar clothing and skin make-up.
10. Getting caught will be terminal and you all will be on your own until extracted.

They were each provided with:

- Somali traditional clothing
- Skin make-up to match local colour tones
- Hand-held GPS communications unit
- Tactical Z-Tac throat mic radio with earpiece and spare batteries
- Portable sat-com radio
- Area maps and aerial photos
- Weather forecast for next ten days
- Reporting schedule, formats and details
- Instructions for HALO jump ingress and with land transport egress to be confirmed
- HALO jumpsuit, face mask with air cylinder
- Tourist-type backpacks complete with:
  o Shade over sheet, camouflage net
  o Food rations
  o Water canteens, bladder type
  o First aid kits
  o Small coils of wire and string
  o Wire cutting pliers
  o Folding spade
  o Basic tool kit

Weapons including:

- .45 Colt shoulder-holstered side arm with two extra loaded magazines
- 1,000 rounds of AK-47 ammunition
- One used AK-47 each
- Six UN-type hand grenades
- One pair of ranging binoculars
- Four smoke grenades
- Machete with leather scabbard

Local transport:

- On two pallets, eight shared Yamaha four-stroke motorcycles, fuelled, camouflaged to look well used plus small tool kits
- Fuel, rations and water – All packaged and supplied on the bike pallet for a ten-day-and-night mission.

Spider huddled with his two squads: 'We will be informed once our helicopter transport staging is ready,' he told them.

After being dismissed from the briefing they were escorted away below decks (one can get lost down there) to freshen up and eat. In one corner Spider motioned over the two leaders with whom he had worked in the past in order to fill in the gaps not provided in the briefings so far. He explained:

1. According to the topographical maps and regional information they had been issued, the terrain would mostly be pretty flat, undulating and dusty with not much cover.
2. Extreme caution was needed as many Somalis were armed to the teeth. They should not be taken on as there were too many.
3. Each would operate independently and must communicate twice daily with the others to ensure operation integrity and request backup.
4. The US expected them to operate a fair distance apart, but as there would be no support if the shit hit the fan the teams should not be more than 10 miles apart.
5. Due to previous experience with the US not providing extraction, a plan 'B' must be available and this would be worked on before leaving the carrier.
6. The drop would be a HALO jump from about 30,000ft, so everyone must make sure they had cross-checked the jumpsuits and breathing masks.

7. The motorbikes would be dropped in two separate crates, including survival rations and tools as needed for each team, so they should keep an eye out for them as the mission would be a bust if they were lost or destroyed. Spider then arranged to have chemical glow sticks attached to the top side of the pallets so they all could spot them on the way to the ground.

8. Each warrior must jump with Z-Tac throat mic and earpiece switched on, with weapons and ammunition plus maps strapped tight.

9. Each must, once on the ground, sort out the bikes (two men per bike), share out the ration packs, check for injuries (disastrous to the mission) and confirm all 'go'.

10. Leaders must share reports on landing their status and GPS location before moving out.

11. If the landing required backup or plan changes, that would be the time to discuss using the satellite phone.

12. If possible the jumpsuits, parachutes and bike crates should be either burned or buried. They must not be found easily.

13. If anyone looked like being caught, were followed or became concerned about anything, they should use the satellite phone to call Spider or vice versa so changes and support could be co-ordinated on the run.

Mission Mobilisation from Carrier – 19 September

On 19 September, the two Australian SAS squads made up of eight men each were ushered up to assemble on the aircraft maintenance deck and suited up ready to go. They cross-checked each other, then the Yamaha trail bikes, spare fuel in rubber tanks and that the bikes would start. Then they counted out the ten days of rations per soldier.

The teams watched as the US naval crew strapped the rations, fuel and bikes down onto the crates with netting, slings and parachute HALO jump packs tightly fastened on top with the glow sticks tied on. The bike and ration crates were then taken on a forklift, the SAS teams following behind, where they were all martialled onto the large aircraft lift. They rose to the upper deck level of the carrier and were directed over to a CH-47 Chinook helicopter by one of the flight deck crew.

All aboard and strapped in to the satisfaction of both flight deck crew and helicopter loadmaster, the chopper started up, lifted to a hover momentarily and then took off sideways away from the flight deck. Once clear, the chopper dropped to about 100ft above the water and began skimming low over the Indian Ocean for about 30 miles until it reached the Somali coastline, where they could see the city of Mogadishu and to its south the main airport where the chopper was heading.

The Chinook lined up and flew in a hover over the main runway as if taxiing on it and then turned off and landed wheels down about 50 yards away from a Boeing C-17 Globemaster aircraft. A forklift arrived by the time they all had alighted from the chopper and the C-17 aircrew directed them to board the very large cargo plane by the side door entry while the crates were loaded by the rear ramp. The aircrew from the chopper assisted the Globemaster aircrew with loading the two bike pallets up into the tail ramp.

Airlift and HALO Jump into Somalia – 19 September

With the pallets now strapped firmly down in the cargo bay and all the SAS warriors strapped in the canvas side seating with their backpacks held firmly between their knees, the aircraft's four jet engines began to spin up. Fifteen minutes later they were speeding along the main runway and climbing up over the unknown and unfriendly Somali countryside. The plane headed over Mogadishu on its initial climb and then headed north inland along the main highway towards Beledweyne, near the southern border of Ethiopia.

Meanwhile, all of them plastered the brown make-up over their faces, hands and arms, tucked the Islamic headwear and traditional shawls inside their jumpsuits for wearing when on the ground to avoid standing out, and then strapped the AK-47s to their side for quick release in case they were spotted on the way down.

The city dwellers may wear pants and tee-shirts but in the countryside it was prudent according to their briefing notes to blend in more traditionally with the head gear, even on a rusty camouflaged motorbike.

When the aircraft levelled out at 32,000ft above Beledweyne, which is about 220km north of Mogadishu, they turned left to head west when over a river and the red (get ready) light was turned on.

It was time for the team to get ready for the HALO jump and follow the bike crates to the ground. The loadmaster came over and advised that it was -52°C outside, so they had better cross-check that their air cylinder valves were fully open and their breathing masks were on tight as the ramp was going to be lowered shortly.

The local barometric pressure was provided for all of them to set the altimeters on their wrists, on their parachute drogue chute automatic releases and the same setting on the bike crates. All the parachutes would then open at the same altitude steps all the way down, with the final full-size chute opening manually at 7,000ft (provided they monitored their altitude on the way down).

That would give them more control of the last few minutes by gliding so as not to get injured. All the team had completed more than 300 jumps at heights including 30,000, 14,000, 1,000 and 700ft. Spider had no apprehension about their skills on the way down to ground, however, they would all need to learn some new skills when on terra firma among the hostile Somalis.

Mission Day One, Beledweyne – 20 September

Precisely at 00:01 hours on 20 September, with only a first quarter moon to light up the fields below, the green 'go' light came on and the two motorbike pallets were released and shoved over the edge of the open rear ramp by the loadmaster and his crew. Following right behind was the first team and then the second team, with Major Spider in the lead exiting the rear ramp.

The freezing turbulent wind ripped past each warrior and caused them to bunch up in a circle within a few yards of each other so they could see and check that all were present, but also monitor the fall and drogue chute openings at 20,000 and 14,000ft. These would slow the decent so the camouflaged night glider chute could be opened manually without getting ripped apart, which would happen if the fall was too fast. That could injure the sky diver or, worse, get him killed. All the drogue chutes did open at the correct altitudes but naturally caused the sky diver soldiers to separate to wider distances apart and at times lose sight of each other and the bike crate below them in the dark. The only sighting in the air was when one or more of the team momentarily checked their luminous altimeters. Looking down, they could see house and vehicle lighting below them about a mile from the landing areas. These sightings would be useful as points to avoid once each got onto the ground and then under way soon after sun up.

Someone once said of paratroopers, 'death from above'. An apt statement!

Fortunately, the crate chutes were white, more easily to spot in the dark of night, and were round, not rectangular glider-type chutes, which meant they should fall fairly straight down subject to a crosswind affecting them. At about 7,000ft, each warrior pulled the glider release and was sharply halted in his free fall as the chute filled out. They began to manually glide in reducing circles until they hit the ground within 10 yards of the bike crates. Several of the crate straps had come loose when the bike suspensions jerked up and down on impact, but there was no damage except to the crates.

It took over an hour for all of them to secure each of the landing sites, gather up the parachutes and jumpsuits and then bury them about half a metre below ground.

The crates were broken up and the debris disposed of by tossing the bits out over a wide area. It was the best they could do in the dark.

First off the rank was the mandatory satellite call to each other to confirm that all men, communications and bike crates with rations on board had arrived undamaged. Spider made the call to the other leader, Brute, who was just finishing up dispersing the crate timbers and checking his team for camouflage make-up and robes.

Everyone carried an AK-47 with canvas bandoleer full of spare ammo magazines. Spider was thinking how he would have loved to have taken group photos right now, but alas it was not a good idea. Brute began to mobilise his team for the ride, about 10 miles to the east of Spider's group. Both squads checked their Z-Tac radios and then turned away and rode off to predetermined observation points well away from the local villages but in sight of the main highway.

The mission amendments sent by satellite radio from the command post on the carrier read as follows:

Mission amendment
1. Work your way down the west side of the Webi Shabeelle river while monitoring the highway between Beledweyne city and Mogadishu and observe the trending of vehicles and people on foot and small vehicles moving towards the south-west in the direction of Mogadishu [where the fighting between indigent Somalis and US troops was under way. The Americans needed to know if this highway was the main supply route and how many and types of people and vehicles were headed their way].
2. Having reached the junction of the road at Buulobarde town and Ceelbuur town:
   a. Hold your position for twenty-four hours to observe and report on the possible confluence of people and traffic movements and directions.
   b. In addition, as there were rough gravel tracks shown on maps emanating from the west village of Tatyyglow among others, observe and report their movements particularly heading east and onto the highway.
3. After observations completed at the junction of the road at Buulobarde town and Ceelbuur town, proceed west towards Baydhabo City and monitor the highway between Luuq town in the north-west down to Baydhabo City as this also leads into Mogadishu.

Each SAS squad moved into a hide position just off local gravel tracks and carried out their assigned observations, shared their observations and reported an alarming number of large mobile groups armed to the teeth with RPGs and AK-47s plus a number of vehicles mounted with machine guns of various sizes and configurations.

The Skinnys (a popular US military slang description of Somalis because of their physical appearance) were pretty chaotic in their haphazard journey towards Mogadishu and they had barely looked sideways at the purportedly motley group of covert fighters on motorbikes wandering on either side of them some short distance out from the highway. They had covered all points of the compass on all three US amended orders.

At times the Americans didn't respond to their satellite communications, so the two independent squads just carried on until otherwise instructed. Both of the Australian SAS squads were totally oblivious to the failing status of the US incursion into Somalia and the strong rebuke it was receiving from the Somali factions for interfering in their local affairs. The fighting around Mogadishu had intensified and the US was receiving unsustainable losses.

Chapter 32

US Forces Debacle in Mogadishu – August to October

Previously, in late August, a US special operations task force of more than 400 men had flown into Somalia with orders to apprehend Mohamed Farrah Aidid. This force conducted six missions against Aidid's forces over the month of September and succeeded in capturing some of his associates.

On 3 October, the US forces staged a seventh attempt to capture Aidid and his top lieutenants. The objective was the Olympic Hotel in Mogadishu, where the targets were thought to be meeting. The mission, which called for a small assault team of Commandos from the US Army's Delta Force to apprehend targets in the hotel while US Army Rangers guarded the area in the streets around the site, did not go as planned.

The trouble began when one of the Black Hawk helicopters used in the mission was shot down near the hotel. Rushing towards the crash site to rescue the crew, other US troops came under a heavy barrage of fire. A second Black Hawk was shot down less than half an hour later. Hundreds of Somali fighters filled the streets and the US soldiers became trapped.

After seventeen hours of continuous fighting, the surviving US troops were finally rescued by an international force. The battle left eighteen US soldiers dead and eighty-four wounded. On the Somali side, at least 300 Skinnys were wounded, many of them civilians caught in the crossfire. Although the mission was technically successful, with several high-ranking Aidid associates apprehended, it was widely perceived as a failure because of its high cost in American lives.

The bodies of several of the helicopter crew were dragged around the streets of Mogadishu by the Skinnys and decimated, to the horror of the American people.

Australian SAS Operation Ending

Two weeks later it was extraction time as both squads' supply of rations and fuel were critically low and the longer they were exposed to the hordes of fighters heading toward Mogadishu, the more likely some or all of them would be caught up in the conflict and brutally killed. Several urgent satellite sit-rep messages were sent, high priority, to the US commander in charge of their mission on board the carrier.

Spider received the first of several incomprehensible communications in return. He sent another message advising:

> The situation here is highly unstable and likely to become an engagement with overwhelming Somali forces.

The US commander responded with:

> Hold your position at all costs.

This was fucking bullshit and not a solution in their circumstances; they were being written off for expediency! Spider sent him another message:

> Situation terminal and am unable to comply without losing entire Australian SAS team with no tactical result – Require urgent/immediate extraction.

Spider also sent a coded copy to Commander Coen. There was no response from the Americans.

Commander Coen's coded response was direct to Spider one hour later:

> Situation understood. US are beginning a pull out of Somalia and you may end up as collateral damage along with some Somali supporters at their base. Are you able to make a plan B?

Spider responded:

> Will check options and advise.

Alternate Plan 'B' – The South Africa Connection

Spider called his old team of three warriors to his side, Brute, Doc and Rat, then explained the shit position the Yanks had dropped them in.

'God fuck me to tears,' Brute mumbled. 'Are they out to get you Spider after you threatened to shoot a rocket up their stinky fucking arses in Cambodia?'

'Dirty rotten fucking pricks,' Doc said. 'Are we just going to be left here to die by the hand of these skinny bastards?'

Rat asked 'What's our options major? Do you have a plan B?'.

Luckily, anticipating the Americans seeing Australia as a minor puppet state to them, he had considered this eventuality among several scenarios. The most obvious one was to be airlifted out by a US chopper but that one wasn't going to happen, although something along the same lines just might work.

'I might have something Rat. Let me follow up on an old connection.'

'Sure hope it's a good one major or we just maybe fucked for good,' Rat responded.

Major Spider had kept the phone number of a South African Commando regiment commander that he had met at a security conference several years ago in Singapore. After a few beers at the time, they had become bosom buddies. There is only one way to grab the bull by the horns in our business and survive the odds, he figured: call him as he can only say 'no'! A 'maybe' won't cut it right now.

The satellite phone call rang on his end phone and after what seemed like an eternity, he answered in Afrikaans.

'Van Der Maas is hare.'

Spider introduced himself quickly and advised him of their predicament in Somalia. The commander remembered Spider and then told him to wait as he looked up the map on the office wall where they were located. He came back to the phone and said 'I vill call you back, give me your sat-phone number'.

Shit, Spider thought to himself, hope he got my return number as it is twelve digits long.

Several hours later, with most of them spread out in a defensive circle waiting to fend off any Somalis that approached, the satellite phone rang and a stern voice started to propose an airlift solution that would involve a South African Air Force Dakota-type aircraft:

- Flying over Tanzania, landing in Kenyan territory to refuel then onward across the western border of Somalia.
- A once only hit-and-run airlift – no waiting for stragglers.
- This option could get under way tomorrow with the aircraft over Somalia in two days hence.
- They would need an open road or good gravel track to land on and immediately carry on after boarding in the same direction to take off.
- There would not be fuel endurance to circle looking for the location, so a GPS position must pinpoint the road and its condition and direction.

Spider checked with Brute and then confirmed agreement: 'Will locate the landing area and advise GPS co-ordinates ASAP.'

Van Der Maas came back 'Oh, and many thanks. You will owe me at least another beer'.

The call ended as abruptly as it began.

As the plan 'B' option was not authorised by the Americans, who had fundamentally sanctioned them to be left behind, Spider decided not to apprise them of the plan and communications would be silent from then on. As for DIO, they were in no position to assist them, but Spider did advise Commander Coen of the crazy plan 'B' using South African resources and at some considerable risk to their two squads and the South Africans.

Commander Coen responded with:

Will try to get our security agencies personal link with the South African Security Agencies for supporting plan 'B' and their Commandos [the old boy's method of doing things outside of informing official circles].

Meantime, Spider and his squad leaders scanned the maps of the countryside that they had previously crossed for a road or track that would take a Douglas DC-3 landing and take-off. They finally picked out a gravel track between Baydhabo City and Diinsoor village.

Both squads set off in a direct north-westerly direction using the GPS to keep them on course away and from recognisable roads and villages.

They had 100km to go and their fuel was limited and may not get them there. If necessary, they would jog the remainder of the way, leaving their dysfunctional motorbikes out in the bush as burning them would attract attention. When each bike eventually conked out one by one, Rat set about emptying the oil from the crankcase, removed the sparkplugs and put sand in the cylinder head and fuel tank. Then he removed the nuts holding the wheels on, cut all the tyres, visible electrical wiring, throttle and brake cables. This surgical operation continued for the next 50 odd kilometres until all of them were on foot and considering what equipment they could afford to shed and they needed to retain.

There was no plan C, so they consumed what rations they had left, retained the water, weapons and grenades and continued onward with their backpacks abandoned and buried.

At the mid-point on the map there was a river and crossing, which would be a good visual navigation point. Previously they had observed that there had not been much vehicle or people traffic. Judging from the tracks, they had not been made by armed militias, only poor farmers taking their wares towards the city and back.

Arriving visually close to the target track and river crossing, Spider ordered both squads to spread out and carry out a reconnaissance of the targeted landing area. After several hours circling the terrain and finding no close inhabitants or traffic, Brute took the initiative, informing Spider on the throat mic that he was going to reconnoitre the track inspecting the gravel surface for deep ruts and potholes. About a mile-long stretch was identified by Brute as reasonable for landing. He then returned to Spider's position on the south side of the track and marked up the map for the best section to make a landing zone.

After a short discussion with all squad members (as this zone would be the one and only extraction point and salvation for all of them), Spider sent the landing area co-ordinates to Commander Van Der Maas.

Van Der Maas replied one hour later with:

- Confirmed gravel road extraction is a 'go'.
- Specified the date and time for pickup after transition two countries plus refuelling as plausible.
- Aircraft just taking off now.

That message left them at least one and half days to ensure that the track remained secure. They all remained hidden from the locals with all rations gone; water from the river would have to sustain them from now onwards.

Everything now depended on the South Africans, whom Spider had not heard a word from since he had agreed on the airlift, and sent the co-ordinates.

Meantime, each squad headed out across the nearby countryside dumping the equipment bit by bit along the way to the river and where the track crossed it and the GPS position specified for the 60-year-old DC-3 landing area.

After disposal actions they set up a hide position and monitored both directions up and down the track at about the middle of the landing zone. As previously observed, civilian farmers used the road from time to time and were not aware of their presence.

The remainder of the day and night passed without incident and morning brought greater vigilance as the rescue ETA was approaching rapidly. They all watched the sky to their west as well as the track and prepared to make a run for the plane the moment it touched the ground.

Somali Technical Vehicle on Patrol

Mid-morning, several hours before airlift time, Brute heard a vehicle engine humming in the distance and signalled everyone to shut up and listen. It was not a plane but a 4×4 motor vehicle slowly coming down the track from the east. It was a Somali militia technical, as they called it. A Toyota utility truck with a machine gun mounted on a stand in the open-tray back. As the vehicle came about a mile closer, Spider and Brute became concerned that it could arrive in the area when the DC-3 landed, begin an attack and disable the plane or worse, destroying it and their chances of extracting from Somalia forever.

Spider advised Brute that it would have to be taken out as the ETA was too close to leave it wandering about on this track. Brute nodded and took his squad low and fast toward the north side of the track ahead of the Toyota.

Spider and his squad moved on the south side parallel to the track and 50 yards towards the direction of the Toyota and the dust cloud rising behind it.

This action would be a pincer movement placing the Toyota into a crossfire and hopefully taking it out with one barrage. Staggering the alignment of both ambush positions would avoid hitting each other in the exchange of bullets. Spider looked past the oncoming enemy vehicle, now only 150 yards away. With no sign of another vehicle, he held up his arm for all to fire at the same time as the vehicle wouldn't be able to stop and aim before they did their deadly work on neutralising it and the fucking Skinnys.

The vehicle came level with Spider's squad first and he lowered his arm, pointing his hand at the vehicle. All hell broke loose for about ten seconds as their AK-47s opened up with automatic fire and several hand grenades exploded. The vehicle swerved as bullets and shrapnel hit the windscreen and driver, then on the sides and back of the vehicle. The Skinnys couldn't get a shot off from their own deadly machine gun and the 4×4 rolled upside down into the ditch on the north side of the road, whereby both SAS squads moved rapidly forward to finish off any live Skinnys.

There were none alive as the four occupants had been sitting in the front of the utility to keep out of the dust they were throwing up. Spider's team set about removing the enemy's weapons and ammunition so that others couldn't use it on anyone else. The stripped weapons and ammo were buried in the wet sands in the river bank to hopefully rot there until useless.

Then, with their two squads regrouped, they monitored for any new movements in either direction along the track for locals or more 4×4 vehicles. However, the dust had settled and all was quiet once more.

The South African plane's ETA had come and gone and the waiting warriors began to get restless. Nearly an hour later, Rat pricked his ears and told everyone to shut up and listen. He was right, the hum of twin-radial engines got closer and closer and the bird slowly sank towards their position. The SAS warriors rushed toward the track with anticipation as the plane would not stop and wait. It touched down and began bouncing on the gravel until it settled up the track about 200 yards away from them. This was the fastest run all of them had done since college sports day.

Tossing their AK-47s into the gaping open cargo doorway, they helped each other to grasp their way into the fuselage and lay flat on the floor. The co-pilot watched with interest until the last one of them flopped down.

The senior pilot then released the brakes, Brute pulled the door shut and locked, and with engines roaring even louder, the bird began bouncing from wheel to wheel until it slowly but surely lifted off the gravel track in the same direction that it had landed. It soon climbed high enough for the co-pilot to retract the undercarriage, while the senior pilot turned the bird towards the west by south-west into the afternoon sun.

The flight took a reciprocal course back across the Somalia border and into Kenya, where it refuelled at the regional airport of Wajir, and it then flew south-west over Tanzania to refuel at the small regional airport of Moshi. After a four-hour flight, they had a short rest, used the toilets and bought some fruit from a small vendor with financial assistance from the co-pilot. They walked about the plane to stretch their legs, then without delay it was onward into Mozambique, over the mountains to a regional airstrip located at Tete to refuel again. This time they were ordered by the senior pilot to keep their heads down as their presence here would be seriously questioned and they might all get arrested.

Arrival – South Africa

They finally headed west into South Africa, then tracked via a non-directional radio signal beacon (NDB) into the tower and radar-controlled airspace by a military airport just forty-five minutes over the border from Mozambique. This had been a very long and convoluted journey, with its success to the credit of the senior pilot and co-pilot.

They both seemed to be a bit amused by their cargo of scruffy Australians wearing Somali clothing and with dark skin colour covering their white complexions underneath. They told them that, having seen them near the gravel track, they almost aborted the landing. These pilots appeared to have done previous sorties over their home country's border using the valued and paid contacts they had at the airports where they refuelled, as no questions had been asked about the human cargo on board, nor where they had come from or their intended destination.

It appeared that the Australian DIO had made contact with their opposites in South Africa because there was a civilian passenger aircraft waiting at the terminal as the DC-3 taxied up. Their saviour and friend Commander Van

Der Maas met them as Brute opened the side door and in his inimitably gruff Afrikaans accent directed them to head for the barrack showers on the other side of the hangars and dump all military ordnance into the hands of their quartermaster. In return he would provide all of them with a pair of flying overalls to wear home to Australia.

On the way to the showers, Brute called everyone to attention and told them all that he had something to say: 'Well, you brave bunch of dirty, smelly Somali-looking bastards, I thank you all for your courage and dedication as soldiers, you all did well. I must say something else. As you all know we were shit on by the Americans, which is nothing new considering their history where allies are concerned. However, what was in our favour was the mission's leader on the ground, Major Pete the Spider. Without him, his knowledge, experience, professionalism and contacts we would all be pushing up Somalia daisies right now.'

He then called 'Attention!'. He and the two eight-man SAS warrior squads faced Spider and saluted.

Spider returned the salute through steely blue eyes that were about to overflow as he turned towards the showers. Rat hollered 'Hip-hip hooray ...'

Once cleaned up, and all wearing wrong-size overalls, Spider and the two squads of elite SAS warrior soldiers were met and fed by the base commander, Jope Van Der Maas, and his officers. The Australians owed him and his DC-3 piloting team a great debt. They toasted their valiant and honourable hosts, with all the SAS soldiers hollering a loud 'right on'. Commander Van Der Maas laughed and said that he would definitely collect on it sometime in the future he was sure of that, but a beer would suffice for now.

As the Australians were actually persona non grata in this country, they didn't outstay their welcome and headed for the waiting passenger plane straight after dinner amid handshakes all around. The Australian Embassy representative had been waiting patiently at the chartered civilian plane since the DC-3 had touched down.

Prior to boarding he provided each of them with temporary passports and supplied one-way tickets out of South Africa. The civilian aircraft had been chartered by the Australian Embassy and it flew all of the SAS warriors in daggy overalls, with no baggage, down to Oliver Tambo (formerly Jan Smuts) International Airport in Johannesburg for boarding a connecting flight direct to Perth, Western Australia. That happened to be Spider's home town but all the other members of this mission had to move on to their homes in the other eastern states. For the regular army soldiers, they went directly to their regiments. For the four contract soldiers, maybe it was now time to settle back, feel the sore spots on their aging bodies, fill up a glass and smile about beating the odds once more, but never knowing when or if the next call would come.

US Capitulation and Departure

Several weeks after the Australian SAS warriors' departure home, and the US military's debacle in Mogadishu, US President Bill Clinton committed to withdraw its troops. Within six months, all its forces had departed. The perceived failure of the Somali mission made the US wary of intervening in future African crises.

A year later, in 1994, the UN troops were also withdrawn, leaving the country engulfed in clan warfare.

Love and war do not follow the ordinary rules of life.

Footnote

By 2019 not much had changed in Somalia. One of the most powerful opposition groups known as Al-Shabaab, an Al-Qaeda affiliate, had the capability of attacking commercial government offices and foreign nationals, and had strongholds throughout the country. Al-Shabaab pursues aggressive recruitment for its child soldier campaign and retaliates with violence against communities that refuse to hand over their young ones. Displaced girls and women are sexually assaulted by armed civilians, some being gang raped, and killings are an everyday occurrence without consequence.

The country is plagued with filthy drinking water, poor sanitation, malnutrition and high infant mortality. Diseases are widespread, with malaria, cholera, tuberculosis, measles, leprosy and intestinal illness all preventable. Most western governments have advised their citizens not to travel to Somalia.

Chapter 33

Civilian Operation – Australian Soil

It was the turn of the decade and Major Pete, alias Spider, or now just plain civilian Pete, had thought that he had finally retired after some twenty-five years of SAS operations around the world. He was thankful he had survived but not all of his men had come home. He was currently living the dream just being a civilian lead mechanical engineer, working on mining and hydrocarbon projects within Australia, Africa, the Persian Gulf and South Asia.

Covert Mission: Anti-Terrorist Assignment

The Israeli security service had contacted ASIO requesting assistance regarding an Islamic jihadist attack they were positive would occur on Australian soil. They required an individual with a military special forces background, possibly retired or on reserve, to support their covert agent, who was deep undercover on an anti-terrorist mission and was currently stationed in Perth.

ASIO immediately forwarded the request to the DIO.

The Israeli security service, also known as The Institute, or Mossad, insisted the DIO did not inform the selected Australian individual (agent) of any Mossad connection and he must remain blind regarding the purpose of his engagement.

When their covert agent was confident, and only then, would the local Australian agent be enlightened. This was of the highest security level. The individual must be unknown within the anti-terrorist world and show no outward knowledge of any terrorist investigation.

Original covert contact between the Mossad agent and the Australian support agent should occur using a well-known dating website, which would require ASIO to monitor.

A Simple Assignment Offered

It seems that trouble finds you even if you aren't looking for it. Late in November, it was already feeling like a hot summer had arrived in Perth when Pete received a phone call from the DIO asking him for a favour on behalf of ASIO, which was looking after Australian internal security.

The DIO said this request was for a simple, make contact, have a sniff around and see if you can meet up with a woman of interest in the suburb of Applecross, Perth, his home town.

Major Pete was immediately wary of such a request as the DIO didn't usually expose its current or previous operatives to civilian operations, particularly for other services.

After some cajoling by his former DIO masters and an introduction to the ASIO representative over the phone (no name given), Major Pete understood that:

- This short assignment would only take a couple of days.
- An older gentleman like himself would fit the bill.
- Availability must be immediate.

Major Pete was advised by ASIO that as recently as yesterday they had been notified by Interpol that there had been phone and email contacts from a possible terrorist organisation member and that this link had to be investigated urgently. The target male with a Palestinian passport had tried and failed to get past Singapore immigration without firstly having applied for a visa to enter Australia. This same male withdrew and it was believed that he had headed to Thailand instead, as the Thais did not require a visa for Palestinian citizens to enter their country. Interpol were currently trying to locate this individual.

An ASIO dedicated contact officer was allocated and a direct landline number provided. The now civilian Pete had not been invited to meet anyone and would be required to wing it as no formal instructions could be provided at this early stage of the operation.

In Pete's past, military operations never mobilised so quickly and without a proper briefing. His instructions were not to raise suspicions with the lady in Applecross or the entire developing game would be up and all contacts might well evaporate.

From the very brief verbal information offered, apparently the lady of interest, who had the username Maybe01 on a well-known dating website, was looking for a gentleman around her own age of 50 located in Perth for dating and a possible longer-term relationship.

Pete was currently living and working in Perth. He contacted his employer and took several weeks compassionate leave, stating his mother was ill and needed his support.

Pete quickly created a profile and uploaded it on the same dating website with the username Mandate, giving the following attributes based upon ASIO's understanding of Maybe01's expectations:

- Single healthy gentleman, no baggage.
- Seriously looking for adventure and travel.
- Businessman, age 55 years, seeking ladies aged between 55 to 60 years.
- Specified minimum height, hair, eye and skin colour.
- Well off with own assets.
- Loves wining and dining and spoiling the lady.

There were a few other sweeteners added to indicate that Pete had plenty of money and interests in a business, properties and investments.

He was to open the website, look up the person Maybe01 using the name search and indicate his interest in this lady's profile. Pete's profile and photo were uploaded onto the dating website and he duly received a notification (kiss) from Maybe01. There were several other ladies who also indicated their interest, but Pete gracefully rebutted them with a 'thank you kindly, but no thank you' response.

The ASIO contact was immediately notified by Pete of the live contact and they in turn advised him that ASIO were aware of the contact message and were tracking both her and his computers and mobile phones. Pete then went back to the website and sent a text message in which he offered his name as Pete and gave a mobile phone number for the lady to contact him directly if she was interested in having an initial chat.

He received a phone call from Maybe01 a day later and after about an hour of getting to know you type of chatting she gave her name as Zelda and confirmed that she did indeed live in Applecross (some ladies don't give out their real name or actual suburb). He kept his cool and tried not to show he was excited to get the call.

So far so good; Zelda had called and they were able to set a day and time to meet the next Saturday morning as she worked during the week. All he had to identify her by was a single photo from the dating website.

Zelda agreed to meet him at the Crown Plaza hotel lobby coffee shop in the centre of Perth. She would be wearing a light blue dress and they could discuss arrangements from there.

Time passed quickly as Saturday rapidly rolled around.

It's now or never, Pete thought to himself as civilian stuff was not his thing. He felt a bit exposed as military operations were more familiar. He had nothing much to go on regarding this assignment and had to shut his thoughts down and tried to relax.

ASIO advised Pete to use his own credit card for expenses and keep receipts for later reimbursement so as not to provide a money trail back to them in case this terrorist organisation was smart about checking on these details.

He was given some business cards for a shelf company that ASIO had control of in case he had to explain his business background.

His job title was engineering manager, which he felt well at ease with and capable of playing the role. The phone number was a direct line to his ASIO handler, who would confirm his identity if a call was received asking for or about him.

On first meeting they greeted each other and chatted briefly before he suggested they head to the coffee shop. Once they were seated and had ordered a cup of hot coffee and shared raisin toast with marmalade jam, Pete began to relax. So far so good. They were getting along all right, both relaxed and smiling. His cover story appeared to have been acceptable and Zelda seemed suitably impressed. He was cautious not to ask her too many prying questions but let her talk and hopefully divulge anything useful between the lines.

So far, he had learned:

- What she looked like and that she was a slim and a fit 50-year-old.
- The coffee she liked.
- Her voice and vocabulary showed she was educated.
- She was employed at the local public hospital in the psychology department.

When Pete heard that she was a psychologist, he became more careful about what he said and how he expressed himself. His body language also needed to be held in check. This was going to be a more constrained meeting than he would have imagined. He needed to avoid overthinking the situation and maintain an open and relaxed composure, even though his gut had tightened.

To ease his tensions, he suggested they take a walk along St Georges Terrace and the Swan River waterfront and let the cool breeze relax him physically and mentally. They walked and chatted for the best part of an hour. Finally, Zelda told him she had another appointment and must go. She then asked him if he would like to come over to her place in Applecross for dinner tonight. He smiled sheepishly and accepted – like a lamb to the slaughter. They said their pleasantries and she left, saying 'See you at 7 tonight'.

We blokes are easily beguiled, he thought to himself while heading to his car. At least the greeting, meeting and coffee conversation had gone well enough to extend the contact until tonight.

Into the Night

Pete was punctual, arriving at 7 p.m.. He knew houses in this neighbourhood ran in the 1 to 1.5 million dollar range. She answered his knock with a pleasant 'Good to see you again, please come in'.

'This is a very nice house,' he told her.

'Oh, it's not my house, I just rent it while I am working at the hospital.'

The house was sparsely furnished, with an open lounge and kitchen area, two bedrooms and bathrooms. Adequate for a single resident. There were some remnants of meal preparation still on the kitchen bench top with the smell of lamb and vegetables coming from the electric cook top.

Zelda had prepared the dinner early, including a setting for two at the table. Pete was invited to sit in the lounge while she dished up the food. He apologised that he had not thought to bring a bottle of wine. Zelda smiled and said that was no problem as she didn't drink alcohol. To Pete, a glass of wine was always his preference before dinner, and during, and maybe a cognac for a night cap. Not tonight Peter, he said to himself.

Dinner was simple and allowed them to talk about their backgrounds. Pete stuck to his engineering field as it was factual; leaving out the military side was easy to do. He showed her his business card, which she put to one side as if accepting it as proof of who he was. The conversation then shifted to her past as he had exhausted his.

The meal was finished, dishes dumped into the sink and his glass of water was now emptied. They moved to the lounge corner to continue the conversation she had started. She told him that:

- She had been born a Jew.
- Her name Zelda was the nickname for the feminine Griselda and meant 'dark battle'.
- She was currently married to a Muslim, who was presently in Cairo.

His mind was flashing up serious questions regarding her originally being born a Jew, then a marriage in Egypt to a Muslim. But he guessed stranger things have happened.

Pete again asked her about her husband and his status with her, given that she had invited him to dinner and he was sitting next to her right now. Were they still together, separated or divorced, he thought to himself. Confusing! After some tea and a biscuit, she began to be more serious and explained their relationship. They had met in Cairo, lived together for a short period and then they got married in a mosque according to the Muslim tradition.

Her husband travelled a lot with the United Nations High Commission for Refugees (UNHCR). She had come to Perth with the intent to help her husband set up a practice here before starting work in the hospital. Pete felt uncomfortable with this marital connection and coaxed out of her her husband's profession:

- He was a medical surgeon.
- Born in Jordan.
- Now located in Cairo, Egypt, but wanting to emigrate to Australia.
- He had a sister and brother-in-law living in Jordan. They had a business there.
- He had been Yasser Arafat's doctor.
- He had worked for the UNHCR in Palestinian and Syrian refugee camps.

From what Pete was able to gather, her husband was a member of the Palestinian Liberation Organisation (PLO) and was a close associate of Arafat, the PLO leader. Arafat had co-ordinated the hijacking and blowing up of a number of airliners full of passengers and hostage taking in the Middle East. It occurred to him this husband of hers was highly likely to still have links to Islamic terrorist organisations. Now he could put two and two together!

Her mood had now changed along with the subject. Apparently, in her words, her husband had returned to Egypt (which he knew was a lie) and needed money to buy an air ticket to come to Australia so they could be with each other. There was no mention of why, how, what or where at this point.

That evening, fairly late, she said that she was expecting a phone call from her husband in Egypt and asked him if he would wait around.

Pete shrugged his shoulders in part disinterest and then she offered to put him up for the night in the spare room. He feigned reluctance and then agreed to stay. (He hoped that ASIO would be tapping her mobile phone call as it may add value later.)

Zelda continued to discuss her relationship with her husband as being somewhat separated by his work, their time apart, contact and his limited income. He was expecting her to pay for his living and travel expenses, including currently attempting to travel to Australia. Then she opened up a little more and said that his sister and brother-in-law would be coming to Sydney from Jordan and bringing a lot of money with them for business purposes.

Pete listened intently, nodding from time to time. She continued opening up about her husband having access to Palestinian and Syrian refugee camps and other refugee locations worldwide.

His mind was ticking over fast as his thinking was that this guy might be a link and bag man for a terrorist group, maybe an offshoot of the former PLO. Zelda mentioned that the Jordanian security services may be monitoring her phone and computer as some files had disappeared and she was worried.

Pete said that it was highly unlikely nowadays because her anti-virus software would block any outside access, hoping that she wasn't computer literate enough to call his bluff. He knew full well that ASIO was listening and watching her communications 24/7. But was she right about others spying on her?

Several hours passed and her mobile phone rang around midnight. She clicked on the speaker so Pete could hear the conversation. Whoever was on the other end of the line had a deep voice, perhaps an older man with an Arab-type accent. It was unusual that neither of them exchanged pleasantries, and the subject immediately turned to where he was in Cairo and that he needed money transferred to him for living expenses and a ticket to Sydney.

There was no mention of him coming to Perth to reunite with his wife. She told him that she couldn't send the funds, whereupon he retorted, 'sell your shoes', which Pete later understood to be a typical Arab or Palestinian way of saying 'get the money, no matter what'. The call ended abruptly at that point, still with no pleasantries between the couple.

Emphasis Change to Sydney Location

Zelda persevered with the discussion about her husband's sister's and brother-in-law's imminent arrival in Sydney. Now that Pete was a bit more alert to the subject, he indicated that he had business appointments coming up in Sydney and could meet and greet her in-laws and organise transport and accommodation if needed. She thought about it while making a pot of now very early Sunday morning tea.

Zelda said that she would let him know and that she would be there particularly if her husband was also arriving with them.

Pete was becoming tired and after a couple of sips of the black tea – there was no milk in the almost empty fridge – he decided to head to the spare bedroom and hit the sack. His brain wouldn't let him sleep and as morning daylight showed its rays through the window, he got up, frustrated and still reeling from information overload, and headed for the shower.

When he wandered into the lounge there was no Zelda, so he headed for her bedroom. The door was wide open, the TV was still on and she was lying on the top of the bed covers fully dressed from yesterday. He asked if she was awake and she rolled over onto her side and said that it would be better if he left now and she would phone him later in the morning for a late breakfast.

Pete took the hint, said, see you later, and headed for the front door and down the short pathway to the street to his car and drove home. Driving along the familiar Perth streets he got to thinking. Now that was one weird and strange night, sleeping alone in the spare room. There was something not jiving with this strange fucking woman. His curiosity was certainly running high.

After Pete left, Zelda sat up on the bed and thought to herself, I hope I didn't overdo it last night with too much information, just enough to rouse his interest. I need him to hang around.

She sent a message to her organisation handler and advised that all was proceeding as planned and believed her Aussie agent had taken the bait and was adequate, even though she knew they were both telling each other lies.

At around 10.45 a.m. Pete's phone rang. It was Zelda suggesting they could go for a walk along the Swan River waterfront and find a little café where they could have breakfast. He was hungry as hell so he didn't procrastinate but drove quickly to the waterfront, parked and met her as she waited near a jetty entrance.

They walked to the café without a word, although they looked at each other a couple of times and she gave him a pleasant smile. They finished their breakfast and coffees and she leant forward and said that she would call him in a few days about the Sydney arrival time and flight number. She said that she would be there at the gate waiting for her in-laws, but there was no mention if her husband was coming or not.

He walked her to the car, where she gave him a hug and whispered in his ear 'Thank you'.

He responded 'Thank you, too'. But he wasn't sure for what.

She climbed in, and as she drove away he took out his pen and wrote down the car registration, make and model details. Oh well, no roses without thorns.

He went for a walk around the block first and then in reverse to spot any tail, and then along the waterfront, where only a few people were walking their dogs.

It was easy to see if a car or person was within 100 yards. If someone was watching him from afar, he took a turn around the boat moorings and buildings and stood in a hotel entrance around back and waited thirty minutes in case someone got inquisitive enough to follow him. None did, so maybe she was alone in this town?

He headed back to his car and drove circuitously for a while just in case he was being tailed.

He wandered into his house. There was no message light on the phone, the security system was still on and no unlawful entry was detected. He guessed that he was home free, although very tired from a lack of sleep the previous night. A dose of paranoia is good for one's personal security. He sat at the small desk and jotted down some notes about this strange encounter before he got to thinking it was some sort of dream or a not-so-clever set-up or scam.

He decided to give his ASIO contact a call and briefly discussed some key points from the meeting with Zelda. They had not been aware of any Jordanian security service involvement but would check their sources as well as Interpol in Cairo as the last information on the husband's movements was that he was supposed to be in Thailand.

Chapter 34

The Plot Thickens

Just like in the movies, Pete's mobile phone rang the moment he fell asleep on the couch, causing him to jump up in surprise with his heart beginning to pound. Focusing his bleary eyes, he saw the caller was the ASIO contact number so he answered a bit groggily 'Hello this is Pete, who am I speaking with?'

There was a pause and then a woman spoke.

'Major Pete alias Spider I presume?' He blinked as this information had not been given to ASIO as Spider was a DIO security code name. Damn, he thought, has my past been compromised?

This lady was short and sharp in conversing with him. He had heard that voice once before but couldn't pick out where exactly? He spoke sharply back:'Who the hell are you and where did you get that tag from?'

He heard a laugh and then she explained that she was the naval lieutenant that he and his team had met at the DIO offices in Sydney some years ago. She had left the navy and later joined ASIO. She saw his army photo on the file and asked to be put on the contact desk (the person on the desk varies by shift, no personal name or details given).

Although he felt his temperature rise and hair curl up on the back of his neck, he held off any chit-chat and simply asked the reason for the call. She read out a message they had received from Interpol:

- Subject with the same face features and height has shown up at the Thai airport check-in with a Qantas flight ticket and no baggage.
- Egyptian passport presented to immigration including a tourist visa for entry into Australia.
- He is currently in the departures area with a four-hour wait until the flight leaves.
- This flight transits in Jakarta, Indonesia, for several hours, then flies directly to Sydney.
- Do we apprehend or observe until he has boarded the flight?

Shit, that was quick he thought; Zelda had only received a contact phone call from her husband just after midnight the previous evening. His mind went into overdrive with questions:

- Where did the phone call to Zelda emanate from?
- Can we have a copy of the Jordanian and Egyptian passport photos?
- Is there any Thai airport CCTV on him that can be downloaded and sent over ASAP?
- In the boarding lounge, did he connect up with anyone, say a woman and a man?
- Were these parties also travelling on the same flight to Sydney?

His curt ex-navy lady from ASIO wasn't able to offer any more details than what she had read out to him. He spat out 'This is not enough to feed my cat with. Find out if Zelda has bought a ticket and headed to the airport aiming for Sydney? And if not, she will; she has to be there waiting for the targets as soon as they get through the exit gate. We could lose them all if you lot can't point them out on arrival and have them individually followed in case they split up.'

Christ this could fuck up right this minute, he thought, then said to her 'Let me know if I should get involved and travel to Sydney to link up with Zelda. If so, I need a one-way ticket Perth to Sydney and just in case I'm packing my bag as I speak.'

Two hours after the ASIO call, Zelda phoned. The background noise sounded like she was at an airport, probably Perth. She asked him if and when he would be heading to Sydney on business. He told her that there was a loose appointment pending a call from his office for a marketing meeting, but probably tomorrow, which was Monday.

She answered 'I wondered if you might be in Sydney tomorrow morning at 11.40 a.m. as my family will be arriving from overseas'.

Pete had already suggested that he would arrange accommodation for them in his name whenever they arrived in Sydney. She gushed 'Could you please do the accommodation thing as they will be very tired? Just two rooms.'

He paused and then agreed in a thoughtful voice 'I believe I can be there but it will cost you a coffee'.

She then offered to meet him in the Sydney airport international arrivals waiting area at 10 a.m., at the coffee shop nearest to the arrivals gate. 'No problem,' he answered, 'and I can provide a company-chartered limousine or minibus if you like.'

She opted for the minibus and offered to pay but he said that he would be using it to get to the airport on the company budget anyway. He let the conversation dry up after that, even though there were a number of questions he need answered regarding:

- What happens when she greets the family members; should he step forward or backwards?

- Will he show them to the minibus and co-ordinate hotel address?
- Whose names will be on the hotel register as the booking of two rooms in advance was in his company's name?
- How will he maintain contact with this group – how does he fit in?
- Will ASIO take over surveillance after:
  - CCTV from Thai airport is received.
  - Copies from Thai airport immigration passport and visa check details of at least one of the male travellers.
  - Tracking of the transit connections via Jakarta.
  - Copies of passports and visas for the three travelling guests are received.
  - Confirmation of arrival into Sydney is confirmed at the immigration desk.
  - The arrival event in Sydney airport as ASIO or Border Force officers will have observed the immigration passage, and CCTV videoed the arrival.

Pete was puzzled by the lack of information (intel) from ASIO. Were they so far behind the ball in play or was he being kept in the dark? His ASIO lady phoned him thirty minutes after the first call and advised that there was a business-class ticket to Sydney waiting for him at Perth airport. He just needed to go to the Qantas desk to pick it up. The flight left at 20:10 tonight and he was told to be on it.

She said 'An ASIO representative will be seated next to you who has been briefed and will co-ordinate your activities prior to landing in Sydney. They will separate from you in the arrivals area. You will be on your own from there onward until someone from ASIO links up with you at an opportune moment. That moment will be dictated by the overseas guests' movements and when we can get to you unnoticed. Whether you continue with the relationship with Zelda and her international guests or break away is not currently known, we will have to work on that.'

Pete was not used to this rigmarole as he was normally the one in charge of a military operation once it went live. So, he was now uncomfortable with having blind handlers that he couldn't see or get in touch with on the run. Reliance on these ASIO people in a civilian environment was something new and he didn't intend to get used to it either. In his mind he was either fully in or fully out of this game of cards.

He had packed business suits and ties, enough kit to keep him well dressed for at least one week. He had no idea where his fictitious office was and if there were any live staff in it. He was also getting the feeling that these guests were not stupid, and Zelda wasn't either or she wouldn't have sucked him into this episode in the first place.

Pete had heard that the Palestinians were pretty rough on their own people, let alone him as a foreign agent. However, bringing in a very large amount of US currency by at least one terrorist link would keep him focused for the time being as he really did want to short circuit any terrorist action on Australian soil. This would be the first action event where he did not have any defensive weapons or protection from a support team. He lay back on the couch to try and sleep before heading to Perth airport for the night flight to Sydney, knowing that it would arrive after midnight (what business travellers call the red-eye flight).

It was now boarding time for his four hours plus flight to Sydney and he got to walk down the priority line, with his boarding card indicating seat Row A, window seat A-3. He had to step past seat A-1, which was occupied by an attractive woman in a grey skirt and matching top with white blouse, and tan stockings to match her beach-tanned skin. It was then the memory came flashing back; that coal-black hair, those flashing green eyes. She looked more beautiful than he remembered.

She simply nodded at him as he passed and then ignored him while he settled into the seat and buckled up. Out of the corner of his eye, he checked her out and was astonished to find the same naval officer woman who used to work for the DIO and now with ASIO sitting there all prim and proper. He wondered if she had requested the free first-class flight to Sydney and whether she would retain her standoffish persona that he had witnessed once upon a time.

There weren't many people paying the first-class price for these seats, so they were almost alone up the front of the aircraft. When the plane had reached altitude, seat belt sign was turned off and the sound and feel of the throbbing jet engines settled, she turned without a word and handed him a folder to read. He nodded, lowered the tray table in front of him and began to absorb the contents page after page.

There were photos from the CCTV in Thailand, then Jakarta airport where the three guests had gathered in the transit waiting area.

There was a note with Thai writing in the title at the top, with handwritten text in English stating that the couple's baggage had been placed on board without going through an X-ray check and placed in the cargo pod by someone working at the airport. However, it had been spotted by a security officer on patrol who reported the bypass of customs to his superior. He in turn was observing the movements of Zelda's husband, his sister and brother-in-law from upstairs.

The officer went down to the cargo pod and verified that the luggage belonged to the two travellers, so they decided to X-ray it for explosives. There were none and they reloaded it into the pod believing there was no threat. However, after the flight had departed, they did make a note of a suspicious activity that was eventually linked to a local suspect and forwarded the note to Interpol. The crime agency then forwarded it to ASIO in case there was either contraband or something else that needed further inspection on arrival in Sydney.

The lady next to him waited quietly while he perused all of the documents and when he handed the folder back to her, she smiled and said 'Long time no see Major Pete. I didn't know if you were alive or dead as there was no mission feedback over my desk. I guess its need-to-know stuff for the DIO commander only.'

He nodded thoughtfully as he had no idea what the workings of the DIO offices were about. It was no time for him to reminisce right now, even though he would have loved to have asked her some pointed questions about her career in the navy and DIO, then here right now with ASIO. All he could do was ask if there was any more intelligence data on the now four targets and if there had been a risk assessment based on all of the shared data including his input of recent times in Perth.

She shook her head and shrugged her shoulders. Unfortunately she was just a folder courier who he may never meet again – typical in his job. Time for in-flight dinner and a glass of red wine, then try to sleep for the rest of the flight.

They exited the aircraft having hardly spoken throughout it. She turned at the end of the exit tunnel and handed him the hotel booking details in an envelope that included a separate room on the floor below where their inbound guests would be accommodated, where he would stay before returning to the international arrivals section.

Then she told him that after the guests had come out with their baggage, he should look for a blue minibus waiting near the taxi stand on the ground-floor car park level.

The driver would know where the hotel was and how many passengers. Pete would have to take a taxi separately after the guests had left the airport. He did not have to check in and his room key was in the envelope.

Sydney Airport Arrivals

The rest of Monday morning saw him trying to sleep, taking swigs of whisky from the bar fridge, watching TV news and ordering room service. The night passed slowly with room service hamburger and chips with a pot of tea, broken sleep not helping him relax and an 8 a.m. wake-up alarm not needed as he was already wide awake, showered and dressed in his best business suit.

He was then off to the airport again for the meet-up with Zelda at the coffee shop. She was sitting at a round table eating a fruit muffin, and he wondered if she had taken the same flight from Perth to Sydney as him. He went to the counter and ordered a coffee, then sat opposite her.

They exchanged greetings and he kept the chat between them to helping her with transport from the airport and the hotel rooms, and not much more. If she had anything to share with him about her guests, she wasn't sharing it right now. He said that he would head off before the flight arrived and she met her guests, stating that he had some business things to sort out back in town. She blinked, possibly wondering why he showed no interest in her guests' arrival. She pouted and asked him to please stay with her until the family came out of the customs gate so he could show them to the transport.

The Qantas flight landed about twenty minutes late and was announced on a large screen. The husband's luggage had miraculously, out of thin air, connected with him during the transit stop in Jakarta; he had no baggage with him when arriving at the Thai airport Qantas check-in counter. However, he now collected a large grey zip-up suitcase.

It was opened and checked on arrival by customs in Sydney but nothing out of the ordinary was found; a dead end – well maybe! The luggage belonging to the sister and brother-in-law was X-rayed out in the incoming cargo bay prior to being loaded onto the baggage carousel. Although there appeared to be either a pile of documents or money mixed in with the clothing contents, the customs staff were instructed by some ASIO officers out back to let the luggage go through without scrutiny for passenger collection without further examination.

The luggage was loaded onto a trolley by the brother-in-law, pushed past the Customs officer checking declaration forms and it rolled out of the arrivals gate. Zelda's husband caught up to them ten minutes later just outside the exit doors.

Zelda had been standing at the back, behind the crowd of people greeting the arrivals. She held her position until she saw her husband and then squeezed her way through the human throng and greeted him. Then she greeted his sister and brother-in-law.

Pete remained at the back and waited for Zelda and the trio to push through toward the external sliding doors leading to the car park elevators and then to the ground floor where the blue minibus was waiting at the kerb.

Zelda's introduction was short and sharp 'This is Pete, he helped me book the hotel and transport. He has a company in Sydney.'

Each of them nodded to each other, not a very friendly greeting but it also suited Pete. He followed them down the elevator, pointed out the minibus and then wished them a happy visit to Sydney. He then turned and left them and their baggage with the driver. He assumed that if Zelda wanted to make contact, she would. If not he would be on his way back home to Perth, more likely in tourist, cattle-class, seating.

Happy that he had done his job without any hitches, he jumped a taxi and headed back into town. He got the driver to drop him off at the park down the road from the hotel. From there he could see the reception area and the tourist group alight from the blue minibus, then check in and head for the elevator up to their room.

It was a nice sunny day, so he decided to go for a walk to shake off the up-close-and-personal meeting with possible terrorists. He reflected on their attitude toward his presence as somewhat hostile with not a smile from any of them – including Zelda. He thought she would have at least have had a hug for her husband or in-laws, which would have been the norm for happy typical families that had not seen each other for a long time.

Chapter 35

Tourist Hotel Arrival and Departure

After an hour or so and a nice salad lunch at the edge of the park, he wandered back in the direction of the hotel, making sure he did not bump into the group, just one floor above his room. Up the elevator accompanied by a hotel porter and a young couple, he got off at his floor and found his door.

Entering the room feeling all relaxed and looking forward to a nap, to his surprise there was the same lady passenger who had sat next to him on the flight from Perth, his ASIO pal. She had the TV on and was sitting back lazily on the couch. This was like a James Bond film scenario. He was thinking wishfully of past movies and women spies. She caught the look on his face and immediately dispelled any romantic thoughts. She stood up, straightened her attire, placed her hands on her hips, looked straight into his face and said 'Where the fucking hell have you been?'.

Not the nicest awakening out of his lucid dreams, but very effective in getting him back onto terra firma. He forced a smile and said pertly 'You weren't invited up here and I'm off duty with our guests now upstairs and no doubt tucked in for the rest of the day. End of mission I believe?'

'Not so,' she rasped. Shit, Pete thought, he was getting a chastising for some unstated set of rules that he was not acquainted with. He liked strong women but this one was fiery and it was not clear whose turf he was standing on, or was it on someone's toes? Apparently, the guests had bugged out of their room, baggage and all, and disappeared while he was out enjoying the sun on the park.

The hotel receptionist had called his room as the bill had not been paid. Hell, what a pickle. Was it his fault or should ASIO have monitored the room, listened to conversations, taken photos and followed the guests, even if they all split up in different directions? Fucking hell, what a bunch of ASIO amateur pricks, he thought to himself. However, there was no point saying it to this witch, who was on the war path.

What a fuck up; ASIO had not bugged the room as it was against the law without justifiable evidence and raising a warrant signed by a judge. His guess was that no ASIO personnel were even in the vicinity of the hotel. That is except for this mean arsehole who thought she had the right to spit chips at him.

Where would they go that wasn't covered by a CCTV camera? It had to be to a private residence, motel or hotel as a train station, bus station or airport would be out of the question. He called the manager of the hotel and asked if he had any CCTV cameras around the building. The manager replied 'Yes four, but who are you?'.

He told the manager they were police and they would be down to see what they had recorded today. He and the ASIO lady then rushed out of the room and trotted down the stairs to see the manager. She showed her ASIO ID as Pete had no authority to ask for a glass of water there. The manager went red in the face and obliged her with a brief glance and nod, then motioned them to follow him to his office at the back of the lobby.

There was a safety deposit room where customers could leave their valuables in a large safe, and where a computer screen sat on top of a CCTV video recorder. Eureka! This was what they needed! The manager also had a schematic plan drawing on the hotel wall showing where the cameras and wiring were located, for maintenance purposes Pete figured.

The video recordings were on CDs and they needed to see today's right now. There were three camera positions covering the rear car park and both laneways left and right facing from back to front. The cameras were originally set up to capture car thieves and vagrants trying to break in.

After a bit of complaining, the manager ejected the current disc from the recorder and inserted a fresh one to keep the recording working. In his office, he had a laptop computer with a disk drive. Pete requested he play the segment from one of the laneways at the side of the building as there were no cameras out front. This was going to take a lot of time, so he asked if he could either skip hours or run the disk at fast speed until they could get to the approximate hour when the guests departed.

The best part of the security camera software was that he could have all the camera recordings shown on one split screen. They spent nearly an hour visually scanning the screen until they saw several vans moving into and out of the lanes and across the blind front of the hotel. Some stopped and some didn't.

Pete requested several reruns of the vans until one van was a lot slower at crossing the front of the building as seen by the left and then the right cameras. They then looked at the rear car park footage. This same van had been parked there for over an hour with someone sitting inside smoking cigarettes before it eventually started up and moved down the right-side lane towards the front of the building.

Pete's not-so-friendly ASIO lady had picked up on what he was trying to achieve and wrote down the registration number of the van from when it had entered the lane towards the car park. The timing was thirty minutes after the group had arrived at the hotel. The number plates could be stolen but they had at least a 50/50 chance they had neglected to do that. Unfortunately, the recording was in black and white, so no colour ID, but it was a late-model Mercedes delivery van with no side or rear windows. Pete requested the manager make a copy of this original CD and they would return to pick it up later on.

He then decided to do what his gut told him not to, he asked the ASIO lady what her name was as Mrs ASIO didn't seem to be appropriate. She smirked sheepishly and said 'Well mate, it's about bloody time we got acquainted, I was beginning to think you would never ask. Call me Sheila.'

He had to laugh as that is the slang term men in Australia call all women, which never made any sense to Pete. It was just one of those stupid Aussie slang things. Fair enough, he didn't ask if she was for real as it would be a waste of time.

Sheila was on her mobile phone for about ten minutes trying to get her colleagues to chase up the number plate details with the police traffic division. More red tape ensued and time was a wasting. They eventually received the data required:

- The owner was a cheap hire company.
- It was up to them to visit the South Sydney–Botany area car hire offices to get:
  - A photocopy of the driver's licence.
  - If possible, a description and gender of the driver.
  - The address of the driver or company stated on the insurance form.
  - The time the vehicle was hired and when it was to be returned.

Pete grabbed the first taxi passing and got it pointed south. Sheila phoned ahead to check if the hire car company was still open – fuck, they were just about to close up shop for the day. He took over the phone and talked the manager into holding the place open so he could hire several vehicles. The manager reluctantly agreed as money always opens doors, for at least another hour anyway. They were on their own on this van chase as it was now 5 p.m. and the end of shift at the ASIO office and the car hire yard.

Pete said 'This might be a late night, young lady'.

She didn't react and kept looking at the traffic bunched up ahead, a frown starting to show on her forehead.

His thoughts flashed forward and he hoped that the car hire place wouldn't alert the van driver. It was another 50/50 hunch so they both were winging it again. Also, Sheila might receive a call from her boss demanding they call off this stunt as overtime was not approved – red tape again.

Pete gave the taxi driver a $50 bill and offered him another $50 as an incentive to get them there a little faster. The man took it seriously and at the next set of traffic lights he entered a bus-only lane and planted his foot. Another thirty minutes and they arrived out front of the car hire office.

Sheila volunteered to do the investigating gig as she had her ASIO ID card in her hand and was halfway out of the taxi before it had stopped. They would need this taxi for the next phase of the chase if she got the information they needed, so Pete asked the taxi driver his name as he gave him another $50 bonus. 'My name is Noel,' he said, then asked Pete if he should stand by. Pete told him 'You bet and keep the meter on'.

Ten minutes later, a bunch of photocopy paper in hand, Sheila jumped back into the taxi and gave Noel an address about 10 miles further south. Noel smiled broadly in the rear-view mirror as the meter was now showing double digits plus, and he had already made $150 for arriving on time. Noel drove out into the peak-hour traffic, this time not at high speed as he was a lousy race car driver anyway and Pete wasn't interested in him giving another bonus or crashing before arriving at the address.

They studied the photocopies and noted that the man who hired the van had an Arabic-sounding name, Rafik Awaz. The car hire manager had insisted that he had never seen this bloke before, plus he had an Irish accent so Sheila had to take him at his word – for now.

It was not yet time to call in the troops for a raid, plus they had no idea if or what this group were up to and raiding innocent tourists' accommodation might not go down well back at the red tape office. The primary thing right now was to locate the group and then report back on what they had discovered.

At least it wasn't raining or bitterly cold out there, so they could arrive in a nearby street, dump the taxi after paying Noel an outrageous fare, and then go for a walk around the local area. On a once-only pass by the house or building, hopefully, they might be lucky enough to spot someone from the group or another vehicle that they could do a trace on the plates via the local police link in Sheila's office.

They split up and separately did a nonchalant walk as if they were coming home from work and just happening to pass an old brick and tile house with a crumbling brick fence and gravel driveway leading to a large shed or garage attached to one side of the house.

There was a small Daihatsu hatchback parked out front on the street, and they were able to note the colour and number plate details for a future check. The lights were on in a front room but they could not see who was inside or how many people as the drapes were closed.

They met up around the next corner and exchanged notes before Sheila began to make a call to her office. Just then, Pete spotted someone getting into the small hatchback. The headlights were turned on and it did an about-turn in their direction. They were out in the open on the corner with nowhere to go, so in a Machiavellian way, Pete pulled Sheila close so the driver couldn't see either of their faces. She was a bit stunned and they stood for a moment staring into each other's eyes with their noses almost touching. She pressed her right hand firmly against his chest and slowly moved him back. Her smell filled up his senses and her breathing was slightly irregular. His heart was thumping.

With that car now heading out of site around the corner, he relaxed his arm around her narrow waist. She said nothing, then slowly raised the phone and keyed a number while he stepped back to look back along the street where the van driver lived and possibly where the group were now staying.

With no movements sighted, he motioned for her to follow him further around the corner in case the car was doing a survey of the local streets. She followed, walking slowly while talking to someone on the phone. They were being instructed to leave the area by train, using a subway station several street blocks away from the house.

Sheila took Pete's arm as they walked toward the station and reminded him not to get any funny ideas as they were merely acting as a couple, no more, no less. He nodded in agreement and they both chilled out as there had been tension in the air back at the corner.

His thoughts wandered back to his SAS operations and the strictly men-only activities. This situation with a woman at his side was very different and new rules would apply. A train was slowly entering the station as he bought two tickets that would carry Sheila and himself back into the Town Hall subway station.

From there they would separate, her by taxi to the ASIO office while he would hoof it on foot across town to his hotel. The thoughts running around his head focused on the group's rapid move from the hotel without notice, and without paying the bill, and the rapid move to a new location. Was this a strategy to evade surveillance or something more innocent?

Pete realised that his stomach was telling him out loud that it was empty and needed tucker. He hadn't eaten since that bowl of fruit for breakfast at the hotel. Seeing a hamburger place along the way, he popped in and sat there to devour it while crowd watching to amuse himself.

There were no phone calls overnight. He slept well and woke at 7 a.m, showered and took a walk around to the back car park of the hotel to visualise where the van had parked and what the driver could see from there. He looked up at the CCTV camera, which was obscured from sight by the broad eves of the building. The driver had possibly not seen the camera on the way in or out.

There were no control gates or barriers blocking service vehicles from entering or leaving the car park. Very convenient and less obvious than the meter parking out on the main street. He would have used the car park at the back himself if he wanted to stay concealed for a while.

He returned to his room and waited for Sheila or someone else to contact him before deciding to again wing it alone. He was thinking of taking the train back to the area where the van driver lived and they had assumed the group was now staying. Just then the hotel phone rang.

Zelda spoke: 'Good morning Pete. We were picked up by a friend yesterday and will be staying with them for a while. Sorry for not contacting you earlier.'

She then hung up without allowing him to get a word in. Was this a way of wiping clean the trail so he wouldn't try to follow up or be concerned about them? Why was he being used and then dumped? Clearly, there was a lot more to this than he had been able to imagine.

Chapter 36

Pete Hijacked by ASIO

An hour later, Pete's mobile phone rang and a gentleman from ASIO advised that he was sitting in the park down the road from the hotel and wanted to have a chat with him. It sounded a bit cloak and dagger, but Pete obliged him and walked out of the hotel, crossed the road between heavy traffic and sauntered down to the park. There were literally dozens of people walking across the lawns, around the monument and fountain, so spotting a lone figure out there would be almost impossible.

He wandered around the outer paths and then arrived back at the main street, where a white four-door car rolled up beside him, the door opened and he was told to get in. He looked inside. The back seat was empty and he took a chance by heaving himself in and shutting the door in one manoeuvre. Sheila was driving and she had a male companion in the front seat.

She gunned the engine and took off like a road rocket, first with a sharp left turn, then along the buses-only lane and right across morning peak-hour traffic. They cut through a narrow laneway and out onto the on ramp for the freeway.

Cool, she can navigate, drive and beat the peak-hour traffic, but who is this bloke sitting beside her and where the fuck are we heading, Pete was wondering.

Neither of them spoke a bloody word and Pete was still trying to fasten his seat belt when the car pulled left off the freeway, then a short distance down a street and into a building undercroft, where Sheila leaned out her window and used a magnetic key to open the gates and enter the car park below.

This was the first time he had ever been kidnapped, so he guessed that he should enjoy it. Those in the front seat didn't react until the vehicle stopped abruptly in a parking bay. They then threw open their doors and the gent in the front seat yanked Pete's open and motioned for him to follow.

They walked briskly over to the single elevator. Sheila used her magnetic key to bring it down to their level, the door opened and, like an obedient dog, he just followed them in. Several floors up, the doors opened and they alighted into a reception area with no signs advertising their arrival at a company or agency.

The male receptionist in front of them had Pete show him his driver's licence, which he photocopied and handed back without a word. He then pressed a button and a glass door unlocked with a sharp click. He was ushered through and into a conference room, where several men sat with documents in front of them. Pete was beckoned to sit between Sheila, her smell filling up his senses once more, and her no-name male companion.

Once seated, he was reminded about the official secrets act and the penalties for divulging anything about this operation outside of the members seated in this room, none of whom had names or job titles either. He was at a disadvantage as all of them had been briefed on who he was and his background.

At the head of the table sat an older gent with greying red hair, who made it obvious that he was in charge by calling the meeting to order. He informed no one in particular but no doubt it was meant for Pete's benefit, that he was the chairman of this team and his name was Roger. Pete looked around the room until there was silence and the shuffling of papers settled. His only thought was: where is the coffee machine?

The formal briefing began by being given details on:

- How he was recruited on loan from DIO.
- His contact by email and phone with Zelda.
- Transcripts of voice communications and phone taps in Perth.
- A list of Zelda's computer files that had been hacked for further review.
- Interpol reports from Egypt, Singapore and Thailand.
- CCTV shots of the husband in Singapore and Thailand airports.
- CCTV shots taken at Sydney airport showing the group, including Zelda and himself.
- CCTV shots from the hotel showing the van in the rear car park.
- A transcript of group voices in the minibus.
- Copies of Sheila's documents from the car hire yard.
- A driver's licence including a picture of the white van driver.
- Ownership papers for the Daihatsu hatchback seen in front of the house in question.
- A driver's licence including a picture of the Daihatsu hatchback owner.
- A statement from Sheila stating what she and Pete had done together on the previous day.

After rummaging through all this paperwork and taking one-sided questions, he was at the point of exploding with a barrage of his own. Lowering his tone while staring down at the pile of paper, he spoke for all to hear 'It's all very well to play catch up overnight for good housekeeping and filing. It's another thing to get ahead of things so there is some semblance of control. What I need to know now is:

- Given all of this detail, what is the game plan going forward?
- Is this group and their associates innocent, with no further need to follow up?
- Do I have a part to play or do I now go home to my peaceful world?
- If there is a concern:
  o Is anyone watching the van driver's house and has there been any movements?
  o Has the Daihatsu hatchback driver's home been checked out?
  o Is there any intel on known associates of all these people?
  o What else do we know about the two drivers' background, ethnicity, police checks etc?
  o Are the phones held by these people being tapped?'

Then Chairman Roger put his hand up to stop Pete's chain of questions and muttered gruffly that all of this was being worked on as they spoke. He then adjourned the meeting abruptly and took his second in command with him out of the room. Good little boys, Pete thought. Leaning back, he looked left then right at his minders, who were still sitting there silently.

Sheila smiled, realising he was pissed off, and asked if a coffee would help him chill out. He responded gruffly, 'Fucking A'. Mr no name from the car followed along behind them for a cup of coffee and a biscuit in the staff cafeteria with a CCTV camera fixed overhead. No privacy in here, and Pete was wondering what security the toilets may have. At least, one could be assured that people here did not steal the toilet rolls, biscuits or sugar.

Meeting over and a fresh coffee under his belt, there was no further discussion. He was taken down the elevator and back to the car park. Sheila again did the driving and he got the impression that she was a lead-footed rally driver. Good on her. They returned precisely to where they had picked him up and told him to jump out, sit tight at the hotel and wait for instructions.

He returned to the hotel room and relaxed watching TV news shows and cat napping. Around midday there was a knock on the door, and on opening it there stood Sheila with some takeaway salad rolls and strong coffee.

She said while walking past him, 'I thought you might be hungry for news and food, I decided to park out back and drop in and bring you up to speed:

- You are still on the case for the moment.
- The Daihatsu driver had been suspected of Palestinian and Syrian people smuggling.
- We believe he is linked to Hezbollah in Lebanon and Palestine according to phone taps of his and several associates.

- Zelda's husband has also been in contact with Hezbollah and he uses several mobile phones. He also has a number of links to people who the CIA, Interpol and other agencies including the Jordanian security services consider to be terrorist groups.
- Zelda appears to be a courier for these groups and, checking back over several months, her mobile phone shows contacts in the Sydney Muslim community, one of which is the van driver.

As for what ASIO is doing right now, thanks to your bull-in-a-china-shop questions to the chairman:

- A telecom team has arrived at the end of the van driver's street and installed a small but powerful CCTV camera up on a power pole, so we are now getting a live CCTV feed back into the office.
- There is now a dedicated team of agents monitoring all mobile phone signals from both driver locations, including specific phone numbers. We will have a synopsis of the chatter later today and every day.
- Several known associates and their phones are also under surveillance.
- A GPS tracker has been attached to the Daihatsu hatchback and as soon as the hired van moves it will be shadowed by several vehicles. Hopefully a GPS tracker can be attached to it at some point if it continues to be used.
- The group of four have not been sighted, which is a concern as they may have moved locations before our resources had mobilised.
- The money, being cash, is also a concern as it is easily moved separate to the group or the known persons of interest.'

Better late than never, he thought to himself, particularly as there was nobody else that he could express himself to. He was sure that Sheila would likely retort in defence of her employer in order to keep him in his place. What an upstart he must be.

His style of getting things done was to take the lead and move ahead firmly with conviction and come up with solutions before they became problems, like his rabbit shooting and trapping days as a kid. On this occasion the solutions were Band-Aids instead of dealing with the problem of catching up. He was for staying in front of one's quarry and possibly sneaking up close and personal. This whole affair had started with him getting up and close to Zelda in Perth and later at Sydney airport.

Reports came in about the little hatchback car's comings and goings to the group house, apparently delivering takeaway food. A week went by and then the Mercedes van reversed out of the shed at the house. This time Sheila was on the ball and radioed for one of her agency's men to be stationed near the hire car yard in case the van was being returned. The agent could get a photo of the driver and possibly enter the office to look at leaflets while he returned the van to find out if the manager there warned him that someone was interested in him and the van.

As anticipated, the van was returned and the extra time paid for with cash after a visual check for damage by the yard mechanic, who also topped up the fuel tank and took the docket up to the office. This was the same driver who had hired the van.

Pete was glad that all of the agency resources weren't forming a convoy behind the van as Zelda left the house after calling a taxi. She headed for the airport with an agent tailing her on a motorcycle. The others in her group were out on the footpath and being picked up, bags and all, and getting into an unmarked Toyota minibus with tinted windows. The driver helped with loading the baggage into the back tailgate and was photographed by an ASIO agent using a long lens while squatting behind a parked car at the other end of the street. That minibus driver had dark skin, was black bearded and wore a long grey smock or kaftan.

A chase team vehicle, with a fake contractor's truck, arrived as the minibus turned the nearest corner. The chase car driver was hailed by the cameraman and both moved off in the direction of the fleeing group. The ASIO chase team were pretty good at tailing suspect's cars and they turned away before the south side of the harbour bridge, while another chase vehicle picked up the tail from the north side using an off-duty taxi disguise.

There were several more changes made and the last one happened to be ahead of the group's minibus as it moved to another house, this time in North Sydney. If the group had been looking over their shoulders for a tail, they were looking the wrong way; the tail car had parked some 100 yards up ahead of them in a petrol station parking spot.

It was time for Pete and Sheila to arrive and they parked right next to the off-duty taxi and got into the back seat. Ten minutes later the photographer arrived from the opposite direction, exited the fake contractor's truck and piled into the front seat of the taxi. They reviewed the photos over his shoulder while the truck driver and taxi driver kept an eye on the minibus and where the group had alighted, an apartment building this time. Both drivers split up and wandered down the road on opposite sides in order to observe which apartment the group had moved into.

Assuming that these observers knew their stuff, Pete asked the photographer to bring them along and follow the minibus as soon as it moved off. At some point they would need to package up this group and their associates, take a good look at what they had in their houses and suitcases and get them charged with some sort of offence like:

- Money laundering
- Importing foreign currency worth more than A$10,000
- Aiding a terrorist group
- Use of false passports
- Entering the country under false pretext
- Weapons or explosive possession – if found
- Perhaps even eating lousy takeaway food for a week

The taxi engine kicked over and they fastened their seat belts as the group's empty minibus pulled away from the kerb in front of the apartment. Sheila pulled out her phone and requested a link up with another chase team. Their taxi pulled up alongside the minibus at the next set of lights, allowing them a look at the driver. He was still the same one with the black beard and a white crochet skull cap.

They let him lead for a while until another chase car signalled that they were several cars ahead of the minivan. Their taxi then veered off at the next left corner. They would now have to wait as separate teams moved into position to observe the group's new lodgings and the minivan driver's final stop.

It was now afternoon and time for stopping off for a coffee and a doughnut and, of course, a chat on what had eventuated so far:

- Clearly the group were moving out at short notice, which meant 24/7 surveillance.
- The drivers had changed. The first one they had the details on, the second one they needed to identify by vehicle registration, home address and photograph matching.
- The driver who returned the hire car didn't return home and went to a small mosque, where he was met by several other men.

Surprisingly, Sheila suggested that they pay a visit to the first house and take a look around. The photographer-cum-taxi driver agreed, so the three of them finished the coffees and doughnuts, got into the taxi and headed for the house. Sheila told the photographer to sit and observe from the end of the street and phone her if someone approached the house. They walked casually along the footpath and passed the house. There was no sign of occupants or lights on in the house, and no vehicle in the driveway.

Sheila nudged Pete's elbow and said 'Let's keep walking closer'. Whereby, she about-turned and walked straight up the front steps, onto the veranda and rang the doorbell. She waited a moment and then tapped on the front window. No answer. She waved to Pete to come back and they simply walked down the side of the garage into the back yard.

Chapter 37

Breaking and Entering

It was an old brick and timber structure with paint peeling, weeds growing through brick paving and a garbage tin without a lid with takeaway food wrappers visible. Pete was taller, so he got the job of looking through the kitchen window. There were no lights on but he still decided to knock on the ragged back flywire door frame. Still no answer, time to try the door. They found it locked but the laundry window was slightly ajar. He heaved at it and, although very tight, it moved to half open. Too small for him to squeeze through.

Without a word, Sheila moved past him and began to climb up. With Pete cupping her firm buttocks, he shoved her slim body upwards until she sat on the windowsill with her feet inside and planted in a cement wash trough.

'I'm in,' she said and dropped down to the floor out of sight until he heard the bolt on the back door clunk loose and the door swung wide open. She looked at him 'You got a little personal there Pete, cupping my bum like that. Don't make it a habit'.

He entered, knowing full well they were breaking the law, so they had better get a move on and get out of here. The rooms were dim due to the sun going down and the drapes being pulled tight, so they used their mobile phones as torches and wandered from room to room photographing anything of interest. It was definitely an Arab Muslim home layout with rugs and cushions on the floors.

A large rice pot on the stove, a typical hijab and men's kaftan robes hanging in closets. No children's toys or clothing at all; this house was solely for adults. The smell of cigarettes permeated the air. Pete began looking for anything that may be evidence and removed several scraps of paper with Arabic script on them.

Nothing much here he thought, until Sheila lifted the corner of a lounge room rug where several diagrams and pages of Arab script had been laid neatly on the wood floor. They carefully photographed them and laid the rug back down.

Sheila was checking the bathroom when her phone beeped and a text arrived: 'Car coming – get out now.' The car pulled into the driveway. They quickly retraced their steps toward the back door, Pete slipped out and waited while

Sheila returned the bolt on the back door, climbed onto the laundry trough and sat on the windowsill with her legs dangling out. Right at that point, she heard a key being placed in the front door lock.

Pete pulled her into his arms, feeling her breasts hard against his chest, and then quickly shoved the window down a bit. Someone had entered the front of the house and turned on a light. They tiptoed across the back yard, past the rubbish tin and around the side of the garage. They stopped as the front porch light was on, shedding an arc of yellow light on the front veranda and up to the brick fence.

There was a Chevy utility vehicle parked in the driveway, with no occupants, so they bent down and scurried along the dark side of the car until they were back on the footpath out front. Still squatting low near the front brick fence, they noted the registration plate on the car, checked the house and veranda, and then looked up and down the street for the possibility of being spotted.

The drapes were still closed and there was nobody on the veranda or the street. All clear, must be good to go then. It was time to head back to the waiting taxi, and they both laughed as they walked away, Sheila grabbed his hand and gave it a gentle squeeze, then they entered the taxi and agreed that a career in cat burglary was not their forte. Their driver couldn't understand their mirth but kept his eyes on the road.

Pete arranged to meet up with Sheila early the following morning as she needed a change of clothes after her window entry had dusted her up some. When the taxi disappeared out of sight, he headed on foot to the subway station and took the train into the city. Then he walked to his hotel, ordered room service hamburger and chips, and took a quick shower to freshen up.

Biting on the half-cold burger, he figured that they sure had a reasonable day with CCTV shots, cars, and vans being trailed around the city and suburbs, house breaking, photos taken and 24/7 surveillance of the group on the go. Time to take a breather and gather his thoughts based on the intelligence data gathered so far.

However, thoughts of Sheila and that very sensual gripping of his hand kept flashing through his mind. This girl was becoming very alluring and clouding his mind with lustful thoughts.

Sheila phoned him from the lobby at 7 the next morning and advised him there was a meeting at her office and that she had been there overnight preparing a report and printing photos and documents for translation. Pete still didn't like their office; no pretty receptionist and they didn't serve coffee at the meetings. Her driving to the office in the traffic was like a rally driver again, and he bared his knuckles holding onto the edge of the seat until they had stopped in the undercroft car park.

They headed up the secure elevator and into the reception area, where he again had to show his driver's licence. They copied it again, then both of them entered the meeting room with Chairman Roger and the same other gentlemen already sitting in the very same seats. Sheila sat right beside him again, her perfume again filling up his senses. Was he going crazy? He was eager to listen to the download briefing of what yesterday's action had yielded.

This time Chairman Roger was a lot friendlier toward him, as he asked how he was coping with the activity. Pete was by no means amused by the question, so he could have taken that comment as an insult. He just smiled and said 'I'm keeping up with your young folk'.

Sheila kicked him in the ankle under the table without looking up from the papers in front of her.

The meeting covered the past, present and the future format, and returned specifically to what Sheila had to say about the sketches and text pages they had found under the lounge room rug and taken photos of with their mobile phones. Apparently, Chairman Roger had a translator write up a briefing overnight on the Arabic text and sketches they had photographed. It was apparent that some sort of operation was being planned and more than one terrorist cell and target would be involved.

The sketches didn't specify where the targets were. They digested the translated intelligence in silence, with most of the attendees sifting through the various photos that by now had handwritten English text on the backs to explain date, time, subject and activity, but not who the actors were to be.

Chairman Roger requested a pin board be brought in and a couple of the no-name attendees went out briefly and rolled in a large one and placed it along the wall behind Pete. It was a bit of a disadvantage to Sheila's and his line of sight but all of them could see it clearly. Chairman Roger got up and began pinning pieces of paper with text on and under the associated photos from CCTV and stills, including some that Sheila and Pete had taken. They now had a pictorial timeline and intelligence uptake, beginning from:

- The date the Singapore customs alerted Interpol about Zelda's husband attempting to enter Australia (he had made a mistake about the need for a visa).
- Singapore CCTV still photos of the husband and a photocopy of his Palestinian passport.
- Phone calls to Zelda in Applecross, Perth, from a Singapore hotel.
- The husband's travel arrangements from Singapore to Thailand (where the link was lost for a period).
- Phone calls from a hotel in Thailand to Zelda in Perth.

- A précis of Pete's report of his time in Perth with Zelda.
- The ASIO contacts via the US CIA with the Jordanian Intelligence Service regarding the backgrounds on the husband's sister and brother-in-law:
  - The Jordanian group were involved in a large trading, import–export business and had no criminal records on file.
  - The brother-in-law is a reservist officer in the Jordanian Air Force.
  - The husband's details showed that he was born in Jordan, not married there. He studied medicine in the USA and after graduation he worked in several American hospitals and became an orthopaedic surgeon. He later joined the UNHCR during the PLO hijacking period.
  - There were limited notes on his movements around the world apart from him being Yasser Arafat's doctor up until Arafat's death from suspected poisoning.
  - There were no records of his activities in Egypt, nor any marriage arrangement.
  - The group's departure flight details from Jordan to Sydney Australia via Indonesia – there was a gap of intelligence links that would have been needed to guarantee that the money was not spotted at each transit stop and final destination.
  - A notice to act from the Jordanian Intelligence Service as they had X-rayed and opened the group's luggage below in the warehouse prior to loading it aboard the aircraft. They counted almost US $3 million in various denominations. As there was no law against taking large sums of money out of the country, no action was taken but it did raise enough concern for them to notify the recipient country.
- With support from Interpol and local authorities in Thailand and Indonesia, the details of the husband's departure flight from Bangkok via Indonesia to Sydney using a Jordanian passport and bringing only carry-on baggage.
- CCTV photos of all three travellers and several of Zelda, including Pete with her in a couple of shots.
- The husband had not yet used his UN passport and there was a watch notice issued this morning in case he tried to use diplomatic immunity to get out of Australia. The rules were, get him before he changes his status from tourist to UN doctor. Each passport used a different name and place of residence

It took an hour of chit-chat around the table before Chairman Roger decided it was sufficient enough in positive returns and it was now time to summarise the past position, which was up on the pin board, then move to the present situation from yesterday's findings forward as he pinned up the translations and sketches.

Chairman Roger thoughtfully wrung his hands in front of him, stood up slowly, looked around the table and announced 'Well lady and gentlemen what the blazes are we going to do moving forward as there is a real threat developing'.

Sitting right back in his chair, turning and facing the pin board, Pete volunteered his thoughts: 'This thing could go badly wrong if the terrorists have the latitude of time to plan and execute a pre-emptive strike on a target or targets unknown. This could also mean that the US $3 million might be getting untraceably distributed all over the country any time soon. We have an emerging picture of whom some of them are and where they live. Let's focus on them much more closely.'

He waited for the attendees to trash his observation, but silence prevailed for a full minute. Then Chairman Roger, still standing, stared at Pete as if he had just materialised in the room. Biting his bottom lip thinking, he swung his head left, then right – no objections heard from his experts. Looking down at the notes he had made, he placed his hands knuckles down onto the table and said 'I partially go along with you Pete regarding the threat and risk from these people, but this thing is still in motion and we need to find out what the targets are, where and who their network affiliates are and then pull the whole bloody lot in all at once and charge them – I'll warm up the Attorney General and a legal counsel.

'Any raids will have to be spearheaded by the Federal Police Anti-Terrorist Unit.'

Everyone in the room sat up alert. This was the objective and the targets set by Chairman Roger. They all needed to put their heads together and come up with the How, When, Where.

The who was doing what would come to the surface from field observations, CCTV installations, phone taps, tracking an expanding list of individuals and using covert building entry actions all around Sydney and wherever the money and people turned up.

At this point, Pete's stomach was rumbling as he hadn't eaten breakfast, so he suggested that they all take a break for coffee and order in some refreshments as this would be a long morning or day and night. There were no objections from the attendees but as Chairman Roger passed him on the way out, he whispered into Pete's ear 'I'm in charge here, not you mister, so don't give out any more orders to my people'.

Pete took the remark on the chin and smiled as he politely opened the door for the chairman. As a reserve major in the SAS, it was always his job to speak up and lead his troops – old habits died hard, particularly on someone else's hallowed turf. However, playing interdepartmental politics right now was not on his radar. Roger would ultimately have to pull him off the operation or suck it up as Pete's forthright manner tended to push these blokes into action rather than wait for their boss to make all the calls.

He needed to know the backgrounds of this crew, operational experience and skill sets before he could settle down to a brainstorming session with them; they should get to know him as well.

With coffees and mixed sandwiches on the table and Chairman Roger away organising the legal side, Pete took it on himself as it looked like he was the oldest in attendance to address the meeting informally. 'Listen people, we need to be clear on who's who in the zoo, your backgrounds, skill sets, specialities, etc., before we embark on brainstorming these next operational moves. Without that there will be gaps, breakdowns in understandings and expectations.'

He pointed to the man at the end of the table, who would have been sitting closest to Chairman Roger earlier, and asked him to start off and inform the room beginning with a first name. Before the fella could open his mouth, Sheila said 'I'll take notes for the record. It will be useful when we get to allocation of who does what later'.

'Good thinking 99,' Pete said, which went over like a fart in church. Guess they were all too young to remember that line from the 1960s TV show *Get Smart*.

Each person in turn introduced themselves and gave a précis of their background and education, years with ASIO and any other service, and specified what skills they could offer to this emerging operation. Now that they all understood their strengths and weaknesses, including Pete's, they could now nominate leaders for:

A. Communications – phone taps – CCTV – two-way radios – supply of listening bugs.
B. Mobile tracking – vehicle GPS tagging – vehicle supply.
C. On the ground – field observations – photography including video – building insertions.
D. Central control desk – 24/7 reception from all the operations sources – additional resources.
E. Authority to proceed – the chairman for central oversight – Legal and media – interface with other services – budget.

Naturally, someone would have to inform Chairman Roger that they had designated him a specific position in the team. If Roger interfered too much any plans of action would go out of the window and they would have to start all over from scratch. Pete had no idea what Roger's credentials were, except that his troops kept their mouth shut most of the time. That meant he was autocratic and was dominating them and thus not getting the best possible performance output. Obviously, it made him feel safe and powerful though.

Pete had seen this type before in the army – useless as leaders, ready to blame others and first to step up for a medal if their people achieved something great by initiative. Politicians behaved exactly the same. Anyway, he hoped that this mob got some fire in their bellies.

Pete noticed the team leaders around the table had warmed to his approach and lights in their heads were turning on with blurts of suggestions emanating from them. Some stuck to the key objective and most proposals were very good. In an hour they could cross-play ideas with each other into a workable matrix until they had a solid game plan worth presenting to Chairman Roger, as his approval was essential or nothing would happen. Pete knew from experience not to give Roger all the details, so he drafted an outline of the plan knowing full well that the chairman would have to make some changes to save face. Let's play this thing out.

One of the blokes went out and brought the Roger back in. Sheila stood up at the opposite end of the table and read out the two-page minutes that had everyone's input covered, man by man including Pete's, in the mix.

Chairman Roger got up with a copy of the recorded notes in his hand and went to leave the room. Pete stood up and said 'Boss, this needs your immediate go or no go right now. As you said earlier, things are in motion.'

Roger stopped in his tracks, mouthing something silently. Then he sat down, re-read the recorded notes and looked around the table and shrugged. Then he mumbled 'This appears to be a well-thought out plan. I do understand that these things must get moving or opportunities will be squandered. I will monitor progress and, if necessary, change the plan.'

Pete spoke up for the team and said 'The changes, if any, must be made by each team leader who is fully aware of the detailed time lines, matrix of skill sets and resources available to them and each other. A general at HQ should only observe progress and provide positive support or the whole damn operation will turn into shit on a shingle and have everyone running around in a circle.'

All those around the table felt their jaws literally drop for a few seconds; nobody told their boss what to do. They all waited for Roger's response. He looked at the recorded notes once again, breathed a deep sigh and nodded.

'Looks like we have a field commander here who will take responsibility for the overall operation on the ground. I will have my hands full back here as noted.

'Sheila, you will co-ordinate the four-hourly reporting to me of progress and all requirements for additional resources or external services support requirements with a forecast for the next four hours.'

She nodded and smiled at Pete, who assumed that Roger meant him as the field commander, which meant Roger was off the hook and the DIO would be blamed if things went pear shaped. Definitely a smart politician.

Chapter 38

Mobilisation of the Action Team

The operation was a go right now, so it was no time to dilly-dally. Pete requested the communications leader set this conference room up as the control centre with more phones, two-way radios to be circulated to all team leaders, lists of contacts within ASIO and external services.

Sheila understood her role so no need to double up on her account. He only told stupid people the same thing twice and she wasn't stupid by any means.

Each of the remaining team members in the room just nodded at him, indicating they knew their next actions, and promptly left the room. That left himself and Sheila standing there looking at the pin board. As he was not familiar with Sydney's streets, he would need a driver and all team leaders would need a few hundred dollars in cash just in case they needed to pay for their travels around town. They wouldn't be creating a taxi service ferrying everybody about.

Sheila nodded and picked up her phone, to the accounts department he guessed, as he left the room, approached the receptionist and requested a temporary ID card and a magnetic key to get into the building on this floor as this was where the control room was being set up. The receptionist picked up the phone, probably to Chairman Roger or an authorised building security officer. Putting the phone down, the receptionist advised Pete to go check with Sheila.

Sheila OK'd his request as she had all his details on her phone. She advised Pete that if any new intelligence data arrived of importance, she would be in contact. He was confident how the ball was rolling, at least confident enough to go back to his hotel, freshen up and eat a late lunch. Then he headed out to where the hatchback driver lived for a walk around, and later went to check out the mosque where he had seen some of the group's associates just to get a feel for the environment.

One of the team leaders was going to check on the first house that the group had moved into, while another met up with the surveillance crew watching the apartment to where the group had been transferred. Someone in the crew would do a walkabout around the entire grounds of that apartment building in case there was a back door; taking a few photos of the entry, exit and fire escapes.

Unable to pinpoint where the money was, or if it had been split up or was still intact, was a concern for Pete at this point in time. Right now there were too many people of interest involved and going in and out in different directions all at once. It was going to be his call on when they pulled the pin and got the Feds to raid all of the premises and pull over the vehicles, drag everyone to a lock-up and allow ASIO teams to fine tooth-comb search everywhere until they came up with the terrorists' intended targets.

He called the communications team leader and checked if there had been any mobile or land line calls made by any of the persons of interest, which included members of the group of four. Pete was advised by the team leader that he had his backroom boys on the job monitoring all of the known mobile phones, illegally at the moment as boss Roger hadn't got the legal warrants signed by a judge in place yet. Maybe the official tapping could begin tomorrow. Pete told him to proceed, send Sheila the transcripts, and he would take the flack if the shit hit the fan. He came back 'Roger that Major Pete'.

Sheila called him on the two-way radio and advised that she had called in a translator to listen in on the mobile phone calls and they were in a Palestinian dialect. The first call had been from the husband to the hatchback driver, named Sidiqi. They had discussed moving the group to a new location in two more days and that he had the address and would advise when the move was under way.

Pete thanked Sheila and suggested that she tell the communications team leader that this was very important data and to keep up the good work and record everything in case it was coded to mean something else. So far it appeared that the group and their associates weren't sophisticated enough to dodge the phone taps by dumping phones and using stolen ones, burners. However, that may change if they got wind of any surveillance presence at any point along the way.

Throughout the night, the mobile phones were active, including several international calls to Egyptian and Syrian phone networks. The IT people were also trying to get into the group's phones, PCs and tablets to monitor texts and emails in and out-going. They already had a copy of Zelda's email contacts off her PC while she was in Perth.

Meanwhile, the field teams kept the surveillance going so they didn't lose any links in the chain. Pete briefed the field surveillance leader on what was happening in the office with the calls and the translators as there was limited activity outside in the streets but plenty going on indoors.

By morning, they had a number of mobile phone transcripts, no legal warrants yet and field reports of car and driver movements with photos of associates and addresses to filter through. Most of the field teams had handed over to a day shift but Pete had only grabbed around four hours' sleep overnight and it looked the same for the team leaders now assembled for a meeting in the control room. Sheila had an assistant to help with her workload, sit in on the meetings, to take notes and fill in when she could get some rest; apparently, she was on duty all night. Pete advised all the team leaders to delegate as they too needed to be firing on all cylinders.

If Chairman Roger wanted to call a meeting, he must pass it through Pete in order not to disrupt the teams' activities unnecessarily. Also, Pete must see every report before Roger saw it, in case Pete could respond to questions, spot any anomalies and cover their arses if needed.

The meeting was short and sharp – the way Pete liked it, with no time wasting. The translations of the overnight phone calls were laid out on the table and studying them led them to believe that there were specific targets planned for attacking. The phone calls also revealed that several associate terrorists had already surveyed the targets and that the newly arrived terrorists needed to do a drive past to familiarise themselves with the locations before the events took place.

Whatever they planned needed funds to obtain whatever they needed to execute their plans. Notes on this and the night's activities would be hand delivered to Chairman Roger, after most of them had left the building. Roger shouldn't be informed of their alternates or he might try redirecting them instead. Pete's belief was 'one captain, one ship'.

Today, it was time to task the day teams to start taking a look inside garbage bins, sheds, garages, storage units and homes; if possible, throughout the day, if not then tonight at the latest. Pete needed to know if they were hoarding any materials that could be used in explosives, or as sharp hand weapons or firearms. If not, they might have to consider that there would be a physical attack using vehicles or things like knives, etc. on random streets. So far, they had no idea, and that would be no cop out if something did happen on their/ Pete's watch. Pete's key unanswered questions were:

- Why are these new arrivals, possibly terrorists, landing here?
- Why the secrecy and shifting from safe house to safe house?
- What is the US $3 million intended for?

So far, they had found nothing out of the ordinary having revisited the original safe house, broken into two cars without damaging anything and monitored at least seven associates, getting their home addresses and following just as many vehicles of different sizes and shapes.

One of the agents sighted several of the associates get off a train from a country town so he called the town's stationmaster. He then rang the martialling yard supervisor to obtain the train's on-board CCTV recordings, used to monitor vandals. The agents would have a copy of the recordings that night and they could take a look at where the associates got on the train and see who got off at the Sydney terminus.

That evening they met in the control room just ahead of the change in shifts to hand over and discuss any changes in objectives for tomorrow's shift.

For Pete things were moving too slowly, but they could not dictate progress. It was up to the visitors and their associates to expose something that would cause them to react – heavily.

They were able to establish the station where the associates got onto the train and that none got off before the city. They were shadowed until the associates arrived at their home addresses. A field agent got out a map of the town where the associates got onto the train to review possible targets of interest.

There was a regional police station, a small hospital, several schools and, out of town, an army base for soldiers preparing to go to Iraq and Afghanistan. The facility also hosted helicopter training exercises. Apart from that, it was a quiet rural wheat and sheep farming town.

Pete knew of the base from past history, so it was appropriate that he contacted his former army colleagues there and ask them if there had been anyone wandering around the perimeter or inside the base over the last couple of days. The base was being used as a training camp and had very few gate checks on people in civilian clothes wandering inside and out again. Security tightened at night only. They did offer to investigate further and get back as there were perimeter guard posts at the main gate and arsenal compound, and some CCTV cameras facing along the main internal roads around the camp.

They also contacted the local police HQ and asked a similar round of questions but came up negative as the local cops thought that there was no need to protect their building or car parks. However, this discussion did evoke some interest and they offered to pop out to the army base and have a look at the CCTV recordings for the previous day. Also, the mess beer was cheaper than in town. This would save ASIO turning up and stirring up the chickens. The cops agreed to give the task a high priority as it affected their turf and they promised to come back with any information the following day at the latest.

They all sat down at the table with a variety of city and regional maps laid out and highlighted anything that looked or smelled like a possible target close to Sydney's city limits. Several stood out as more likely, so they set up a team to go visit them and talk to the folks within the facilities. There were three industrial chemical plants, a naval base and an air force base. Pete maintained the surveillance crews on the bunch of known associates and the apartment where the group were currently located, expecting some or all to start moving about. Additional agents were requested to visit the Sydney sites, interview the security guards on strangers hanging about and report back if there was lax security.

As there was nothing more Pete could do until morning, he dismissed the day shift team leaders and agreed that they meet the night and day shift leaders at 7 a.m. sharp the following morning. Sheila handed him that day's draft report, which included what they had researched up to the end of this meeting. It was a bloody accurate synopsis, with not too much detail for Chairman Roger to fiddle with. They had received several phone tapping warrants from Roger's secretary and enough cash to feed out to the day and night teams to cover the next few days.

Late that night, as Pete had just got his head on the pillow, the mobile phone rang. It was Chairman Roger on the line, doesn't he like to sleep? Pete made an effort to talk without croaking his voice. Roger wanted to know which assets would be attacked by these terrorists. Obviously, he had not read the report properly, so Pete unravelled what it stated even though he had no copy with him:

1. There appeared to be no imminent threat of an attack.
2. Several associates were in a rural town that had a police HQ and an army base but at this time there was no evidence of any surveillance by them, CCTV is being checked.
3. A number of possible targets have been researched in that town and out in the countryside, no specific target stands out apart from military bases.
4. During tomorrow and next two days all agents will visit potential target sites and gather security post interviews and CCTV recordings which may or may not highlight attention by the known associates or group members.
5. Surveillance of all known parties and vehicles is ongoing.
6. Entry to various storage assets is under way.

Pete wasn't sure if Roger was satisfied with his response, but he reminded the chairman that all was under control, and said he had full confidence in the agents to do their job and there was no reason for concern. Then Pete said 'Good night boss' and hung up.

Chapter 39

The Take Down

The following morning's report and meeting covered the overnight observations, but apart from some associates' cars being seen moving about and several storage sheds and units being opened and checked there was nothing new to report. Pete anticipated that the group would move safe houses either overnight or during peak hours today, so additional resources were made ready on several streets in opposite directions away from the safe house apartment.

Right on time, in the tightest peak hour at 8.30 a.m., the group had a visitor and they all bugged out using the rear fire escape with all of their baggage into a mobile home vehicle.

The obvious checks on the vehicle began instantly. The registration number, make and model were received and a number of long-distance photos taken and forwarded to the control room. The plates didn't belong to the vehicle and the driver was known as one of the associates from the mosque. The surveillance team that had followed this guy from his home to pick up the mobile home hadn't notified them of the change in vehicles, so Pete told their team leader to wake them up and read them the riot act. There could not be any slip-ups due to laxity.

If their surveillance teams near the apartment had not spotted the mobile home enter the rear car park, and agents on foot had not seen the movement down the fire escape, they might have lost the whole group – again.

Sheila had phoned the country town regional police contact and pressed him for any information that his cops had gleaned from the local army base security guards that were now off duty and if their officers had looked at the CCTV. They were informed that the CCTV recordings had been loaded on one of the police computers and two officers were currently reviewing. This was of no use to anyone as the cops did not know who the suspects were, what they were wearing or what they looked like. Sheila requested them to send a copy of the recordings electronically to her ASAP.

Their chase teams maintained surveillance of the motor home containing the international group plus Zelda. They were heading south in the direction of the regional town and the army base. Pete chose not to inform the local police in case they jumped in and stopped the vehicle. At present they had no case against anyone, so all parties under surveillance were free to come and go as they pleased right now.

They were hoping for more intelligence coming in from the vehicles under surveillance, the remaining sheds and storage units, and after entering houses and inserting listening bugs. Meantime, their translators were working overtime keeping up with translating and documenting phone communications.

Pete and a couple of available day shift team leaders laid out the new phone transcripts along with the earlier ones to try their best to work out any commonality. All the transcripts appeared to have common words, and similar inferences also appeared. Sheila documented these into a facsimile of a storyline. One was emerging as it appeared that there were two or three similar targets and the best guess at this time was the army and naval bases because of their involvement with the USA, supporting Israel and having troops in Iraq, Syria and Afghanistan.

It was now getting closer to the time that they would need to call in Chairman Roger and arrange to formally brief the Federal Police Anti-Terrorist Unit leaders, begin plans for setting up simultaneous raids on the houses of all associates, pull over the mobile home and go through everything until they came up with sufficient evidence to charge all of them with conspiring to commit terrorist acts.

They weren't quite there yet, but they were preparing in advance planning for the best result while covering themselves for the worst result, meaning that some of the targets might get away. For the best result, they had to be patient and try to catch the terrorists fully prepared to act or as they started to act. That could risk their people or the community but the Feds were specialists in these exercises and ASIO agents were not. Pete's SAS pals would probably make a bloodbath of it.

There was a lot more communications chatter between both international and local sources and the interpreter could not translate in real time anymore. There would be a time gap that would slow their reactions down to a walk, plus it was taking time for the team to go through the CCTV as there were a number of camera recordings to evaluate. Sheila contacted Chairman Roger and requested more resources or they might drop the ball.

Roger came into the control room eager to assess what resources they needed and bring in those not on critical assignments to support this operation. They got two more translators into the cluster, plus four more men and women looking at associate photos and comparing them to the CCTV footage on several computers.

The team leaders huddled in the control room over each translation and updated the matrix of common words or phrases. Then one of the CCTV review teams hollered out for them to come see some of the associates walking through the front gate of the regional army base taking photographs of guard houses, buildings and barracks.

This photography was against Commonwealth laws, so they could apprehend them simply for that. Roger contacted his legal team and began co-ordinating the verbiage to be used in warrants, including reasons to raid the associates' premises and impound vehicles etc. He cautioned them that these operational actions all had to be done legally or they could get kicked out of court and their arses would be kicked from above.

More CCTV recordings arrived thanks to their field officers visiting the naval base and other nearby army bases. More computers and personnel were set up and reviewing the recordings continued with intensity. They soon had more recordings of more associates wandering about inside or around the perimeters of military bases or outside the fences, taking photos as they went.

Sheila radioed the surveillance teams shadowing the motor home to ascertain exactly where it was and where it appeared to be headed. The call came back immediately; the motor home was now on the Hume Highway heading towards the Victoria border.

Pete figured that they still had most of the money with them and, although they had an interest in promoting the proposed attacks on army bases, they had other business around the country. More likely, some of the money had already been handed over to the Sydney-based terrorist cells and more pay days could be expected in Melbourne or other states and territories.

He asked the communications team leader if there were any interstate phone calls made by the group members in the mobile home vehicle. The team leader checked his register of calls by caller number and found several calls to a Melbourne land line and several mobile phones. Transcripts were being drafted but needed the translators' input. Sheila then spoke to the chairman about the calls and the links to the international group from Melbourne. Things were widening and could get out of control. Should they go after the Victoria connections or stop the motor home in New South Wales and bring them all back to Sydney? Australian stateliness required communication with authorities across a border or a turf war could start up and information could then be blocked or delayed by red tape.

Chairman Roger thought about the predicament for several minutes and then decided to call in some favours from his colleagues in ASIO offices in Melbourne and other cities in Victoria. The decision meant that they would pull back at the border and allow the Victorian ASIO resources to shadow the motor home and observe the contacts with the associates. Then, before the terrorists had a chance to settle in, plan or act, they would pull them all into custody as an integral part of a terrorist group.

The waiting time was on the clock now as it would only take another day for the group to arrive in Melbourne and meet up with their associates. As soon as they got the word from ASIO there, they would jointly mount a simultaneous Federal Police Anti-Terrorist Unit raid in Sydney and Melbourne, thus neutralising the entire operation and shutting down sleeper cells in both major states.

The team leaders were tasked with co-ordinating with the Feds for synchronising the raids and arrests of all of the groups and individuals to happen at the same time, shutting down their entire ability to communicate or go to ground. The simultaneous raids were set for the following morning at 2 a.m., irrespective of where the terrorists were at the time.

Chairman Roger was ecstatic and, of course, he would take all the credit if it went well or blame Pete and the DIO for incompetence if it hit the fan.

Pete was sure that because of their team's hard work and the way they documented all the evidence, the Feds would have more than enough meat on the bone for a major hit against imported terrorism. Pete was constrained to monitor the show and provide advice to the field teams, so he had no direct part in the raids that yielded a number of shotguns and rifles, ammunition and out of shelf life mining explosives in stick form. Several dummy explosives vests were also found with machetes and masks. A large amount of electronic and printed material was also captured at the various locations. The best find of all was close to US $1 million in a woman's car; she was the wife of the first safe house owner.

The report from Melbourne's ASIO commander listed all names, according to passports, of the international group and a list of charges laid. There were only five associates picked up in Melbourne based on phone taps from communications with the group, but there were investigations ongoing based on phone contact lists. Similar raids were executed on the Sydney-based associates' homes.

Chapter 40

Mossad and Moles

They met the following day at noon and learned the results of the raids with a lot of smiles all around. However, something was bothering Pete and he whispered into Sheila's ear 'Let's go have a coffee'.

They left the building and walked a block to Alannah's Coffee and Cakes, a cute little café with half a dozen tables adjacent to the footpath. They choose a table and he ordered two coffees and a couple of lamingtons.

'What's bothering you Spider? May I call you Spider? It just sounds so intriguing.'

'Of course, you may, I will explain how it came about one day, maybe. Anyhow, my concern is just where the hell is Zelda? I have not seen or heard any information of her being captured, arrested, or her whereabouts, have you?'

'No, I haven't and it had crossed my mind. Tell you what, I'll go back to the office and ask around. Maybe somebody has some info and I will meet you at your hotel around 5 p.m.. How does that sound?'

'Sounds like a plan Sheila, five o'clock it is. These lamingtons taste bonzer.'

They sat silently for a couple of minutes considering the past events and where things currently stood as they slowly sipped the coffee. Sheila then stood up abruptly and said 'Catch you later Spider'.

She simply turned without looking back and walked briskly down the street in the direction of her office. Looks like the bill will be on me, he thought with a smile.

He decided to go for a walk into town and then back to his hotel room, where he had lunch and relaxed as his head was still spinning from all of the events and reactions over the last few weeks on this civilian operation. He wouldn't recommend this shit to any of his army mates; it was too bloody dangerous not knowing who the bad guys are.

He went down and sat in the lobby just people watching, and as 5 p.m. rolled around Sheila walked through the door. Surprisingly, she gave him a hug, with her perfume once more filling up those male senses.

He asked her if she would like to go to the restaurant for dinner and she readily agreed. They ordered the meal and a couple of glasses of white Yellow Tail wine, from the vineyards of the Riverina district in the state of New South Wales.

Back to business, he asked Sheila if she had any dope on Zelda's whereabouts. Sheila frowned.

'Spider I asked everyone I could find, even made a couple of phone calls but no luck. I even spoke to Chairman Roger but he brushed it off saying "Looks like she's the one that got away". Which to my way of thinking was just a little too casual, do you know what I mean?'

'I do Sheila, I tried Zelda's mobile several times but no luck. It's dead. I am not sure where we go from here but I am guessing my assignment is basically over.'

They finished the meal and he asked if she would care to join him in his room for a nightcap as he had a bottle of ten-year-old Napoleon Cognac, XO blend.

At 7 a.m., Pete's phone jarred him awake. He looked across at Sheila, it had stirred her as well.

'Hello, good morning, this is Pete.'

'Pete, this is Zelda.'

'Zelda!'

He sat up in the bed, while Sheila headed for the bathroom in all her sensual nakedness.

'Just where the hell are you, Zelda? I tried calling you.'

'Pete, I need to see you its urgent, can you meet me now?'

'Of course, where are you?'

'I am down in the lobby, can I come to your room?'

He thought to himself, no that would not be a wise move. He could hear the shower in the bathroom, so he told her 'Zelda, I had a bit of a wild night and need to shower. Can you give me fifteen minutes and I will meet you in the hotel coffee shop.'

'Fine, thank you Pete.'

He gently knocked on the bathroom door and spoke her name.

'Come in Spider.' He opened the door and kissed her bare shoulder as she was using a towel to dry her hair. She asked 'Did I hear you say Zelda?'

'Yes, she is down in the hotel coffee shop waiting to meet with me. I will just have a quick shower and join her. What do you think Sheila, would it be wise if you joined us?'

'No, Spider I don't think that would be wise right now. I will dress, leave and please call me after your meeting, is that OK?'

'Sure, that will be fine. Sheila last night, you and me. Well, it was magic.'

'Have your shower and call me later.' She winked and kissed him. He stepped into the shower and drew the curtain.

Fifteen minutes later he spotted Zelda sitting at a table staring out through the plate glass window.

'Good morning Zelda.'

She spun her head and looked in what seemed like a nervous reaction.

'Pete, please sit with me. I have things I must tell you.'

He ordered a coffee and waited for her to unwind.

'I am not sure just where I should start.'

'From the beginning would probably be wise,' he answered.

'OK Pete, here goes. I am a special agent with the Israeli Secret Service, Mossad, sometimes called The Institute. I work with a counter-terrorist unit.

'When we first learned some years ago that Australia was a potential Islamic target because of its support of, and participation in, the United States' wars in the Gulf, Iraq and Afghanistan I was assigned to go covert and get deep under cover and get as close to our objective as possible, whom we suspected would head up the Islamic jihadist attacks in Australia. I had to do what had to be done. His name is Abdul. He is my so-called doctor husband.'

She paused and sipped her coffee, then continued, 'Pete, we have agents, some may call them moles, others may use the term spies. Whatever the label, they are embedded within the DIO, ASIO and the Federal Police, even in major businesses and the broader community. I will tell you this, the Israeli intelligence-gathering system that exists throughout Australia far outstrips that of ASIO and the Federal Police. The intelligence we have gathered has now pinpointed Abdul as the leader of the Islamic jihadist movement in Australia.

'For this assignment we, Mossad, required backup by someone in Australia who was completely unknown in the counter-terrorist world with a very strong and capable military background and also unarmed combat abilities.

'An individual whom we believed would not hesitate to pull the trigger if warranted but had to be kept blind to my activities and who I was. If for some unknown reason you accidently exposed me or my actions, I would be exterminated.

'Moving forward we have to be extremely careful, but it is time you had full understanding of my mission.

'Through our agents we received dossiers of half a dozen SAS warriors to choose from to fulfil our requirements. You, with DIO support, were chosen major.'

He was surprised to hear his former rank of major quoted and almost choked on his coffee.

'I find that very intriguing Zelda. From what you are saying the whole dating game, Perth, meet your family in Sydney was all bullshit, simply a cover to get me involved in up to my neck. So how am I supposed to know if you are being truthful now? Maybe you are trying to sucker punch me again for your own purpose.'

Ignoring his words, she continued, 'This man, Abdul, is a PLO agent and a Yasser Arafat stooge. Along with other members of this terror cell whom he claims is his sister and brother-in-law they are in this country, your country Pete, to do nothing but harm.

'Mossad Intelligence is aware that Abdul has powerful connections within Hezbollah, Hamas and ISIS. He is suspected of being an intricate part of several Tel Aviv suicide bombings, the Shawarma Restaurant bombing and of a bus passing through the centre of the Tel Aviv central business district on Shaul HaMelech Street. Pete, more than thirty Israeli citizens were killed and a hundred plus were injured.

'I am a proud Israeli Pete. I lay with my legs apart for a filthy Muslim who demanded I go through some disgusting mosque wedding to satisfy his sexual gratification. I did this for the country I love and am willing to die for.

'These Islamic Jihads will tell you, it is good to die as a martyr for Allah.

'Abdul is currently on a "most wanted" enemy list. He will eventually be eliminated and for that your assistance may be required.

'Right now, I am on their dark side. I was informed by our agent in ASIO that raids in Melbourne and Sydney would occur several days before the events.

'I knew I had to go to ground so I used an excuse to return to Perth for business purposes, which means they may now suspect me of not being an Allah worshipper, particularly as immediately after I left them the ASIO/ Federal Police raids took place. They will likely put two and two together. It is imperative I move cautiously. Do you understand?'

'I do understand everything you have said, as graphic as it is, but it proves nothing. What I suggest we do is leave here, right now, and head to the ASIO office and meet with the chairman who has been my controller to satisfy my curiosity. What do you say?'

'If that's what you require Pete, let's go!' she said matter of factly, but he could see in her eyes a spark of reaction.

He picked up his mobile phone and texted Sheila and Chairman Roger that he was heading to the ASIO office for a debrief. However, he got no response from Sheila or Chairman Roger but decided to carry on anyway.

He hailed a taxi out front of the hotel and they headed for the ASIO offices. The morning peak hour traffic was bunched up and it took at least half an hour to get there. As he and Zelda entered the ASIO office, one of the team leaders was waiting in the building's foyer, which meant Chairman Roger knew he was on his way and had had one of his people meet him, but there was still nothing from Sheila.

Without a word, the team leader curtly opened the elevator doors and escorted them to the upper-floor reception desk, where he left them without a word spoken.

Pete took Zelda through the identification process with him as her referee, then when the security door clicked open, they walked towards the conference room.

Inside the room, Chairman Roger and his crew were standing around making a lot of noise. When Roger looked up and saw him, he then stared at Zelda.

'Pete, where have you been? Who is this? Why is she here? We have a serious incident meeting. Please everyone sit down.'

Roger abruptly strode up to Zelda and spoke. 'Please sit here next to Pete. I am the chairman of this unit and I need to know who you are, and what is your purpose in coming here?'

Zelda appeared to be quite relaxed and said with a slight smile on her lips 'Maybe Pete should enlighten you'.

Pete stood and looked at Chairman Roger and then at Zelda 'Are you sure Zelda?'.

'Yes, tell them everything that you believe is important to this gathering, Major Pete.'

Chairman Roger looked impatiently at Pete, grimaced in discomfort and then took his seat at the head of the table. Pete then, as briefly as possible, sequentially laid out most of what Zelda had told him, beginning with the first meeting in Perth. He glanced around the room of ASIO folk staring at him with almost disbelief on their faces.

Chairman Roger sharply requested proof and Zelda silently leant forward and wrote on the notepad in front of her. She gave him a name and a telephone number, and then said 'It would be far too dangerous for me to carry a hard copy of proof. Just call that number and tell the individual my name.'

He was not amused at all and stood up 'Excuse me, I'll go and make the call. Everyone sit tight.'

A couple of minutes later he returned and announced that Zelda was indeed whom she claimed to be. Both the ASIO and the DIO commanders were aware of her presence. He then announced she would be assisting with the current situation.

Ransom Message

Chairman Roger then announced 'Everyone listen up. For those of you who don't already know, we were contacted by a person about half an hour ago who identified himself as a member of an Islamic jihadist group informing us that our colleague, Sheila, is being held for a US $1 million ransom in revenge for the raids in Melbourne and Sydney.

'From what this individual said we gather she was snapped off the street near the hotel where you are staying Pete at around 7.30 a.m.. We have no way of knowing how the hell they would have known who Sheila was or her ASIO connection.'

Zelda raised her hand and said 'Mr Chairman, Sir, let me tell you this. You and your committee have utilised Arabic interpreters these past weeks. My organisation has evidence that one or more of those same interpreters are Islamic jihadist sympathisers and have no doubt passed on names and photographs where possible to the jihadists of as many members of your organisation as they possibly can.'

Chairman Roger's face turned ashen as he said 'My God, have we become so slack that we have no idea who the hell we have working with us. Thank you for your input Zelda and be assured I will follow up on your information.'

Roger continued 'Of course, it goes without saying we have all our assets on alert, the federal police, along with the state police. We are currently awaiting further instructions from the bastards who have her.'

Fuck me, Pete thought. That's why there was no response from my text; this is precisely when I was sitting talking to Zelda in the hotel coffee shop. Sheila would have exited out of the side door of the hotel.

He knew his jaw had dropped and he felt like he had been kicked in the nuts. He tried to control his emotions. Chairman Roger was about to continue, when Pete interrupted 'Do we have any idea at all as to where they may be holding her?'.

'No, we don't Pete, however, we are rounding up the ransom dollars as we speak and will be ready, willing, and able to make the drop as soon as we have the word.'

'I would like to be a part of this show, boss.'

He thought Chairman Roger was being a bit too cautious as he said 'I would prefer you to go back to your hotel and have your phone turned on and with you at all times so we can have immediate contact. Is that clear Pete?'

'Clear as mud boss. OK, I am outta here.'

'Hold on one minute Pete,' Zelda spoke up. 'Sir, I am leaving as well. It is my intention to try and pick up with these terrorists where I left off. Give me someone's number I can call anytime twenty-four hours.'

Chairman Roger responded 'Here's mine Zelda. Please call any hour that you may have something, anything.'

'Thank you, sir.'

As Spider and Zelda rode down to the foyer in the elevator, Spider looked at her and said 'I am calling in backup, an old SAS mate. This could get nasty.'

'I fully agree. Keep your phone handy. I will call you first rather than into Chairman Roger's office, too many ears there. I saw your reaction when you learned of this girl being kidnapped. She mean something to you Spider?'

'She does Zelda, she means a lot.'

As they left the building in opposite directions. Zelda hollered 'Later Spider'. She turned the corner and was gone. Pete had to hang about for a peak-hour taxi ride back to his hotel, all the while feeling extremely helpless while waiting for others to initiate any reaction or action.

Chapter 41

Brute

SAS Backup

Slamming the hotel room door open, Spider grabbed his phone and impatiently dialled a well-known number: 'Brute, it's Spider. How are you mate?'

'I am fine Spider. Just laying around the beach here at Surfers Paradise eyeballing all these topless chicks. You know what they say: living well is the best revenge.'

'Brute, I got some shit happening and need some urgent backup.'

'Time and place Spider. I am on my way.'

'Mercantile Hotel, 25 George Street, Sydney, Room # 2208'.

'Book me a room, I will text my ETA, over and out.'

Six hours later, at 4 p.m. Sydney time, Brute knocked on door 2208 and bear-hugged his mate when he opened it. Brute put both Spider and his duffel bag down and plopped his huge frame down on the couch.

'Damn good to see you Spider. Now, what's this shit you are in?'

Spider explained the whole scenario from when he was contacted by the DIO, up until the present moment and his dealings with ASIO Chairman Roger.

'Oh, one other thing Brute, as this mission is on my quid, I didn't bother with another room. This suite has two queen-size beds.'

'No problem. Wow, you sure can pick your shit. Now two questions Spider, tell me about this Zelda. Can she be trusted, does she have your back, and did I detect a soft spot for Sheila?'

'Zelda is a solid Mossad agent and those people don't fuck around, so yes, I trust her – to a point – as she has other puppet masters. I think I am in love with Sheila, Brute, well at least totally infatuated. Don't ask me how, it's just one of those things and I pray to God nothing or no one hurts her or by God Brute I will fucking kill every last one of those fucking rag head terrorists.'

'OK Spider, just relax and congratulations on your new found love. If anyone deserves it you do. Remember this life is no fucking rehearsal, enjoy it now. Our next move, weapons, can you organise any? And let's gear up. I feel there may be a shootout with these rat bastards in the cards. Also is this ASIO boss man, Roger the Dodger, any good? Can he be trusted, and is he really gathering the dough?'

'To the best of my knowledge, I do trust that he will protect one of his own. As far as weapons go, he is a politician and will have to rely on the Federal Police armed unit for backup. There are pretty tough gun laws here and we sure don't want to get arrested.'

Spider phoned Chairman Roger and informed him he had a support weapons specialist with him. He then asked specifically about armed response and obtaining special ministerial authorisation. Spider advised Roger he had been working on it with the DIO, and gave him a list of what he and Brute would need. The chairman sputtered a few expletives and said OK and that he would email a response. Several hours later an email arrived on Spider's mobile phone:

We have ministerial authorisation to use calibrated force if and when necessary, keeping in mind public interests. In other words – do it without adverse publicity.

As requested, weapons and equipment are on the way via permission Federal Police armoury:

- Three Sig Sauer short-barrel silenced automatic rifles
- Three Glock 33 compact hand weapons with sound suppressors
- Spare 9mm ammo with 4 spare magazines each for both weapon types
- Six flash bang grenades
- Three Kevlar bullet-proof vests
- Three Z-Tac throat mic and tube earphone radios
- Three black balaclavas
- Three sets of military full-fingered tactical gloves

Having studied the email, Spider looked at Brute and said with relief 'I think that should just about do it'.

'Holy fuck Spider, that's an arsenal. Where did you get all that on such short notice here in fucking Sydney and why sets of three?'

From our old DIO Commander Coen from past covert adventures. He is still active right here in Sydney. The third set is for backup, not sure yet for whom if anybody but it's always good to have spares. As a matter of fact, they should be delivered in the boot of a rental car any moment.

Brute winked and said 'One thing we always knew about our SAS Major Pete, the Spider – he was fucking organised!'.

Spider's phone rang. It was Chairman Roger. 'Pete, we just received an email with a video message from the kidnappers. I have downloaded it and e-mailed it to your laptop. Watch it and call me back.'

Spider opened his laptop and indicated for Brute to come and watch.

The video was a little shaky at first and out of focus but then it stabilised and focused. Sheila was seated in a chair with her legs duct-taped to the chair legs, her wrists duck-taped to the arm rests, and with duct tape across her mouth. Behind her was a man dressed in black with a balaclava covering his head and a long-bladed knife in his right hand. Draped on the wall behind him was the ISIS flag.

He grabbed a handful of Sheila's coal-black hair and brutally pulled her head back, exposing her neck. He then raised the knife and held it to her throat. Hanging around her neck by a piece of string was a strip of cardboard with the words 'US $1 Million' scrawled on it.

He then ripped the duct tape from her mouth and ordered her to plead for mercy as he drew the knife gently across her throat, leaving a small pinkish trail behind it.

Sheila screamed two words, 'Spider, Spider!' Then someone placed another strip of duct tape across her mouth. Tears streamed down her cheeks.

Brute put his hand on his mate's shoulder. Spider was shaking with rage and torment.

'Easy major, let's see that again.' Brute could see Spider was shook up like he had never seen before.

'Have a seat Spider and sip a little of this Cognac. Looking at that video, there is nothing that can be distinguished regarding location.'

There was a knock on the door, Brute answered it. Before him stood a young, female Australian naval lieutenant in dress uniform.

'Major Pete?' she asked. Brute shook his head and called for Spider.

She handed Spider the keys to the rental car and said 'Sir, Commander Coen sends his regards. The vehicle is in the hotel parking lot, level #3. Your items of request are in the boot, and it is a late-model, four-door, red Commodore.'

Before Spider could utter a word, she saluted, turned and walked towards the elevators. Spider grabbed his phone and called the ASIO boss.

'Pete here Boss, I watched the video. This is an extremely dangerous situation and Sheila's life is in the balance. Have you been contacted about delivering the ransom money? And do you have it? Also, I have received the equipment as requested.'

'Pete all noted. Yes, the gravity of the situation is very well understood and our people are doing everything possible. So far, I have not been contacted by Zelda or the kidnappers regarding the ransom cash and, yes, we have it in several satchels ready for delivery. Pete, I have a question, maybe you can clear up about Sheila's words on the video "Spider, Spider"?'

'Yes boss, that is my tag. It relates back to my active military days in the SAS.'

'So, she was calling for you?'

'Yes, she was, boss. I have to go, I have an incoming call. I will contact you when and if I have any info.'

'Pete, this is Zelda. We need to meet. I have important information regarding the perpetrators and the location of where they are holding Sheila.'

'Zelda, where are you?'

'I am on my way to your hotel see you in ten.'

'Brute, Zelda is coming here and says she knows who has Sheila and where they have her stashed.'

'That is good news. Why don't I go down to the rental car, check out the weapons and make sure everything is there, secure and operational.'

Two minutes after Zelda arrived at Spider's room, Brute returned and gave the thumbs up to Spider, who then introduced them.

'Glad to meet you Zelda. Spider tells me you have solid intel on our kidnapped victim.'

'I do, I wangled my way back in and Abdul, my so-called husband, is leading this group, which includes his maybe sister and her husband. Plus, he said he has six more radicalised Hamas ISIS sympathisers that the authorities are looking for with him. Sheila is being held in a terrorist safe house here in Sydney but is being moved around to other safe houses every eight to ten hours.'

'That's one hell of a lot of intel. Have you seen Sheila? Have you informed ASIO?'

'I have not actually seen Sheila or informed ASIO because, as I informed you all at the meeting including Chairman Roger, we have information that ASIO has Arab interpreters, one or more of whom may be ISIS sympathisers and if they discovered I was an informant … well I am sure you two SAS warriors with Middle East experience know the consequence of my fate.'

'Sorry Zelda, yes, we do. So what are your plans now?'

'Pete, my own plans depend on what the terrorists decide, so I can't plan much right now. The decision of if or when to inform ASIO I am going to leave strictly for you, but I ask please, if you can, don't mention my name. What I have to do right now is swallow my hatred and pride, spread my legs and solidify my solidarity with Abdul and his group. I do this not for you Pete, not for Sheila, not for Australia. I do this for Israel.

'I do know it is their intention to have the ransom cash within the next forty-eight hours. I must be a part of this. I will text only you Pete as and when I become aware of their plans. I will be using a burner phone, only in a life-or-death situation should you try to contact me on my mobile.

'I will have information for you before the terrorists take action and I would ask you Pete, please do not inform ASIO that you and I have communicated.

Always remember ASIO have moles who pass information to our enemies. Now I must go.'

'Thank you, Zelda, we will stand by.'

After she had left, the two SAS warriors put their heads together to layout the strategy for the rescue mission.

'Brute, what do you think of Zelda now that you have met her and listened to her explanations of the matters at hand?'

'I believe she is currently on our side. I sure hope for Sheila's sake she is on our side, but I also understand her loyalties to Mossad, which could place us in the dispensable category if things go wrong. I don't for a moment believe that Zelda or Mossad care about you, me, the money or about Sheila but their interest is solely about taking out the terrorists that have hurt Israel.'

'Good assumption. As soon as she relays some intel we will mobilise. Here's what I am thinking. The alignment with ASIO and the Federal Police armed response unit needs to be staged only after we have gone in to recover Sheila. The services can then do the clean-up and reporting bit so we can stay, as always, invisible.

'Right now, there are three factions with differing objectives and timelines that need to be managed:

1. Terrorists in two locations.
2. Mossad – we have no idea what strength, action or how, why, what intended.
3. Zelda – who knows if she will be caught with the terrorists, help us, or disappear again.
4. Spider and Brute – loose cannons, armed to the teeth, retrieving the hostage.
5. ASIO and Feds out on the road following the ransom money and terrorists, will catch up at the hostage site when notified.

Chapter 42

Ransom and Rescue

The following morning Spider was up walking the floor at 4 a.m., his mobile close by on the coffee table and plugged into the charger; it buzzed at 4.30 a.m.. Spider snapped it up and read a copy of the text sent to ASIO by the terrorists.

Ransom drop:

1 p.m. tomorrow – Sydney Tower
4 backpacks to be delivered with ransom $ $.
2 on level 1 – 360 bar & Dining
2 on level 2 – Sydney Tower Buffet
Both drop exchange in toilets
ASIO mules to return to their seats at table/bar

Another text message hit Spider's phone, this one from Zelda stating:

Sheila alive, intel on hostage location will be forwarded soonest – Zelda.

Spider handed the phone to Brute, who read both texts.

'It's happening mate, all we need now is Sheila's location. Looks like Zelda is holding up her end so far. Let's quickly go and oil the machinery.'

'I am just gonna give the ASIO boss a call to find out what more he knows. See you down in the coffee shop.'

'Roger that.'

Ten minutes later Spider joined Brute. He had already ordered breakfast of sausages, eggs, toast and coffee for them both.

'What's the news major?'

'ASIO has the intel, a little more detailed than ours but mainly the same. The drop is to be in the shitters on each of the two levels of the Sydney Tower. Each mule drops at the same time of 1 p.m. tomorrow. Then the mules are to return to their seats in the restaurants and wait for the all clear from their boss, who will receive a text when the terrorists are clear of the tower. The boss tells me there are three exits. The main entrance/exit for the Tower is on Market Street, one is in the Pitt Street Mall and one on Castlereagh Street.

'Surveillance teams will have a long-distance cover on all three exits but will not interfere with the perpetrators. The streets will be covered by ASIO mobile tag teams spread out across the city plus choppers in the air. He was also informed that Sheila would be released when all four backpacks are away and safe with the kidnappers. Then and only then will Sheila's location be revealed by text message to the ASIO boss, who said he would stay in touch with me.'

'Spider, I hate to say this mate, but we have to rescue Sheila before those fucking rag heads get their ransom and bugger off leaving us empty handed, or worse case, with a dead hostage body. You and I both know what will happen to her if we don't act first. Those rat bastards will torture and rape and sodomise her. They will never release her alive.'

'That I do know Brute. I will give Zelda a couple of minutes after the ransom pickup. If she hasn't contacted me by then I will call her, what else can I do. Fuck me Brute, I am all twisted up inside.'

'Love will do that me old mate. Just stay cool, I believe we have an ace with Zelda. She will come through. If you call and her associates spot it, she is dead meat on a stick and so is Sheila.

At 8.15 a.m. Spider's phone buzzed; it was another text from Zelda:

Arrived the Royal National Park
Terrorists rented Trekker cottage # 3 Webo Blvd.
1 hour drive south of Sydney
Contains 3 bedrooms, 2 bathrooms, 1 kitchen, 1 lounge
Cottage rectangular
Veranda along west side.
1 rear door, 1 front door
Bedrooms – large, windows – steel vertical security bars.
Waterway or river located a hundred yards west from cottage
Prisoner has ankle bracelet chain, anchored to bed frame
Bedroom on south-west corner of cottage
9 terrorists present – Zelda

Spider spat out 'Here Brute, read this text while I upload Google Maps for this Royal National Park. I've got it. Shit there is even photographs and all. Look Brute, that is most likely the cabin near the edge of a waterway and a footnote says that tourists play on the water with jet skis and canoes.'

'Time to lock and load Spider. We have a lady to rescue, the car is fuelled up so what highway do we take?'

'South down the Princess highway. We will recon the layout and hit them ASAP. We are running down the clock.'

'Chill Spider. If there's nine of these fuckers we will have a battle at short range. The odds are in their favour if they are all inside the building. Of course, we could always light up the front of the cottage with flash bang grenades; you hit the rear door as it is right next to the bedroom where Zelda says Sheila is being held.'

Brute added 'Spider do you think there would be any way we could have a face-to-face with Zelda. I am sure she is versatile with weapons, I'd sure like to have a third gun on our side.'

'Good idea, I will try after we arrive, but don't bet on her help as she may be occupied with the ransom pickup. But we have a third kit for her just in case.'

On the journey south, Spider received a text message from ASIO. It stated:

Ransom exchange 1 p.m. tomorrow – confirmed
ASIO request live video of victim with TV channel broadcasting news –
ABC Channel 2, at 12.30 p.m.. Before ransom drop
4 backpacks confirmed – each US $250,000.
Exchange confirmed – Sydney Tower – Toilets x 2.

Spider read the message out loud to Brute.

'That's good news mate, it almost guarantees they have to keep her alive until 12:30 tomorrow afternoon. Also, they are likely to split up their group so half do the pickup and half are left to hold the captive. If the good Lord is willing and the creeks don't rise, we will have Sheila safe and sound and back in Sydney before sunrise tomorrow.'

'Ya know Brute, I was looking on the park's web page. These fuckers charge $12 just to drive through the gate, then another $11 dollars to park your vehicle. This fucking world is becoming nothing but a rip-off. All they have to do now is find a way to tax you every time ya fart!'

Spider paid the total of $23 and they drove through the gate and decided to recon the park and waterway as tourists until they located Trekker Cottage, nonchalantly passing number 3 on Webo Blvd. It was likely that there may be a spotter if they were smart enough. He'd be sitting out here separately watching for any suspicious cars or people moving near the cottage.

'OK there it is. Let's park about 100 yards back and go walkies in the park and wide of the target. Our best recon will be to circle the cabin heading in different directions and meet back here at the car. We need to consider how to approach the cottage from the front, side or rear, how close are other cottages, cover such as trees and bushes. Can we toss flash bangs inside, check for window bars, obstacles, locate south-west corner, how far to the water's edge?'

'Roger that major, see you back here in an hour or so. Any problems, I'll phone you.'

While they were out scouting, Spider received another text message from Zelda.

On the highway to Sydney
Will assist with ransom pickup
5 enemies with me including the brother-in-law.
3 men, 1 woman including Abdul at cottage
Abdul will send ASIO a live video of Sheila just before ransom pickup
If pickup successful, Abdul will send video to social media of himself standing in front of ISIS flag. Sheila in orange jumpsuit being murdered by throat cutting.
Urgent you eliminate with extreme prejudice
Will text Sydney address when known
Good luck – Zelda

A little better than an hour later the two SAS warriors met up, sat on the park grass lawn and discussed their observations. No terrorist spotter had been seen by either warrior. Spider marked up a copy of the park map for planning their step-by-step attack on the cottage, then immediately handed Brute his phone with Zelda's last text message. After Brute read the message, he looked directly into Spider's eyes, which showed hatred and anger.

'Fuck me to tears, Spider. I knew these fucking mongrels would pull this shit. You and I both know they will rape, sodomise and literally torture Sheila before they cut her throat. Don't know if I ever told you but one of those Kuwaitis we were hunting Iraqis with in Kuwait City told me he had stayed in his homeland during the Iraqi occupation and saw some of his fellow country women raped and then they had their tits hacked from their bodies and strung up in downtown Kuwait City from street traffic lights.'

'No, I don't recall you ever telling me that. Fucking savages.'

'OK, let's initiate a plan. We have done our shit all over the world but this time this is our fucking homeland and by God Spider not one of these rag head cunts walks away from this. I don't give a fuck if I have to do time over this, they are dead, dead, fucking dead! Better them than Sheila!'

'I know Brute but as you said we have to stay cool, control our emotions then we slowly plan and execute. Here's my suggestion. Thanks to Zelda we now know there are four targets in the cottage: Abdul, his sister, and two other perpetrators.

'We have good brush and tree coverage around the cottage, the blinds are pulled on the windows and there didn't seem to be much movement. Other buildings are a good hundred yards away. I don't think flash bangs will work, just the Glocks with sound suppressors and our night goggles.

'If we wait until after dark, say around 8 p.m., then move to the cottage and lay low and do a little surveillance for an hour or so. Watch if anything is moving, then you attack from the front veranda door and I will attack through the rear door. How does that sound?'

'Sounds like a plan major, let's do it. But that's a couple of hours away. I say we grab a bite. I seen a little fish and chip joint on the way into the park, it looked appetising. Relax a bit, then action.'

At 8 p.m. the special forces soldiers opened their kit bags and put on their black Kevlar bullet-proof vests, balaclavas and military full-finger tactical gloves.

The warriors were getting close to attack mode. They lay in the thick brush next to the pathway that led from the veranda steps 25 to 30 yards down to the water's edge.

At around 9 p.m., the front door leading onto the veranda opened and two of the terrorists walked out, down the steps and followed the path. They stopped several feet from where Spider and Brute lay hidden under the cover of the bushes.

They both lit what smelled like camel shit cigarettes, then squatted and began smoking and speaking softly in Arabic; Brute nudged Spider as he began to rise slowly, Spider followed suit. Several minutes later the two Muslim jihadists lay dead from bloodless neck injuries.

Their bodies were silently and quickly moved into the brush alongside the cottage. Silently the warriors returned to their hide, waited and watched. Ten minutes passed, until Spider whispered 'I am going to work my way around to the rear door. I will click the "press to talk" button twice on the Z-Tac when I am in position, and you click one time if you receive. When you are ready to attack just say "clear" and I will respond "clear" using our Z-Tac and we will go in simultaneously.'

'Roger major.'

Spider slowly and cautiously moved towards the rear door, ten minutes later Brute heard the two finger clicks and responded appropriately. He waited another ten to twelve minutes and had slowly stood up and stretched his legs ready for action when the front door leading onto the veranda opened and a tall slim man, close to 6ft, walked out onto the veranda and stood by the railing peering into the darkness and spoke: 'Ali, Mohammad, what are you doing, where are you?' He repeated this several times and Brute realised he was calling his two cohorts. He flipped down his night vision goggle, raised his hand-held weapon, sighted, and squeezed the trigger at the same time as he hollered into his Z-Tac, 'clear'!

The hollow point entered the forehead of the tall thin man and exited, splattering the back of Abdul's head over the cottage wall. Still gripping the veranda railing, his body slid slowly to the deck. With three or four steps Brute was through the open door and into the lounge room. Seated on the couch was a jihadist woman dressed in a black hijab with an AK-47 rifle on the couch beside her. She began to reach for it when a hollow point tore through her chest and she tumbled forward like a rag doll, blood dribbling from her mouth as she crumbled face down onto the floor.

At the same moment Spider crashed through the rear door and looked at Brute, who was moving towards him. They both reached the bedroom at the same time, and Brute hit the locked door with his shoulder busting the lock and tearing it off the top hinge. Spider burst into the room, Sheila screamed, the duct tape had been removed from her mouth. Spider rushed to the bed and gently placed his hand over the terrified woman's mouth saying 'Sheila, it's Spider, it's Spider. Everything is OK. You are safe now.'

Sheila looked at Spider with terror and tear-filled eyes. He was still wearing the balaclava. He pulled it up exposing his face as he hugged her and soothed her. She cried uncontrollably while he held her.

Brute about-faced and re-entered the lounge room. He checked the remaining two bedrooms, all clear, then returned to the veranda and pulled Abdul's remains into the lounge room. He kicked the door to the veranda closed with his foot, then searched the terrorist's pockets for keys. He found them, then rushed to Spider, tossing them in his direction and shouted 'keys'! Spider grabbed them in mid-air and fumbled through the keys until he found the one he was looking for that unlocked the ankle bracelet.

Returning to the lounge room, Brute removed the pistol from Abdul's waist belt and placed it in his right hand and curled his dead fingers around the hand grip. He took out his phone and snapped several pictures, then he rolled the jihadist woman wearing the black hijab onto her back and laid the AK-47 rifle along her body with her right hand on the trigger mechanism. Then he took several photos of her.

Brute photographed the video camera on its tripod facing a chair and the ISIS flag on the wall. He also snapped two AK-47 rifles and a machete that were leaning up against the wall next to the flag. On the coffee table was a bunch of documents with Arabic writing and a long-bladed knife. Lying beside the knife was a page written in English, the heading said 'Statement for social media'. Brute picked it up and, glancing through it, realised this was the statement Abdul would have read into the camera before the beheading of Sheila. He ran two of his gloved fingers through Abdul's blood, then wiped the blood on the bottom of the statement. This he figured was DNA evidence if it was required. He rolled it up and slipped it into the leg pocket of his black cargo pants, then turned off all the lights in the cottage.

'Come on Spider, we have to move. Grab the lady and let's haul arse. Does Sheila require medical attention?'

'I am OK. Just get me away from here please.'

Five minutes later they were in the red Commodore and, respecting the speed limit, Brute drove out of the park. Spider and Shelia were in the rear seat, with Sheila totally bewildered and Spider trying to explain the day's events.

2 Bullets, 4 down

Sheila laid her head on Spider's lap and was out like a light. Spider removed his phone from his shirt pocket and dialled Zelda's number. She answered on the second ring.

'Zelda, this is Pete. Sheila is safe. All occupants of cabin # 3 are deceased. I suggest you text the ASIO boss and tell him what I have just told you. Give him the address of the safe house, also the Trekker cottage, then get out of there as fast as you can. The cops will raid it. You should go to my hotel and wait in the lobby for Brute. He will explain everything. Do you understand?'

'Yes, Pete. I will follow your instructions and go to your hotel and wait for Brute. Pete, thank you.'

'I thank you Zelda. Without you Sheila would have been murdered. We will speak later, over and out.'

'Brute, when you get within a couple of blocks of the hotel pull over and I will take the wheel, no point in you becoming involved with these ASIO people at this time. Walk to the hotel where Zelda should be waiting for you in the lobby. Also, we should swap weapons just in case I am searched and ASIO snatch it. They will find it will match ballistics as the weapon used to neutralise the terrorists, if they are stupid enough to take it that far. Do you have a key card for the hotel room?'

'Yep, I do major and one other thing, I have a written statement with Abdul's blood on it if DNA is required. It was to be the social media statement praising ISIS and Al-Qaeda condemning the Australian infidel for supporting the Great Satan and its wars on the Muslim world. He would have read it into the camera before the beheading.

'Also, I took photographs of the whole fucking scene in the bedroom and lounge room; bodies, weapons, camera and that arse wipe flag.'

'Good work, just like a true warrior. But just what kind of people are these fuckers. What good would murdering an innocent human being in real time on TV in such a barbaric manner have done for their cause. It's beyond me, ya know what I mean Brute?'

'Only too well, me old mate.'

'I have to call the ASIO boss and fill him in.'

'Boss, Pete here. Have you heard from Zelda?'

'Yes, I just finished reading her text. What the fuck have you been up to? She said Sheila is safe and is with you and there are dead terrorists in a park cottage.'

'Sheila is with me, no physical damage, I suggest you meet me in the hotel parking lot, level #3 of my hotel, in about twenty minutes and make sure you have a medic with you to check out Sheila. Yes, there have been a few casualties.'

'Pete, we have a Federal Police armed unit on the way to the safe house and hopefully will have captured every last one of these jihadist bastards. Our forensic people are on their way to secure the Trekker cottage in the national park. I am guessing that there is a mess for them to clean up. So glad Sheila is with you and alive.'

Brute pulled the vehicle into the nearest kerb down the road from the hotel and stepped out.

'OK Spider, it's all yours.'

Spider shook Sheila awake as he helped her sit up.

'Sheila, how are you feeling? We will be at my hotel in a couple of minutes and Chairman Roger and his crew will be there to meet us. They will also have a medic to check you over. I will leave you in their hands.'

'I am OK, still in shock I think. When will I see you again?'

'I am hoping we can all meet in the ASIO office sometime soon. Call me anytime and if you can, without putting yourself in a difficult position, please leave Brute out of any conversations or report. If not, just do what you have to do. Now let's get this seat belt on you.'

'Brute turned away without looking back and then took off on foot in the direction of the hotel.'

Zelda was seated in the lobby and Brute spotted her as soon as he entered. She stood up and surprised him with a hug. He responded likewise.

After she received the last call from Spider saying he and Brute were successful at the cottage situation, she just simply picked up her small overnight bag and looked at the two younger Muslims who were now happily watching a girlie show on TV. The other three were sleeping. Zelda said nothing, she just opened the front door to the safe house that very soon would not be safe for these jihadist shits as ASIO and the Feds were on their way. She walked out into the street, flagged down a taxi and headed for the hotel.

'Zelda, good to see you again. Come on let's get to Pete's room and order in something to eat. It's been one hell of an evening.'

'You must tell me all about it,' she said with a wry smile creeping across her lips.

As Spider pulled the red Commodore into the hotel parking stall it was surrounded by ASIO and Federal Police personnel along with a couple of medics. He stepped out, opened the rear passenger door and assisted Sheila. The two medics immediately rushed to her side and assisted her to their EMS vehicle.

Chairman Roger greeted Spider with a warm handshake and spoke: 'We have taken into custody the five terrorists from their so-called safe house and the Feds have secured the cottage with the four deceased terrorists. I am not sure just how you and Zelda pulled this off but believe me when I tell you we are grateful.

'There is one other thing; we would like to know who was with you when you rescued Sheila. Park CCTV shows you with a rather large male companion whom we believe is one of your SAS compatriots. ASIO is very interested in making acquaintance of this individual. We do not wish at this time to involve Commander Cohen of the DIO.

'Boss, thank you for meeting us and bringing the medics. Good to hear you have those jihadist pricks alive and in custody. If I am not in trouble right now, can we leave these questions until tomorrow and can we all meet in your office around 1 p.m.? I have had one fuck of an evening and need booze, food and sleep.'

Brute asked Zelda to have a seat and asked what she would like to eat, telling her he was going to order in room service, then he would explain the evening's events when Pete arrived. They finished their hamburger and chips and were sipping on their second can of cola when Zelda said 'It feels like a huge load has been lifted from my shoulders knowing that dirty filthy Arab bastard Abdul is well and truly dead, I just feel so free after all these years. I don't need to know all the details but thank you so much Brute. Both you and Pete did the world a huge favour tonight, Israel thanks you.'

The hotel room door opened and Spider walked in. 'Good to see you Zelda. You will be glad to hear all five terrorists at the not-so-safe house are in custody and will appear in a closed court tomorrow morning. They have CCTV footage of us at the park, Brute, and ASIO wish to make your acquaintance, if you agree. We will all meet at the ASIO office at 1 p.m. tomorrow. Is that OK with you Zelda?'

'That's fine with me. Well it's late so I am heading back to my little flat in Potts Point. Thank you Brute for the hamburger and soda and thank you Major Pete or Spider, for everything, you too Brute, both of you. Good night, or should I say good morning. Anyhow, see you at one tomorrow.'

Sheila was treated for dehydration, a shallow cut on her throat and shock, then allowed to go home on the understanding she would attend the meeting at the ASIO office the following day. A car would be sent for her.

Next afternoon back at the ASIO office, Chairman Roger called the meeting to order at 1 p.m.. All present were introduced including Brute, then he thanked all of those present for attending. He stated this report draft would be tabled here today and if no errors or omissions were raised into the kidnapping of special agent Sheila, the ransom demands and the demise of the Muslim jihadist cell then the report would be forwarded to those in the upper echelons of ASIO and the Minister, of course:

Those in attendance at the ASIO special meeting were:

- ASIO Chairman Roger
- An ASIO stenographer
- ASIO special officer Sheila
- Mossad special agent Zelda
- Major Pete, former SAS officer
- Sergeant Major Brute, former SAS officer

The report was read out by the stenographer:

A special agent of the Australian Security and Intelligence Organisation (ASIO) was kidnapped and held against her will for a total fifty-six hours with ransom demands of one million dollars, United States currency. After fifty-six hours of detention the ASIO special agent was rescued by combat experienced personnel on loan from the Defence Intelligence Organisation (DIO). Owing to their successful intervention this ransom demand was never paid.

During the rescue mission several members of the jihadist terrorist cell were killed inside the cottage, two other members of the cell were later discovered dead at the side of the cottage located in the Royal National Park where the kidnapped victim was being detained.

Evidence obtained at the scene proved this terrorist cell was intent on causing grievous bodily harm to the kidnapped victim and had in their possession ISIS paraphernalia, military-style weapons, a large knife, a video recording device, Islamic jihadist documents and a statement for social media condemning the United States and Australia of waging war on the Muslim world.

The remaining five members involved in receiving the ransom money were captured alive at a safe house and taken into custody by ASIO agents assisted by Federal Police and appeared in a Sydney closed court session this morning. They faced a barrage of charges which included, kidnapping, holding a person against their will, torture, ransom demands from a Federal Agency and Islamic jihad terrorism. Other charges are forthcoming.

That ends the report.

ASIO Chairman Roger then thanked all present for their actions and stated Special Agent Sheila would be taking a leave of absence for several months to recover from her terrifying experience and would be receiving a commendation for her bravery.

Major Pete's assignment with ASIO was now complete and he would be returning to his home in Perth with a letter of appreciation sent to Commander Cohen of the DIO.

A personal letter of appreciation from ASIO would be issued to Sergeant Major Brute for his assistance in the rescue mission of one of its special agents.

ASIO Chairman Roger stood and wished them all the best, then asked if anyone had anything they wished to add.

Zelda stood and addressed the gathering, saying 'I, on behalf of Israel, want to say a heartfelt thank you to all of you for all that has been done in the elimination of this horrific terrorist cell. I will be returning to Tel Aviv in several days just as soon as I take care of some personal business both here in Sydney and in Perth. I wish each and every one of you a happy life and Sheila I am so sorry for your ordeal. However, I know you are a strong person and a survivor. Thank you.'

Does anyone else have anything to say?

Sheila stood and spoke, 'There are so many things I would like to say but I guess the most important is thank you to the three very brave people that saved my life, Zelda, Spider and Brute. There is no way I can ever thank you enough but to say I love all three of you and I will forever be eternally grateful, thank you.'

'Is there is anything else from anyone? OK, thank you. This meeting is closed.'

They all left the ASIO building and said their goodbyes. One by one they hugged Zelda, who then climbed into a taxi and was gone. Brute hugged Sheila and wished her well, then told Spider he would see him back at the hotel, turned and walked away.

Sheila and Spider hugged for a long while, then Sheila asked 'Spider would it be OK if I came to Perth and visited with you for a while during my leave of absence?'.

Spider looked into her green eyes and responded 'I would really like that; just hope you make it soon'.

'I will, I have to go now. I have an appointment with a counsellor.'

They kissed and she climbed into a taxi and was gone. As Spider walked back to the hotel, he called Commander Cohen and thanked him for his assistance and advised him he was finished with the red Commodore. The car was now ready for pickup and the keys were with the hotel concierge. Also, all the items that were requested were securely locked in the boot and only a couple of them had been utilised. He finished by saying 'You have my number'.

Back at the hotel, Brute had packed his duffel bag and was sipping on a can of cola when Spider entered.

'Well, you old SAS warrior what you gonna do now? I see you are packed and ready to roll.'

'Yea, I have a flight out in about three hours, not much sense hanging around Sydney. I'll go back to eyeballing titties on the Gold Coast beaches and soak up some of that Queensland sun.'

'Sounds like a plan.'

'Spider, you wanna hear a theory of mine?'

'Sure, why not.'

'I been sitting here drinking this can of lolly water and I got to thinking about Zelda. Seems to me she is somewhat of a mystery woman.'

'How do you mean?'

'Well, from what you have told me, at the very same time on the morning Sheila was kidnapped you were meeting with Zelda and that was when she informed you that she was a special agent with Mossad and that her organisation had agents or moles, whatever you want to call them embedded within the DIO, ASIO, the Federal cops and God knows where else.'

'What are you getting at Brute?'

'As you explained to me, she told you that her organisation had acquired several dossiers on SAS soldiers, including you, who had very strong military background with unarmed combat abilities and would not hesitate to pull the trigger in a critical situation and they chose you. With all the privileged information she had she would have known that you and Sheila had a thing going.'

'Where is this going mate?'

'OK hypothetically, we both know Mossad are no fools. What if they decided to bring this terrorist shit to a quick and bloody end? Wouldn't it make operational sense to have Zelda finger Sheila for a kidnapping knowing full well you would be pissed off and more than likely bring in the cavalry and waste those rag head, anti-Israeli jihadist bastards? I mean she fed you all the correct intel so we could and would exterminate quickly with extreme prejudice.'

'Fuck me Brute. If that is true then I was, I mean we were, used by Zelda and her organisation as nothing more than hired assassins.'

'Well, if that was the case, don't seem like there is much we can do about it anyhow. Spider, it was good for the soul working with you once more. Who knows, maybe we will get to do it again, hired assassins. I don't know, maybe I'll go do a little trekking in Southeast Asia, never know what may turn up. Anyhow, what about you?'

'I am off to Perth tonight. Sheila said she will come visit during her leave of absence, so I have that to look forward to. But ya never know, I may wind up joining up with you for that Southeast Asia trek.'

Brute finished his cola, tossed the empty can into the garbage bin, picked up his duffel bag, gave Spider another bear hug then shook his hand. He opened the door and said 'See ya later, mate'.

Then he headed for the elevator doors.

Don't worry about those things you have no control over.

The end (for now).